SKOKIE PUB LIBR (IHG)

REQUEST ID 184991786

AUTHOR Segaloff, Nat
TITLE   Arthur Penn : American director

DUE DATE 02/16/2018   **BORROWER** IV@
                             LENDER   IHG

RETURN INFORMATION

NOTE TO PATRON   **BORROWING LIBRARY**
Please return to: *Please return to:*
ILL   Interlibrary Loan
VERNON AREA PUBLIC   Skokie Public Library-XWH
300 OLDE HALF DAY RD.   5215 Oakton St
LINCOLNSHIRE, IL US 60069   Skokie, IL US 60077-3680

Arthur Penn

Screen Classics

Screen Classics is a series of critical biographies, film histories, and analytical studies focusing on neglected filmmakers and important screen artists and subjects, from the era of silent cinema to the golden age of Hollywood to the international generation of today. Books in the Screen Classics series are intended for scholars and general readers alike. The contributing authors are established figures in their respective fields. This series also serves the purpose of advancing scholarship on film personalities and themes with ties to Kentucky.

Series Editor

Patrick McGilligan

Books in the Series

Hedy Lamarr: The Most Beautiful Woman in Film
Ruth Barton

Von Sternberg
John Baxter

The Marxist and the Movies: A Biography of Paul Jarrico
Larry Ceplair

Warren Oates: A Wild Life
Susan Compo

Being Hal Ashby: Life of a Hollywood Rebel
Nick Dawson

Raoul Walsh: The True Adventures of Hollywood's Legendary Director
Marilyn Ann Moss

Some Like It Wilder: The Life and Controversial Films of Billy Wilder
Gene D. Phillips

Claude Rains: An Actor's Voice
David J. Skal with Jessica Rains

Buzz: The Life and Art of Busby Berkeley
Jeffrey Spivak

Arthur Penn

American Director

Nat Segaloff

Foreword by
Jonathan Demme

THE UNIVERSITY PRESS OF KENTUCKY

Published by The University Press of Kentucky
scholarly publisher for the Commonwealth,
serving Bellarmine University, Berea College, Centre College of Kentucky,
Eastern Kentucky University, The Filson Historical Society, Georgetown
College, Kentucky Historical Society, Kentucky State University, Morehead
State University, Murray State University, Northern Kentucky University,
Transylvania University, University of Kentucky, University of Louisville,
and Western Kentucky University.
All rights reserved.

Editorial and Sales Offices: The University Press of Kentucky
663 South Limestone Street, Lexington, Kentucky 40508-4008
www.kentuckypress.com

15 14 13 12 11   5 4 3 2 1

Library of Congress Cataloging-in-Publication Data

Segaloff, Nat.
  Arthur Penn : American director / Nat Segaloff ; foreword by Jonathan
Demme.
      p. cm. — (Screen classics)
  Includes bibliographical references and index.
  Includes filmography and television credits for directing.
  ISBN 978-0-8131-2976-1 (alk. paper)
  ISBN 978-0-8131-2981-5 (ebook)
  1. Penn, Arthur, 1922–2010. 2. Motion picture producers and directors—
United States—Biography. I. Title.
  PN1998.3.P4525S46 2011
  791.4302'33092—dc22   2010047399

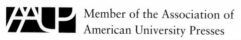

For Arthur, of course

Contents

Illustrations follow page 142

Foreword

In the middle of Arthur Penn's magnifico *Four Friends* there arrives the now justly immortalized, cosmically American moment where we find ourselves with an American family playing outside with their adopted Vietnamese child, while inside the house the television broadcasts news of the first landing on the moon by U.S. astronauts. It's fair to call this a quintessentially American moment, brilliantly conceived and crafted by my dear friend and not infrequent mentor, the quintessentially American filmmaker, artist, and all-around great guy, Mr. Arthur Penn. (It's not lost on me that I have already used one particular word—*American*—way too many times, but when it comes to Penn, this word will just pop up again and again and again because that's who and what this man is.)

The book you are holding is rich in all the vital details and insights pertinent to the filmmaker in question, and I have the high honor of providing a few words of introduction here. Because my relationship with Arthur is so deep and long running, I'm introducing him through the prism of my experience of meeting the man first onscreen through his films, and eventually in person as a fellow New Yorker and as a brother in the Directors Guild of America.

I first met Arthur in the early 1960s at the Dixie Drive-In Theatre on the outskirts of Miami, Florida, where the usual crew of my movie-obsessed buddies and I, beers in hand and under the stars, watched this western called *The Left Handed Gun* at our favorite venue. We were all bowled over by this western, way more intimately scaled than we ordinarily cared for; in black and white, which we were not at all partial to; and, what's more, painfully lacking in the gunplay and brawls we had reasonably come to expect and demand from a western. Yet we were collectively mesmerized and deeply gripped by this utterly unique motion picture! Everything about this movie was different from what we were comfortably accustomed to in this, our collective favorite genre—even (and especially) the claustrophobic and elliptical visual style in which the story was presented. So even though as a teenager in love with movies I should arguably have known better, and despite the fact that I didn't give a hoot about what a director was or did anyway, Arthur Penn had already had an impact on me so powerful that I can still recall in vivid detail the thrill of being swept up in Paul Newman's Billy the Kid the night I first met Arthur Penn at the Dixie Drive-In.

As the midsixties arrived, I was plugging in to the French nouvelle vague, and I had come to learn—more than anything by having my mind blown by Truffaut's *Shoot the Piano Player* and Godard's *Breathless*—what a director "did." In the midst of my feverish embrace of these rule-breaking new films from France, Penn's *Mickey One* showed up, and I was knocked out by its challenging, fractured, existential portrait of Warren Beatty's paranoid film noir flight from the threatening powers that be. The excitement I felt in seeing this terrific American film out-nouvelle vague-ing the French can only be described as patriotic—a truly surprising reaction for a young person of my generation in the tumultuous America of the 1960s.

I think we might imagine that, inspired by what he was seeing from France, Arthur was emulating the stylistic approach of his overseas contemporaries, but we now know that this was in no way the case. Penn was in the midst of his very own process of actor-driven, boundary-breaking personal evolution that had begun with his early work in live television (where "seizing the moment" was what it was all about), had come to light on the big screen with *The Left Handed Gun,* and now, with *Mickey One,* was proceeding more boldly and effectively forward with this daring film that—far from copying the French—was in fact challenging and inspiring his contemporaries, such as Godard, Resnais, Varda, and Truffaut, who were among those leading the stylistic revolution in Europe. Having heard this directly from François Truffaut while working as a publicist on *The Bride Wore Black,* I can vouch for it with glee and conviction.

Then along came the masterful *The Chase,* which absolutely floored me with the overwhelming power of Penn's now trademark gold-standard performances from a brilliantly assembled cast, including Marlon Brando's extraordinary and extraordinarily controlled tragic sheriff and a brand-new-to-the-scene Robert Redford in a portrayal that left no doubt of the magnitude his subsequent career was destined to have. This absurdly rich ensemble cast also included Jane Fonda, Janice Rule, E. G. Marshall, Angie Dickinson, and Robert Duvall, to name but a few. However, it was the new epic scope of Penn's canvas, populated by his customary vivid performances, that left me reeling and believing that this edgy outsider, first encountered at the Dixie Drive-In, stood there revealed to be an emerging cinematic giant. In few other films of the time had violence been staged with such appalling and devastating impact as the beating administered to Brando; we witness not only the horrid spectacle of a decent individual going down but also, along with him, the entire rule of law as a community is summarily dismantled before our very eyes. I loved and marveled at that profoundly moving film then, and I love it even more today. For me, seeing *The Chase* for the first time was to experience a whole new broadening of the possibilities of American film.

I was working as a publicist on the New York film distribution scene in 1967 when the buzz surrounding *Bonnie and Clyde* first started rolling across the border from the Montreal Film Festival where the film premiered, igniting a firestorm of controversy, sharply dividing critics, and generally freaking out ecstatic moviegoers with its revolutionary approach to . . . everything! For this ardent young cinéaste, *Bonnie and Clyde* was nothing less than a two-hour sustained cinematic hallucination that truly honored the American films that had come before while utterly reinventing the language of the medium. With its groundbreaking in-your-face style and overwhelming emotional power, *Bonnie and Clyde* was an *Avatar*-level game-changer, but it did it all in 2-D.

When you see *Bonnie and Clyde* today, its brilliance remains vividly intact. But to see this picture in the late summer of '67, it was truly shocking and joy-inspiring to witness this expansion of the possibilities of the medium, and people were shocked in different ways. Bosley Crowther, the justifiably esteemed, all-powerful critic for the *New York Times,* had been at the forefront of those who had found *Bonnie and Clyde* appalling at the Montreal Film Festival. In the following weeks, as *Bonnie and Clyde* became more and more of a cultural phenomenon, Mr. Crowther revisited the film in print, this time now finding fault with the colossal popularity the film was experiencing and with American moviegoers for embracing it. When Mr. Crowther later retired from the *Times,* there were those who saw his departure as tied to his passionately negative reviews of *Bonnie and Clyde.* As my dear friend Marshall Lewis, American representative to the Montreal Film Festival and manager of the Bleecker Street Cinema, said at the time, "Bosley made the fatal mistake for a critic: he panned the audience."

This, then, is the power of Arthur Penn: he can create a masterpiece that not only redefines the possibilities of the medium but can also dethrone the most powerful film critic on the planet.

By the time Arthur was making *Alice's Restaurant,* I was a closet hippie and in true film-buff heaven working as the newspaper contact for United Artists, the hottest and boldest American distribution company of the day. I was given the assignment of escorting the incredibly sharp *Newsday* critic Joe Gelmis to Stockbridge, Massachusetts, to visit the *Alice* set! Gelmis introduced me to Penn; I shook hands with my hero. Their interview dinner was the first time I heard Arthur speak of his deeply collaborative approach to working with actors and his unflappable faith in the "shared discovery" dynamic of filmmaking. I remember thinking how much this flew in the face of what the literature told us about the director's pivotal role in the process: directors had visions! They showed up with every detail of the final movie etched in their head and basically told all, "This is what you will do!" It seemed that the Penn approach was about showing up and saying, basically, "Okay, let's take a look at this and see what happens." Over the years, the thrill of first tasting Arthur's commitment to the actors has remained vividly with me.

When I started making my own films, I definitely went through a difficult period defined by the old imprinted notion that the director's job was to tell everybody what to do and how to do it. (Despite the fact that I was a working student enrolled at the Roger Corman school of filmmaking, I still had so very much to learn.) Then one morning in 1976 I went to Bruce McGill as he arrived on the set of *Citizen's Band* to tell him that I had decided the night before to drop the face slap from the scene we were about to shoot because I had determined that it wouldn't work. Bruce looked at me with a mixture of horror and confusion and said that he had based his preparation for the scene on that smack. Thankfully, my first impulse to defend my "vision" and insist that the slap was history was derailed by the arrival of a retrieved memory of Stockbridge a decade earlier. I took a deep breath and dared to say, in my best approximation of how Arthur Penn might sound, "Okay, go for the slap and let's see what happens." What happened was that this fine young actor, freed from the limitations of the director's preconceived notions of what would and wouldn't "work," set the scene on fire, and the power and excitement of the "Arthur Penn idea" of deep trust and shared explorations with actors became an inspiration and a goal for me that has continued to grow in my head and my heart to this day.

Over the years I have been privileged to get to know Arthur and Peggy Penn quite well. From my first "meeting" with Arthur at the Dixie Drive-In via *The Left Handed Gun* to now, being fellow filmmakers who work and live in New York, I daresay that we have become friends. It is also true that my undiminished awe of Arthur's work still leaves me a little gaga for the first few minutes of our encounters, and I am once again the wide-eyed hippie publicist meeting my hero for the first time on the set of *Alice's Restaurant*.

I love Arthur so much as a human being, and I love hearing him talk about many things, but maybe, most especially, actors. He reveres and adores actors. He speaks about them like a devoted father, like a fiercely loyal friend, like a passionate lover, like a two-fisted protector, like a happily baffled alchemist who has been front and center at the creation of true magic, yet he still finds the phenomenon absolutely astonishing. It tickles me to this day that the mere mention of the word *actor* causes this stunned look to come over Arthur's face; his head begins to shake in amazement, and I swear to you, I've seen tears of joy and adoration mist his eyes at the very thought of the power of what these mercurial artists of stage and screen are capable of doing to the viewers' hearts and minds. That power is at its greatest when Arthur Penn is on the set.

Jonathan Demme
Academy Award–winning director of
The Silence of the Lambs,
Philadelphia,
Citizens Band,
Something Wild,
Melvin and Howard,
and *Stop Making Sense*

Preface

Arthur Penn was a contradiction among American filmmakers. He was a founding father of the "Movie Generation" of the 1960s and '70s that produced Steven Spielberg, Francis Coppola, and George Lucas, yet he neither hung out with their crowd nor was he seduced by the Hollywood system they rose to dominate. He was an award-winning theater director, yet found Broadway increasingly irrelevant. He was a powerful force in the "golden age" of television yet, unlike his colleagues, never considered it merely a stepping-stone to movies. Indeed, for fifty years he moved effortlessly between film, television, and stage, directing only what drew his interest, and mastering all of them.

Arthur Penn died on September 28, 2010, in New York, one day after his eighty-eighth birthday. I had phoned him from Los Angeles on the morning of September 27, not only to wish him well but also to tell him that this book, on which we had enjoyed so many hours of collaboration over a five-year period, had just gone for typesetting "and nothing can stop it now." He said he was pleased and relieved. That night, over dinner with his family, he opened his gifts, one of which was a framed print I'd sent him of the cover of this book. On the back I had written, "For Arthur: For your birthday and the rebirth you gave cinema." Twenty-four hours later he was gone. Neither of us was spiritual, but I can't help but think that once he knew his legacy was assured, he felt free to move on.

Arthur's life and art were tinged with irony: he was able to hold onto his ideals when few in the entertainment industry seemed to have any ideals at all; he remained an intensely devoted family man who never directed a work about a functional family;

he was a peace activist who triggered the trend in screen violence; he was a writing collaborator who took only one co-credit despite nurturing dozens of scripts; and he drew a formidable portrait of the American experience, yet never made a "message" picture, unless sympathy with, and hope for, the human condition counts as a message.

During his creative heyday in the 1970s—which is widely considered the last great era in American filmmaking—audiences and critics anticipated each new Arthur Penn film. Sometimes they were shocked (*Bonnie and Clyde*), charmed (*Alice's Restaurant*), seduced (*Little Big Man*), stunned (*Night Moves*), and baffled (*The Missouri Breaks*). But they were always challenged.

This book began as an exploration of Penn's creative process and the elements in his life that influenced it. I originally wanted his story to unfold in many voices until I realized that it was ultimately his voice that was clearest. I also worried that, if I didn't get his words on paper, no one else would have the chance. Sadly, I was right. I deeply thank those who spoke with me, forgive those who wouldn't (except for studios), and apologize to those whom I did not approach. I leave it to future scholars to deconstruct and analyze his work. Here I analyze the man.

In an effort to make this book readable, I occasionally edited quotes to reflect what a subject *meant* rather than what he or she may have *said*. This is what directors do when they choose the best moments from several takes to construct a scene, and I attempted no less. Completists will find full interview transcripts in the Margaret Herrick Library.

Finally, where people disagree on events, well, let's think of Truth as a destination, not an itinerary.

Acknowledgments

Although he was interviewed extensively throughout his career, Penn has never, I believe, been as forthcoming as in these pages. This book owes its existence to his openness, Peggy Penn's resolve, and the perseverance of my agent and friend, Agnes Birnbaum. The Penns' children, Molly and Matthew, have been unfailingly gracious. In addition to those who gave me their thoughts and quotes in interviews (on and off the record), I owe a great debt to Philip Porcella, who provided access to his early unpublished interviews with Arthur Penn, Dede Allen, and Robert Benton, which appear here for the first time. Philip got the ball rolling, and my colleagues Paul Cronin and Patrick Harrison helped it roll faster. Thanks as well to Elizabeth Adams, Shirin Amini, Liane Brandon, Claire Brandt, Donovan Brandt, Lauren Buisson, Beth Cannon, Lionel Chetwynd, Mary Cross, Christopher Darling, Dom and Carol DeLuise, Stephen Fleischman, Tenell George, Anna Maria Geraldino, Allan Glaser, William Goldman, Robert L. Goodman, Martin Gostanian, Robert Greenwald, Gary H. Grossman, Haden Guest, Barbara Hogenson, Carla Brooks Johnston, Philip Kleinbart, Alexander Kogan Jr. of Showcase Productions, Inc., Jon Krampner, Blake Lucas, J. V. Martin, Jenni Matz, Rick McKay, Myron Meisel, Callie O'Brien, Rochelle O'Gorman, James Robert Parish, Estelle Parsons, Harriet Sharp, Jorge Suárez, Allan Taylor, Marilyn Tessen, Katharine Vile, Ted Walch, Robb Weller, John Wildman, and Doris Wood.

Institutions providing important access include the Margaret Herrick Library at the Academy of Motion Picture Arts and Sciences Center for Advanced Film Study (Linda Harris Mehr, director; Barbara Hall, special collections archivist; Howard

Prouty, acquisitions archivist; Faye Thompson, photo archivist); the Archive of American Television at the Emmy Foundation of the Academy of Television Arts and Sciences; the Paley Center in Beverly Hills, California (formerly the Museum of Television and Radio); the UCLA Arts Library Special Collections; USC/Warner Bros. Archives; and the Museum of Broadcast Communication.

Writing is a lonely profession but that doesn't mean that it's done alone. The University Press of Kentucky is to be commended for their knowledgeable and aggressive presence in the field of published film history. Gratitude goes to Anne Dean Watkins, Melinda Wirkus, Ila McEntire, Richard Farkas (go Blue Devils!), John P. Hussey, Mack McCormick, and the people who work with them. Special thanks to Robin duBlanc for her editorial and diplomatic expertise and to Patrick McGilligan for a history of history.

The Micturating Mogul

Jack L. Warner had to pee. He didn't know he was watching the movie that would change movies. He just had to pee.

The picture was taking forever and it was only the first reel. It was in his private projection room, in his mansion, in his town that his vision and his tenacity had helped build. The filmmakers were sitting there with him, not that he cared. He just had to pee.

He'd warned everyone before the lights went down that if he had to leave for the bathroom during the screening, the picture was, as he branded it, "lousy."

Over at Columbia, Warner's rival Harry Cohn used to say his ass was his barometer ("If I squirm in my seat . . ."). But Cohn and his ass had died nine years ago, and Jack Warner's bladder, at seventy-five, was still going strong.

Too bad the picture wasn't; the boy was just meeting the girl and the bladder was already calling time-out. Several rows behind the legendary mogul, the film's director and producer sank into their seats, strategically avoiding his line of sight. A few of Warner's executives were also there in case he needed somebody to say Yes.

The picture began with two strikes against it. One, Warner didn't much care for the actor who played the male lead, even though he had already starred him in two films. The kid was a pain in the ass. Talented, bright, and handsome, sure, but he was one of those Method types who wanted to discuss everything.

Plus, he was also the film's producer; J. L. hated producers almost as much as he hated actors, and this kid was both.

Then there was the actress who played the girl. She was stunning, but her first two films had flopped, and nobody had ever heard of her anyway.

Not only that, their "meet cute" scene wasn't cute at all; it was some kind of artsy-fartsy symbolism where the girl was in heat and the boy came on to her by showing her a handgun like it was his dick. Warner—who could be blindingly vulgar in person—didn't want that kind of filth on the screen.

Warner would never have stood for this if he were still running his studio. But he wasn't. Oh, his name may have remained on the water tower that overlooked the Burbank lot, but Warner himself was now an echo. This screening was only a courtesy. Eight months earlier—in November of 1966—he had sold the place lock, stock, and water tower to Seven Arts Productions, a TV company—the enemy—after covert machinations contrived to cut his surviving brother, Albert, out of the deal. It brought J. L. $32 million from the sale of stock alone, not counting capital gains. But it also earned him the sickening status of "former mogul" and, with it, the stench of tolerance that Hollywood grants those whom it sees only in its rearview mirror. From the moment he signed the sale papers, Warner knew that he would be—as he groused to his son-in-law, Milton Sperling—"just another rich Jew." His star-making days were over. No longer would he inspire fear, only nauseating respect.

The filmmakers sweating in J. L.'s screening room showed their respect by bringing him the finished picture. *Finished,* as in rendering Warner superfluous, even though he was the one who had green-lighted it a year ago.

He went to the can three times before the picture ended. When the lights finally came up, the group retired to the library, where Warner wheeled on the filmmakers and asked, with his customary subtlety, "What the fuck was *that?*"

The director blanched and deferred to the producer, who turned up his actorly charm. "You see, Jack," he said, pretending to search for words he had carefully prepared, "you know what this really is? You know all those great gangster pictures that you and your brothers made in the past?" Warner listened cautiously. "Well, this is a kind of an *homage* to your body of work, to all those gangster pictures that were so extraordinary."

Warner weighed the compliment, then snarled, "What the fuck is an *homage*?"

The producer, Warren Beatty, smiled and left the room with studio operations manager Walter MacEwan, head of distribution Benny Kalmenson, and the other brass to haggle over the film's advertising budget and release pattern, leaving Warner alone with the film's forty-four-year-old director, Arthur Penn. The walls of his library boasted plaques, trophies, and other honors that he had received, by achievement or contrivance, over the decades. Lining the shelves were J. L.'s personal leather-bound copies of the scripts of all the Warner Bros. films, from 1918's *My Four Years in Germany*, whose grosses built the studio, to such milestones as *The Jazz Singer, Casablanca, A Star Is Born*, and the recent Oscar winner *My Fair Lady*.

Warner lit a cigar and blew its smoke toward the collection in a gesture of unmistakable pride. The diminutive Penn, struggling to make conversation with the combative Warner, could only summon a rote question: "Jack, of all the pictures you've made, which one is your favorite?"

The mogul's eyes turned to steel. "You're from the theater, right?" he asked Penn.

"Yeah."

"Come here. I'll show you."

Narrowing his eyes against the smoke, Warner reached between two titles and withdrew a thin pamphlet that didn't even have a binding. "*This* is my favorite," he said with a tinge of anger, not nostalgia.

It was *Girl of the Golden West*, a 1905 David Belasco potboiler about a young woman who gives herself to the town sheriff to save the life of her true love. Cecil B. DeMille had first filmed it in 1915, and in 1923 Jack Warner thought it would confer legitimacy on his new studio if he could acquire it. The cost was something his ego neither forgave nor forgot.

"You fuckin' bastards in the theater," he began, saddling Penn, a Broadway prodigy, with all the sins of Thespis. "When we were starting out, you guys wouldn't sell us any of these plays. *Any of them.* This—" he waved the pages in Penn's face— "belonged to David Belasco. I had to get down on my hands and knees to that cocksucker and *beg* him for it. *That's* how I got him to sell this to me." The mogul beamed at the memory of his ancient triumph. "*That's* the picture I'm most proud of."

As Warner gloated over long-conquered foes, his successors in the next room were waging a new fight: how to sell the public a film that its own studio hated (Kalmenson called it "a piece of shit") and thought would fail, and that they would ultimately try to destroy before it was rescued from the shelf in one of the most remarkable turnarounds in Hollywood history.

What none of them could know at the time was that the picture they were dismissing, *Bonnie and Clyde,* would not only become an international commercial success, but it would also revolutionize the American motion picture industry. It would change not only the art of film but also the way a burgeoning new generation of film-savvy audiences would review, attend, and appreciate motion pictures.

Especially those of Arthur Penn.

1

A Boy of Two Cities

Sonia Greenberg and Harry Penn had little in common before they got married and less by the time their sons were born.

Sonia had arrived as a teenager in New York with her older brother, Joseph, during the great wave of pogrom-inspired eastern European immigration early in the second decade of the twentieth century. But the Greenberg children were not fleeing Cossacks as much as seeking their father, who they thought had preceded them from Lithuania with vague plans of sending for them once he'd established himself. His summons never came, but his children did, not knowing that he had gone, not to America, but to the Warsaw ghetto, where he remarried and sired a second family.

In Lithuania—which was at the time under Russian domination—the paternal Greenberg had been an accountant. He was apparently a good one, for under the czar, no Jew could practice a profession without royal consent. But he was also an itinerant, and the family relocated time and again to follow his work. Often he would leave them behind; sometimes he would return to wherever they had last lived, and other times their mother would pack up Sonia and Joseph and pursue him to some new town. This last time he never returned, and his children, assuming he had sailed for America, left to find him, never to see their mother again.

Once in New York, Joseph, headstrong before and even more so in the land of opportunity, announced to Sonia that he was going to be married and went off to New Rochelle, consigning his sister to whatever survival devices she possessed. These turned out to be considerable: Sonia had blossomed into a bright, garrulous, and extremely attractive young woman who had no trouble drawing men. The problem was keeping them. Having thus been deserted twice by the males closest to her, she developed into a prickly combination of neediness and independence. Though she desperately wanted a man to love, respect, and support her, she simultaneously insulated herself against further abandonment by becoming self-reliant and manipulative.

She was also a prisoner of her intelligence. Smarter than the men she met in her blue-collar world (quite literally; she worked in a shirt factory), Sonia read widely, learned easily, and, had it not been for the chauvinism of the era, would have advanced far beyond her station. An opera devotee who could never afford to attend performances (but who learned the music from radio broadcasts), she was also an early proponent of health foods, a holistic interest that would lead her to seek work in the medical profession.

Sonia's future husband, Gregory Penn, emigrated from Lithuania on the same wave that carried the Greenbergs. A skilled watchmaker and engraver, Gregory—who, upon his arrival, changed his name to Harry for unspecified reasons—was as emotionally remote as Sonia was effusive. One of several males in a large Jewish family, he was apprenticed in the old country at age eight to a traveling watchmaker, and allowed only occasionally to return home. When he reached the age of military conscription, his parents sent him to live with another family that had only daughters as a ploy to avoid the army on the grounds that he was the sole heir to a family name. The scheme worked, but at the price of alienation from his own kin; the story is told that, during a visit to his birth family, Gregory/Harry got into a scrap with his actual siblings and complained to his mother, "Mother, your children are hitting me." These words of estrangement were so shattering that she burst into tears.

Arriving in New York, the newly minted Harry Penn found employment as a jeweler. It will never be known where or how this reticent craftsman met the ebullient Sonia, but the two of them married and moved to Plainfield, New Jersey. On June 16, 1917, their first son, Irving, was born.

By the time their second son, Arthur, arrived on September 27, 1922, the Penns had moved to Philadelphia; Harry had opened his own shop in Jewelers Row on Sansom Street, and the marriage was beginning to melt. When Arthur was three, they divorced, and Sonia returned to Plainfield with the boys.

"They were not compatible at every level, sexually or temperamentally," Arthur Penn recalls with a deep sigh. "My mother was a beautiful woman physically and I suspect that men figured in the divorce, though I don't know it for a fact. I know that, at some point, she took me by train to California to visit parts of her family who were living out there. And I think there was a gentleman. But again, I don't have any real memory of it. I was barely out of arms."

If divorce was unusual in 1925 America, Jewish divorce was even more so. Strictly speaking, Judaism does not recognize civil divorce; only a formal document called a *get* can dissolve what God has joined. But the Penns were not strict Jews, and Harry and Sonia Penn enjoyed the advantage of their Christian-sounding last name.[1]

Harry remained in Philadelphia while Sonia moved with Arthur and Irving to New York. Before the decade was over, the trio would move at least half a dozen more times. The peripatetic Penns didn't exactly live out of suitcases, but neither did they completely unpack the barrels of belongings that they carted from basement to basement on their residential tour of the city's boroughs. As the Great Depression gripped America, Arthur spent more and more time in the streets and, on one singular occasion when he was six, in a movie theater.

"It was just a film, not a horror film," he strains to recall, "but I just got scared." It so frightened the boy that he didn't venture back into the darkness of a movie house for years.

Her marriage over, Sonia sought absolution. Recalls Penn, "Throughout early childhood, my mother used to enlist me to be her co-victim. She would start weeping and I was supposed to weep with her about how my father was so uncaring, cruel, et cetera. That went on for a couple of years, and then I remember vividly the day when it started on one occasion and I thought, 'Wait a minute, I don't feel this way!' I just put the brakes on and stopped crying. I realized that there was an event going on inside the event: she wanted a partner in self-pity and grief."

Harry's business was not strong, and his marginal existence made it difficult, if not impossible, for him to send child support. This caused Sonia to resent him even more. There were occasions when she would place seven-year-old Arthur on the train from New York to Philadelphia, enlist an adult in the next seat to watch over him, and let Harry deal with the boy at the other end. Arthur felt like a stranger in his own father's apartment. Except for such visits, Sonia struggled to raise her sons alone.

"She was a lonely, rather beautiful woman who was filled with a certain kind of despair at having fallen in love with somebody else," Penn reflects generously. "It was a more noble life than I gave her credit for. It was the depth of the Depression. Her generation was largely immigrant, so they were carpenters and so forth. These men were illiterate or knew Yiddish but not English. I don't know why she never sought out men who were her intellectual equal. On the other hand, she just simply couldn't do it all. It's a sad story. But she did have the power to say, 'I want out of this marriage.'"

Sonia craved the financial independence that could come from owning a business. One attempt was a corset and stocking shop. Arthur would clerk the counter after school, but had to send for his mother when a female customer needed a fitting. Another was a food store in Plainfield that catered to what she hoped would be a growing awareness of the value of an organic diet. It, too, failed, but her interest in nutrition and health led her to success at the Good Samaritan Dispensary, a charity clinic. She was hired as a janitress, but her personality and demonstrable learning ability soon made her a nurse's assistant, in which position she was noticed by the head doctor, who took her as his assistant. This meant a $12 weekly stipend, a goodly Depression-era sum.

Wherever they lived, the Penns shared close living quarters.

The strain showed. When Irving was thirteen, he fell ill with rheumatic fever, and soon the tension of working, moving, and raising both boys became too much for Sonia to bear alone. When Irving recovered, he was sent to live with friends in Plainfield.

Despite their separation, Sonia and Harry were both concerned that their younger son was learning more in the streets than at school. Years of moving had denied him a continuity of friendships and, although the wiry and athletic boy had little trouble attracting new playmates at each venue, their character varied with the neighborhood. Gangs were the order of the day, and on Fox Street in the Bronx, they played a rough game. "They used to go down in the basement, take coal cinders out of the big furnaces, put them in a sock, and use that as a weapon," Penn remembers, cringing. "It wouldn't tear your head off, but it would tear the scalp. It was really dangerous."

When Arthur was ten and the Depression was at its worst, a solution of sorts knocked at Sonia's door. Professor and Mrs. Videll were evangelicals who had been run out of Spain for trying to convert Catholics to Protestantism. He was sixty and humorless; she was considerably younger and, Penn recalls, "was blonde, wore her hair in a crown of braids, and was really quite beautiful." The Vidells ran a camp in New Hampshire and were recruiting young people to spend the summer there. Sonia looked at Arthur and said, "Take him."

"It was a very painful experience and has probably left untold marks on me," Penn now says without a dram of sarcasm. "I stayed in barracks with the other kids but they wouldn't let me into the main house. I took my meals in the kitchen. At the end of the summer all the other kids went home, but my mother never sent for me."

Abandoned, he spent the next year absorbing the clean air and fresh food, but—pointedly—not his hosts' religion. "I have had no religious training in my life," he says. "I will tell you what I think is one of its most appealing aspects: it's one of the few areas of modern life that is genuinely theatrical. I like that impulse, and on finding it missing, I grieve for it. I have never held any religious beliefs."

The Videll gambit broadened Penn's horizons in other ways. They had brought with them from Spain a man named Eduadro whom they employed as their handyman, and it was he who fed young Arthur's burgeoning interest in sex. "Mrs. Videll would be cooking at the big iron wood-burning stove," Penn says, "and Eduadro would get behind her and go all the way down and look up her dress, and then would look across at me, and I had to keep from giving anything away." Decades later Mrs. Videll would find her screen counterpart in Louise Pendrake, the horny wife of the pompous preacher Silas Pendrake in *Little Big Man*.

By the time he was twelve, Arthur was recalled from the Vidells and sent to stay with Sonia's friends Fanny and Wally Plotkin in Bayonne, New Jersey. It was the Plotkins who ushered Arthur into his adolescence, including him in such grown-up rites as discussions, parties, and even joke-telling. A school-teacher, Fanny enrolled Arthur at her school and saw to it that he attended.

When he was fourteen, the Plotkins deposited him back with his mother. It was not a happy reunion. Sonia by then had moved to Brighton Beach and taken up with another carpenter, a man named Davidoff, who resented young Penn's presence. Davidoff, who was living on workmen's comp and Sonia's salary, per-suaded her to invest her savings in a candy store on Neptune Avenue in New Lots, the last stop on Brooklyn's elevated transit. The trio lived uneasily over the store until one morning Sonia found a stash of adult magazines that teenage Arthur had hid-den. In the fallout, Arthur was shipped off yet again, this time to live with his father and brother, whose influence, Sonia believed, would set Arthur back on course. Instead, it threw Harry and Irving into disarray.

Irving, while with Harry, had been progressing academically and professionally; he had distinguished himself at Olney High School, where he was one of the new institution's first gradu-ates, and won a scholarship to the Philadelphia Museum School of Industrial Art, where he studied under Alexi Brodovitch from 1934 to 1936. The two Penns had been living comfortably in a small apartment in a residential hotel. Arthur's arrival forced the trio to find larger quarters and hire a cook, an expansion that strained their finances.

"One of the terrible things that happens in a family like that is that it goes out of balance," Penn analyzes. "Here was Irving, this very good artist with all this adroitness who did very well in school, and here I was, not doing well in school and with no discernable talent. So my father, in classic European view, thought, 'He should have a trade to fall back on.'"

That trade was watchmaking, and fourteen-year-old Arthur joined Harry in his Sansom Street shop. The teenager accepted his fate and made the effort to at last get to know his father. He found him "a gentleman, an autodidact—but of high literary taste—and, interestingly enough, an ethical culturalist."[2] But he continued to find him emotionally remote. "I wish I'd known him better," Penn laments. "He was rather a mystery to me. Not an emotionally available man at all. I really know less about him than I should."

More to his liking was the joy of bonding with his brother. "We've always been very close and fond of each other and respectful of each other's work," he appraises. "Indeed, more than respectful. Admiring."

Arthur's apprenticeship was not a success. Although Harry's skills were widely respected, Arthur's were not, and he still needed to finish his formal schooling, an uphill march. He made it through Jay Cooke Junior High, but when he tried to enter Olney High School he discovered that his latest change of address removed him from the school's enrollment jurisdiction. The Penns' new apartment was in the jewelry district in Center City; Olney High was in North Philly. To solve the problem, Arthur used the address of family friends named Nissenbaum who lived in North Philadelphia. With the Penns at Eighth and Pine, it meant that Arthur had to travel from the center of the city to its outskirts every day.

Though he essentially had no neighborhood, a tiny glimmer of belonging soon presented itself through the efforts of Arthur's French teacher. Impressed with the teenager's clear, rich voice, she asked him to shout a few offstage lines for a play she was presenting. Waiting backstage for his cue, he became entranced by the workings of scenery, curtains, and other theatrical accoutrements. When he spoke, his vocal delivery drew the attention of a producer from WCAU radio who was casting a local knock-off of *The March of Time* news broadcasts. WCAU paid him a few needed dollars to impersonate Hitler, Stalin, and other figures in dramatized newscasts and exposed him to the discipline of show business.

An even greater influence was the Neighborhood Playhouse.[3] A combination school, performance center, and settlement, it became Arthur's second home and its denizens his adoptive family. One day it was announced that there was to be a directing contest. Surprisingly, he had no interest in entering. Then he happened to hear an Arch Oboler radio broadcast that gripped him enough to want to adapt and direct it himself. As he worked on the project, all the elements he had been absorbing backstage came together, and he won the competition.

The exigencies of day-to-day survival took precedence, however, and Arthur returned to the Sansom Street shop, where Harry's dismay at his son's inability to learn watchmaking devolved into chilly indifference. Feeling this, Arthur spent as much time as possible with his older—and by now quite independent—brother. "Irving taught me everything," Arthur muses. "He taught me not to spit on the street (what did I know? I was a street kid; it's what you did). At that time, he was going with a terrific woman named Nonny,[4] whom he would later marry, who sort of took me under her wing." Nonny had studied costume design at England's historic Dartington Hall and insisted on bringing Arthur to museums where modern art was making its controversial debut. "It was nuts to me," Penn now blushes, adding, "I was just sixteen." With Irving and Nonny living together, it allowed Arthur to avoid his father, preferring his brother and Nonny's Bohemian crowd.

"I was sort of funny and saucy and snotty," he remembers, "but not with them. It was a nice experience to suddenly be in a kind of community, albeit that they were five or six years older than I was." Together they explored the rapidly changing

American creative scene, including WPA [Works Progress Administration] productions of *One Third of a Nation* and the cautionary anti-venereal disease play *Spirochete*. Seeing theater at professional levels further nudged Arthur in that direction.

It was while in Irving and Nonny's thrall that Arthur had his first girlfriend. "She was a woman I'd met through one of their friends," he says distantly. "She was older than I was, and we had my first real sexual encounter. She got pregnant. 'Don't worry about it,' she said, 'I'll take care of it.' She did."

Then Harry got cancer. It was Nonny who knew it first, even though Arthur was living with him. "She went to the doctor without my father," Penn reports. "She was a wonderful take-charge woman, and eventually that's what ended their marriage. But she was a blessing as far as I was concerned because I had no education of any kind and she really helped me."

The diagnosis was bladder cancer, a malady with a particularly unforgiving prognosis. Harry was not told, and neither was Irving. "Because Irving had been sick with rheumatic fever," Penn analyzes, "the myth in the family was that he had to be protected from bad news. She told me but she didn't tell Irving, and she certainly didn't tell my father. But he knew he had *something*."

No longer able to work, Harry stayed at home, tended by Arthur. Satisfied that Harry was in good hands, Nonny and Irving went off to live in Mexico. Confined to the apartment, Harry took up painting and evinced a distinct talent that Arthur describes as "Jewish-American-Lithuanian primitive" but remarkably accomplished.

Eventually his father had to be hospitalized, forcing Arthur to make a circuit almost daily from failing school to failing the jewelry shop to failing his father. Then Harry became verbally abusive. "The abuse was directed at me," Penn says, "because I was dissembling and acting as if nothing serious was going on with him. I would come bouncing into his hospital room, which led to him one day saying to me, 'What the hell are you doing, you look like a fairy.'"

"The bladder cancer induced a kind of uremic poisoning which affects the brain," Penn later learned. "My father decided that I was taking money. It was extremely painful to go up to see him, because when he asked, 'how much this week?' it would be a pittance. He didn't know I had sold the furniture. I had to give up the apartment and move into a furnished room, and my father was getting worse and worse, and we're getting more and more distant. Finally, one day, he took my hand and said, 'I'm so afraid, I'm so afraid.' It was the only time I'd held his hand or seen him weep. It was the first time I'd seen *any* demonstration of feeling toward me."[5]

Next Harry was taken in by the Nissenbaums, whose household staff could look after the dying man. In the summer of 1942 he died, and Irving and Nonny were called back from Mexico. Only after he was gone and cremated did Sonia deign to see her sons again. It was a frigid reunion. According to Penn, she still expected them to take her side long after the divorce. Neither boy would give her that satisfaction. Later, in private, the brothers discussed their father, at which time Arthur said, "I really have to confess, I didn't like that man."

Agreed Irving, "I didn't, either."

When Harry's will was read there were few assets, but he did make a provision for his paintings. Except for one of Arthur's choosing, he left them all to Irving. At first Irving talked about giving his late father a show. "But as that discussion took place," Arthur says, "I detected a real reluctance in Irving to have a show for my father. He was enthusiastic but restrained. My view of it is that he was seeing his own sophistication measured against the naiveté of my father's work. Here was Irving getting increasingly exact while my father had amusing street scenes, baseball, et cetera. And to this day the paintings are in a vault."

It was a dark time for the Penn boys, not only because they had effectively lost both parents but also because their world was plunging into war. "If you were a certain age and healthy, it was inevitable that you were going to go," Penn says. Being both, Penn bided his time at the Neighborhood Playhouse while waiting to be called up for service. His father's will had specified that he be cared for by legal guardians in New York, and one of them, Irene Rose, encouraged his stage pursuits by billeting him around New York City with her theatrical friends, one of whom was Canada Lee, who opened his Harlem home to the precocious youth.

Work was hard to find in prewar New York. "I was a liability," he says. "I was 1-A and knew I was going in, so you can't get a job because who's going to hire you?" He changed his draft locale from Philadelphia to New York and awaited his fate in the company of three friends who shared his interest in theater. "I came to New York with Kathy Cunningham, Shirley Grayson, and Vito Christi," he says. "Kathy and Shirley, two beautiful women, can't get a job [acting]. Vito walks in and gets a part [in *Pickup Girl*]. Vito knew he was not going to be drafted. The tragedy was that he went nuts later, totally schizophrenic. He opened and ran with the show, and that was the last I saw of him until I was successful in television, and then he arrived saying, 'I need money.'"

When Penn's inevitable draft notice arrived, he reported for induction and was sent first to Fort Dix, New Jersey, then to Fort Jackson in South Carolina, and then to the European theater. What awaited him was another kind of theater.

2

The Theater of War

By the time he was drafted, Arthur Penn had decided that theater would be his future if Hitler allowed him to have one. World War II held everything at bay. America's "Arsenal of Democracy," which scrambled to arm itself after Pearl Harbor, was far from victory when twenty-year-old Private Penn reported for induction at Fort Dix, New Jersey, in early January of 1943. News reports from the battle lines were gloomy, and word quickly spread among the recruits that they were being groomed as "replacements"—"repos"—army slang for GIs who would be shipped to the front lines to replenish fallen troops.

After being sworn in at Dix, Penn was shipped for basic training to Fort Jackson, South Carolina where, predictably, he was marked for the infantry. He and his fellow troops were trained for a year, unaware that they were headed for the D-Day invasion, which was being planned in secret. It was while on a pass from the base that he encountered a slightly older man who, three years earlier, had decided to postpone his graduate studies at Yale to take over the Town Theatre in nearby Columbia. As codirector of the playhouse, Fred Coe and his wife, Alice, not only mounted seven shows a season, but they also became surrogate parents to many of the enlisted men who served as actors, stagehands, painters, and whatever else the shoestring operation might need. Called the Fort Boys, these young men—all of them poised to be shipped abroad to combat—were accorded their own upstairs lounge in the Sumter Street structure.

Coe was an easy man to respect but a hard man to know. Born in 1914 in Alligator, Mississippi, not far from the Arkansas border, he embodied a combination of southern courtliness and agrarian work ethic, simultaneously smooth and coarse. He had no trouble reconciling the two temperaments, but others did, especially when alcohol fueled his flinty temper. According to his biographer,[1] Coe didn't talk until he was two, developed a heart murmur from rheumatic fever, and had colitis. Raised by his widowed mother in a household of uncertain security, he was a mediocre student who, by the time he went to Yale Drama School, was torn between a career in teaching and one in stage directing. He would succeed mightily in both as a producer of genius who would mentor an entire industry. Not surprisingly, the fatherless Penn became one of the Coes' most devoted Fort Boys, working at the theater on the infrequent occasions when he had a pass. "Whenever anybody would get a three-day pass, you'd go to Columbia," Penn says. "The streets were filled with soldiers either vomiting or trying to get laid. At least Fred's theatre was sensible and you could talk to people. I got to know Fred. Fred was very generous; he and Alice would open the house where they lived, and we'd sleep stacked in corners. Of course, there were also women whose husbands were overseas . . ."

As nurturing as Coe was, he could also be mercilessly demanding and colorfully mercurial. The story is told about a performance of *My Sister Eileen* at the Town. Ten minutes into the first act, Coe ran down the aisle, frothing at the mouth and yelling, "That was the *worst* thing I've ever seen! That can absolutely *not* be done in front of these people in that manner. I won't *have* it!" He then ordered the company to start the play over from the beginning. "It seemed to me, at that time, a piece of wild nuttiness, but wonderful," Penn says wistfully. "Years later I realized that Fred Coe was fearless in behalf of the art. He taught us all a great deal."

Before he finished basic training, Penn's aptitude test scores caught up with him. The same Arthur Penn who had barely graduated Olney High School was discovered to have performed exceptionally well on the army's intelligence exam. The brass were so impressed that they pressured him to join their ranks. He resisted. "They kept saying to me, 'We want you to go to officers' training school.' I said, 'Not while I'm in the infantry.' I wanted to be in the Army Air Corps. It was clear you'd get your ass shot off by being first guy over the top. They tried a lot of ways, and I wouldn't respond. I got to the point where I was sent up to Staten Island, given all my shots, supposed to go over as an infantry replacement, then got orders to report to Texas."

Fort Sam Houston, to be precise, where the Fifteenth Army was just being assembled. What rescued Penn was that, with military logic, somebody saw the word *theater* on his induction papers and seconded him to a newly formed unit that was to create entertainment for the soldiers. With those orders, he was sent to Europe in the company of a major who was in charge but thoroughly adrift on stage as well as in battle. "I was the guy who knew what *he* should have known," says Penn charitably. "He was an interesting guy but didn't know from diddly. The big problem was, there were two of us from the infantry, and when the Battle of the Bulge hit, we were in the King's Hunting Lodge in the Ardennes Forest. That's where this Fifteenth Army was put. And *boom!* come the Germans."

It was the winter of 1944–45, one of the fiercest on record, and a hunting lodge was no place to fire up a furnace if one wanted to stay hidden from the German Army. While waiting for orders to evacuate, Penn and his party found themselves in the Nazis' path. "The Germans, fortunately, were not gonna stop for any little nonsense of this size," he continues. "They were heading to Antwerp so they would have a port on the North Sea and be able to swing into Belgium and recapture Paris and own Europe again. Finally, the word came: 'Get out of there.' So we zoomed out, this whole group. We get, I don't know, twenty miles away, and we discover that we had left behind a Spanish couple who were the housekeepers. We were dubious about whether they were fascists, but had left some papers about the Fifteenth Army. We wanted some volunteers to go back. No volunteers. So: 'Penn!'

"'Yes?'

"'Go back.'

"So we went back again—the major, the sergeant, and I—choosing back roads, ever wary of the German armor still roaring by. We got to the place. They went inside to get the couple and all the papers that had been left behind, leaving me on a sort of guard duty. While I was there I thought, 'Why not hitch a trailer to our jeep and load the stuff in there, plus whatever baggage the couple would have?' I was at the side of the building doing the hitching when around the corner comes the major with his pistol drawn. He was scared, thinking that I was gone, and when he saw me he said, 'Don't ever go away like that again,' as if we would be back in the morning! We herded the two Spanish servants into the command car with the major. The sergeant and I got into the jeep and we started the evening drive back toward Brussels."

The 106th, Penn's initial assignment, took profound casualties in the Bulge; two of its three regiments were forced to surrender to the Germans while, overall, some seventy-seven thousand Allied soldiers were killed, wounded, or captured before they rebuffed Hitler's attempt to seize Antwerp. During the campaign, Penn and the major took the suspect Spanish couple to Brussels, where G-2 headquarters had commandeered the Hôtel des Colonies. "It was full of journalists," Penn recalls. "We came in with full arms and loaded weapons and they started running for the typewriters. Jump ahead: years later I finish *The Left Handed Gun* and I'm in New York doing *Two for the Seesaw.* I hear from the Belgian film critics that I have won the award for Best First Picture. I couldn't believe it. Then they started sending me articles by André Bazin and others from *Cahiers du cinéma* about *Le gaucher* [*The Left-Hander*]. I thought, 'This is weird,' because Warner's dumped it at the bottom half of a double bill with no advertising. They didn't think Paul Newman had a future. But all of a sudden this takes off. It was the first time that Belgian film critics decided that they would award this prize, and we got it. So Peggy [Mrs. Arthur Penn] and I go to Brussels and we go into the hotel where they were putting us up and it's the Hôtel des Colonies! My jaw dropped."

The war in Europe had ended, but the war in the Pacific had not. Allied military discipline in liberated Europe began to crumble to the extent that MPs were picking up more drunken GIs than surrendering Nazis. In response, the War Department revived a program of Soldiers' Shows designed to keep the occupying troops, well, occupied. Because of his theatrical background, which still barely existed, Penn was assigned in 1944 to the Soldiers' Shows unit. "The incoming army of occupation should not be playing around with *fräuleins*," he was instructed. As part of the program, Penn was transferred from Germany to Saint-Cyr-le-Chatoux, not far from Paris, with orders to report to the Hotel Lancaster and present his papers to the captain in charge. The captain turned out to be Alan Campbell, the husband of famed writer and wit Dorothy Parker.

"Alan was having an early morning gin and bitters," Penn recalls, "and when I reported to him, he said, 'You want one?' I said, 'No, thanks.' He pointed to a safety pin that was holding my jacket together and said, 'What's that on your jacket?' I said, 'A safety pin, sir.' He said, 'I've *seen* them before; what's it *doing?*' I said, 'I never had a chance to fix it; we were moving.' We got to be quite chatty."

As a bright man floating in a sea of mundanity, Campbell appreciated Penn's insouciance as much as the gin. He introduced him to an old friend with whom he had enlisted, stage director Josh Logan. "Of course it was '*Captain* Logan,'" Penn adds dryly. "He was still very much army, but it relaxed at a certain point. I started looking around and there were Mickey Rooney, Bobby Breen, Billy Hallop, as well as a lot of actors on the margin that I'd seen in movies, plus a lot of other people, including Paddy Chayefsky.[2] There were writers and there were movie stars, but the main thing was that they brought over a hundred American actresses to be in the shows."

French theater was just emerging from Nazi shadows, Théâtre-Libre[3] was being reborn, and such shows were being performed as *La folle de Chaillot* with Louis Jouvet, and Albert Camus's adaptation of *Caligula* with Gérard Philipe. In the midst of this renaissance, Logan and Campbell rented a Parisian pied-à-terre and, on several occasions, let Penn and Chayefsky have the prized key. "We did our socks in the bidet," Penn says. "I had a pencil-scribbled pass from Captain Alan Campbell, and don't you know, I get stopped on the street by one of those pricky MPs because it wasn't typed out and signed in ink, and I got put in jail in a dungeon in the Paris Opera! The smell of piss was serious. They let me out at two or three in the morning."

Soldiers' Shows took Penn to Cologne, Duren, Wiesbaden, Hamburg, Frankfurt, Stuttgart, and Aachen, finally depositing him in the village of Baden-Neubauer, a German bath spa. When the war ended in August of 1945, Penn got a pass (typed this time) and went back to Paris. As those around him started returning home to the States, he was struck by the unsettling fact that he had no home to return to. "Going back to New York didn't make any sense to me," he reasons. "I wanted to go to college, but I didn't have a dime. So when the army offered me a job as a civilian, I was delighted to take it." Penn applied for discharge the day it was offered, filed his papers in Heidelberg, and was handed the army's entertainment unit, headquartered in the Wiesbaden opera house. "I knew better than they did how to get a show on," he smiles, "to say nothing of the women. Everybody left in a flash, and I was running things without any supervision, plus I was getting a check from the U.S. government."

For the next year he traveled throughout Europe on government planes and jeeps with a government stipend, supervising the far-flung Soldiers' Show companies. For material, he confesses, "we ripped off New York musicals. We'd make up a story that we could use that was partly their story, but we weren't paying royalties or anything like that. We did *On the Town*. I started them on straight dramas and comedies, and then I would come back, because I was traveling around." As an American he could go anywhere, including Nuremberg. "I was at the Nuremberg trial," he recalls, still in awe. "How can you be in Nuremberg and *not* go to the trial? But who do I have to know to get in? Well, it was a snap. I just got in. There was some minimal credentialing, but there was nothing to it."

In an effort to show the world that their victory was an

example not only of military might but of moral rectitude, the Allied forces convened tribunals in the town where Hitler had held his triumphant Sixth Party Conference in 1934. Now the triumph belonged to America, Britain, and Russia, which tried the Third Reich's surviving ringleaders for crimes against humanity.[4] "They were sitting on two benches, right there," Penn describes. "Fat little Hermann Göring was now skinny with flesh dangling. It was really quite something. I was there for two or three days. I watched the testimony of Baldur von Schirach who was the head of the Hitler Youth. The attorneys were Telford Taylor, the leading American attorney; then the British and the French and the Russians. Everything had to be done in four languages so the pace, naturally, was very different.

"It was a rather smallish room, but I wouldn't think there were more than a couple of hundred spectators. And then there were the ranks of the attorneys a little bit over to the side. There were prevailing justices and the defendants. It was amazing.[5]

"Germany was very strange that first year right after the war because nobody knew who was a Nazi, nobody would trust nobody, nothing. But with this group there was no question about who was a Nazi. That was the absolute heart of the Nazi Party. I was staring right into it."

Back in America, Penn's family was falling into disarray. Irving had, because of his heart, been rejected by the army, so he joined the American Field Service and drove an ambulance in North Africa and Italy. Returning to New York, he resumed his ascension to becoming America's premiere fashion/designer photographer with innovative work for *Vogue* magazine. By this time, he and Nonny were no longer together. In fact, she had disappeared. "You have to put it in the war environment," Arthur explains. "Nonny wanted to have a baby. Irving was determined to get into the war. When he returned, Nonny had left. No forwarding address or anything."

As for Sonia, for nearly ten years she maintained contact with her younger son by letter, asking in one of them if she could move in with him. By then he was married to Peggy Maurer, had children, and knew it would be disastrous if his mother were to live under his roof. He arranged for her care in a nursing home but insists that he doesn't know what happened to her after that, not even when she died. "I don't really keep records of that," he says dismissively. But then he remembers. "Peggy and I were in Stockbridge," he says, his mind searching into an inner past. "I was in the barn working on the tractor when Peggy came in and told me she died. Surprisingly, I found tears in my eyes."

3

The Teachable Moment

Unlike mainstream colleges, the GI Bill of Rights recognized the experimental curricula that John Andrew Rice and Theodore Dreier established at Black Mountain College, fifteen miles east of Asheville, North Carolina, on Black Mountain, and paid for Arthur Penn to go there.

Founded in 1933 at the nadir of the Depression and born of rebellion (Rice and Dreier had left Florida's Rollins College without looking back), Black Mountain College welcomed the disenfranchised. Before its doors closed twenty-three years later, the school had attracted and nurtured an array of iconoclasts who would challenge, change, and inspire the world for the rest of the century.

"It was a very little school," explains Penn, who attended Black Mountain on returning stateside in 1947. "It was not accredited, you didn't have classes, it was a sort of Socratic atmosphere of, at maximum, maybe 150 faculty and students. It was a very barebones, threadbare place with no endowment. The great, great good fortune that happened during my period there was that the Bauhaus had been obliterated by the Nazis and a few people from the Bauhaus came to the States."

Hitler's loss was America's gain. Alas, U.S. immigration policy, then as now, was to reject lumpen huddled masses in favor of selected émigrés, and artists, scholars, and scientists (unless they knew rockets or atoms) were told that they were welcome but their credentials were not. Denied positions at America's

24

colleges, several Bauhaus artists gravitated to Black Mountain College.

"What happened was that it became *the* place," Penn continues, recalling the excitement of being a member of the group that was there when history happened. "Here's this little place down there, and somebody had the genius to say, 'Now look, Mr. Gropius, we'll give you a house, small salary, food, and insurance; will you come?' Gropius came. Albers came. Now these two giants are down there, and the word begins to spread among the unconventional people, and we start to get John Cage, Merce Cunningham, Bucky Fuller, Willem de Kooning, Alfred Kazin, Isaac Rosenfeld, and the top literary guys. It was a hotbed; it was so alive."

By the time Penn enrolled, the school had settled into its Lake Eden campus, which had opened in 1941. "It was a commune," Penn avers. "We lived together, we ate together at a common dining room. Everybody had a study built out over the lake, designed by Gropius. You didn't have a private room, but you had a small place that nobody else could come into without invitation."

Consistent with Rice and Dreier's philosophy of educating the whole student—mind, body, and spirit—there were no formal classes. Instead, it was a voyage of mutual discovery: "The classes were, 'Hey, what do you know about Russian literature? You want to read some together? Let's read some together.'" Since accreditation wasn't a factor, neither were grades, although marks were contrived for official transcript purposes. "You did what you did because you were curious," Penn says. "It was wonderful. I was so damn uneducated that I sort of self-taught myself. I'd done some reading when I was in the army, but I didn't know anything; it was all *The Book of Knowledge.*[1] I really didn't know what relationship Dostoevsky had to Tolstoy and what they both had to the French writers, any of that. So I said to M. C. Richards, who was a wonderful teacher, 'What should I do first?' She said, 'You should learn to read. Let's read together.' That was it. I'd read, and she'd ask, 'What was this book about?' and I would tell the narrative, and she said, 'No, no . . . ' and we would explore its full meaning.

"We were this funny group. Most of us were GIs, mostly on the GI Bill. But the atmosphere was such that you could walk in and go to Albers and ask, 'Why the hell did you have to go to Mexico to paint three rectangles?'"

It might be said that Josef Albers personified the Black Mountain College experience. A student at Bauhaus and a protégé of Klee, Kandinsky, Mies van der Rohe, and Gropius, Albers is most noted for his paintings of color and shape, primarily as represented by the geometric form of the square. The first Bauhaus graduate to be asked to teach at the school, he began exploring new media at Black Mountain. "Albers was talking about the power of certain colors,[2] and as an example, he opened up a can of tomato juice and left it outdoors until it was quite rancid," Penn describes. "Then he pierced it, and inside was this spectacular green mold and the fierce red of tomato juice burst through, demonstrating the power of the interaction of color. This happened in one particular class of his, but it stuck in my mind."

While America at large was settling into postwar conformity, the mood at Black Mountain was exuberantly revolutionary. Composer John Cage was exploring the avant-garde, although he had not yet begun writing his famous silent compositions. Instead, he was planning a free-form experience for which everyone in the room had the best seat for the performance because each of them *was* the performance; in 1952 it was the first "happening." Merce Cunningham formed his first dance company and developed the demanding yet exhilarating physical vocabulary that would distinguish his choreography. Painter/collagist Robert Rauschenberg began his transition from abstract impressionism to "pop." And an introverted, eccentric inventor named R. Buckminster Fuller emerged from his own shell to create another kind of shell: his first geodesic dome. "It was built out of Venetian blind slats," reports Penn, who watched Fuller and his students struggle to put it together in the school's lakeside yard. "Then it collapsed, as Fuller knew it would."

With so much freedom and such affection for the arts, it's no surprise that Penn's fellow students, on hearing of his background in the Soldiers' Shows, asked him to help them put on plays. His protestations that he didn't know how to direct fell on deaf ears, and so, in keeping with the school's ethic, he learned by doing. He told everyone to get a copy of Konstantin Stanislavski's *An Actor Prepares* and they would all read it together. When the date arrived, he says, "half the school showed up," all of them wanting to be actors. "We did exercises from the book. I would do exercises in tension and relaxation, stuff that we would then spin off from. Then, of course, as always happens, somebody finally said, 'We gotta actually *do* the play.'"

That led to *The Ruse of Medusa* (*Le piège de Méduse*), written by composer Erik Satie in 1913. John Cage was obsessed with it from the moment he arrived at the school in 1948 and prevailed upon M. C. Richards to translate Satie's French text into English. He persuaded Willem and Elaine de Kooning to create sets, and Elaine to play Frisette, Baron Medusa's daughter; Merce Cunningham to play the "costly mechanical monkey"; and the entire school to tolerate his constant playing of Satie's repertoire right up to the performance date. Finally, he unaccountably cast the diminutive, bespectacled Fuller as Medusa and asked student Helen Livingston to direct. Recalls Penn, "Buckminster Fuller, at that point, was shy, withdrawn, and not comfortable in public. Nobody who heard him lecture since then can believe that,[3] but it was true. He was terrified, absolutely terrified."

The troupe rehearsed in the dining hall. When Livingston was unable to coax Fuller into emoting, Cage begged Penn to help. "I realized what the nature of his self-consciousness was," Penn remembers, "which is [that] he kept looking at himself from the outside, and he had nothing that was really engaging him in the play except waiting for cues and waiting for lines. You know, all the things that all early actors experience, but for him it was a totally alien setting with John and Merce carrying on.[4] I realized that there was no hope of just talking him through it, so I said, 'Let's start doing it.' We got down on the floor and I'd roll over, and Bucky'd roll over. I'd start laughing, and he'd start laughing. It was phony laughter, but pretty soon it began to have a life of its own. We rolled around to the point where [his] inhibition began to fall. That was it. He got up and started laughing by himself instead of imitating me."

It was an example of what Fuller and Penn would call "the teachable moment"—that instant when the pieces come together and something that was previously unknowable suddenly makes sense. It also broke Fuller's public speaking logjam, a distinction that came back to haunt Penn in light of Bucky's later legendary four-, five-, and six-hour lectures. "People say to me, 'You started that? *You started that?* Tell him to shut up!'"

By the 1950s, conventional schools finally awoke to the innovation that was taking place at Black Mountain. Harvard bravely invited Gropius to be its dean of art and architecture. Josef Albers received a teaching post at Yale along with his brilliant weaver/wife, Annie. Fuller became a professor at Southern Illinois University in Carbondale, when he wasn't making four hundred speeches a year and amassing forty-eight honorary degrees.

Even aside from its talent being poached, though, Black Mountain was feeling a crunch. Its community of contemplative scholars knew little about how to keep the school's head above the financial waters. Unable to attract investors, its board of directors instructed then-rector Charles Olson to close the school in 1956. One year later Black Mountain College stopped making history and became a part of it.

Penn had left in 1949. Footloose and twenty-seven, with two years remaining on his GI Bill benefits, he went to Italy, where he studied the language. "I wanted to read Dante in the Italian because T. S. Eliot had said how meaningful and great it was," he says. He was living on the remnants of his army pay and the occasional stipend from Irving, who was by this time established in his career. Moreover, "everything was cheap, really cheap. I wasn't living well, but I was living."

He landed at Naples, bought a third-class train ticket to Rome, then went to Perugia, where he enrolled in the university. Needing housing, he was shown to a group of *pensiones*. "I went to one run by four maiden sisters," he says, "daughters of a former military officer of not a very high grade. They were like the women you read about in those wonderful European novels: their life was already determined by their father's status, they were not marriageable, so they chose an excess of religion, although they weren't of the cloth. They opened their house to students. In this pensione it was all just Italians and 'Arturo.'"

He stayed in Perugia for a year trying to read Dante, then went to the University of Florence. "Florence, in the winter, no matter what anybody tells you, is the coldest fucking place in the world," he warns. "The floors are marble or terrazzo, there's no heating, and you never get warm. It got so cold that my best Italian friend, who was a travel agent, said, 'Go to Austria. They've got it all. They've got ski lifts. They've got coal.' He booked me to Austria and got me a room over a bakery. In the morning I would get a basket of rolls. It was ironic: from rather impoverished Italy, where people were still hurting, to Austria, where they've got the Marshall Plan. I would ski, I would read Dante, I would have this marvelous breakfast of wonderful coffee and fresh-baked rolls, all on seventy-five bucks a month army pay."

In the spring of 1950 the money ran out, and Penn took a boat to New York City, choosing finally to call it home. He found an apartment on Cornelia Street in Greenwich Village for $16 a month and began looking for work. At first he tried to gain employment as a stage manager in one of the city's many live theaters, but nothing was available. Instead, following rumors of job openings, he found his way to 30 Rockefeller Plaza and was excited to be hired as a stage manager at NBC television. It wasn't the job that excited him, though. It was the fact that it paid $80 a week. It was only the beginning.

4

Up at Eight, Off at Nine

When he stepped off the elevator at 30 Rock in the spring of 1950, Arthur Penn wasn't looking for a career, just a job. "I came back thinking, 'What do I know how to do?'" he mulls. "I can fake reading Dante and I can stage manage. But it was my history of having run the Soldiers' Show program for the army that got me swiftly hired."

Instead of live theater, he started in live TV.

Modern television began, not with an explosion, but with a test pattern. Although visual transmission existed experimentally, it made its public debut at the 1939 New York World's Fair when NBC televised the opening ceremonies to the hundred or so experimental receivers that were placed around Flushing Meadow. Commercial broadcasts, such as they were, took hold by the end of the 1940s. Few advertisers initially saw the potential. At the time there were barely seven thousand receivers in use, they were expensive, and there were no technical standards. Besides, 50 million radio sets, in 80 percent of American homes, still dominated. The spread of television was further hampered by World War II, when electronics factories were ordered to produce parts for the military, not civilians. War's end brought a revitalized economy, and by October of 1946 the Television Broadcasters Association, a trade group, declared that its medium was once again ready to deliver a commercial message.

The nation's topography and its four time zones, however, posed an obstacle. Unlike AM radio, whose signals could be recorded by transcription, TV had to rely on clumsy film kin-escopes shot off monitors in New York and shipped west for delayed broadcast.

Differences in audiences were even more profound. Initially, broadcasting and advertising executives saw television viewers as separate from radio audiences, whom they had long since written off as imbeciles. The first TV sets were expensive ($200 to $600, a month's wages), so it was presumed that those who could afford to buy them were better paid, better educated, and better bred, so there was a greater interest in appealing to these upscale viewers. This, many believe, is what gave birth to the "golden age" of television dramas.

But there was also room for Milton Berle. General David Sarnoff may have been president of the National Broadcasting Company, but Milton Berle was its king. Equally at home in women's clothing or with other people's material (he was affec-tionately called "the Thief of Bad Gags"), "Uncle Miltie" would do anything for a laugh. He also knew what he was worth: when NBC wanted to sign him to an exclusive contract in 1951, he demanded one that ran thirty years and paid him $100,000 annually whether he performed or not. Despite his success, Berle was an insecure and competitive entertainer with a need to upstage his guest stars and abuse those who served him. When NBC saw that Penn exuded the self-confidence that could tame Uncle Miltie, it hired him on the spot.

"My first day at work, I got the job holding cue cards for Milton Berle," Penn says, adding, "Comics are like thorough-breds. You have to calm them and cool them before they go on. So I started talking to him. 'Listen,' I'd say, 'you're about the fun-niest guy I've ever met. You're going to be wonderful tonight.' When they saw that I could survive Uncle Miltie, they switched me to *The Colgate Comedy Hour.*"

Colgate debuted on September 10, 1950. It originated from the Colonial Theatre, a former New York legit house that NBC bought. It had rotating hosts and shifted its personality each week to accommodate them: the droll and acerbic Fred Allen, the energetic Bobby Clark (whose trademark was painted-on eyeglasses), and Eddie "Banjo Eyes" Cantor. Other hosts in subsequent seasons (the series ran until 1955) would include Abbott & Costello, bandleader Spike Jones, hoofer Donald O'Connor, Bob Hope, Jimmy Durante, and Gordon MacRae.

Despite its seasoned lineup, *Colgate* might have become just another variety show if its second installment hadn't featured a pair of brash new kids who were knocking them dead at New York's Copacabana nightclub on Thirty-fourth Street: Dean Martin and Jerry Lewis. "Pat Weaver was the head of NBC Programming," Jerry Lewis explained, "and Pat Weaver had a great idea. He talked to us about doing a weekly show, and I turned it down and said no. We're going to get burned out with a weekly show; I won't do that. Well, the interesting thing is, he got the same response from Abbott & Costello and Eddie Cantor. So his idea was, 'I'll tell you what. Here's what we'll do: we'll put you on every six weeks. You'll do eight shows in the season and you'll do it with Abbott & Costello, Eddie Cantor, Donald O'Connor, Ed Wynn . . . ' and that's how *The Colgate Comedy Hour* started."[1]

Dean and Jerry's debut was Sunday, September 17, 1950, on NBC, opposite the indestructible Ed Sullivan on CBS. They caused a sensation. "I had never heard of Dean Martin and Jerry Lewis until I was assigned to the show," Penn admits, "and I thought, 'These two snot-noses from the Copacabana. I couldn't care less!' But after the rehearsal, the next thing I knew was that I was sitting on the floor trying to recover my breath."

"It's hard to remember a time when, the next day, that part of America that had seen the show would be talking about it to the part of America that hadn't seen it," recalls producer Norman Lear who, with Ed Simmons, wrote Martin & Lewis's material. "Jerry was a piece of real genius at that time and together they were an explosion." It was on *Colgate* that Lear met Bud Yorkin, with whom he would form Tandem Productions, which would, in 1971, launch *All in the Family*. "It was a very, very special period that we all grew up in," agrees Yorkin who, like Penn, served as an NBC floor director before moving into the control room to direct. "It really set the path for where the future of television went."

The crucible of *The Colgate Comedy Hour* was made hotter by the volatile personalities of the comedians. "They were powerful guys and they exerted power," Penn says. "There was an incident. Jerry Lewis used to cut off [director-producer] Ernie Glucksman's tie. I never knew what prompted it. And Ernie would say, 'C'mon, Jerry, someone gave me this tie.' On one occasion I think Jerry took a fountain pen from Ernie, and Ernie said, 'Oh, please, that was given to me by . . . ' and Jerry went around and finally threw it as a dart and broke it. It was so evident that Ernie was stricken that Jerry snapped his fingers and one of his gofers went out and came back with six pens or twelve pens. Now, at the same time, you understand, Ernie's life hung with Jerry, so the entrapment of one with the other was terrible. And it was true of almost each comedian. Each comedian had his group whom he exploited but who, at the same time, wildly depended on him. With Abbott & Costello, Abbott would get something screwed up, and Lou would look out in the audience as if to say, 'Do you see what I have to live with?' All of them were, to a greater or lesser degree, real-life Sunshine Boys."

"I've seen this with comedians," says Lear, who has known his share of them. "I don't know what the phenomenon is, but suddenly they become so knowledgeable about everything that they have to control everything and start spouting things they know nothing about."

If anybody was winging it, though, it was the people behind the cameras. They were unflappable. "You couldn't throw us," Penn says of the directors who emerged during this period. "We had just been through a war. We were not kids, we were battle-tested veterans with strong feelings. There's nothing that could happen in a TV studio that could surprise us." They were also de facto filmmakers. "The thing about live TV," he continues, "is that we were editors. We were thinking at a rate that was simply unimaginable. Every once in a while a camera would go, and then you would have to reconfigure ahead these four lenses, and who had what. It was a feat! The guys who could succeed at it were relatively precious because it was so damn hard. A lot of guys didn't make it. One of my early breaks on *Colgate* came when I'd finally moved from stage manager into the control room and I was getting the next shot ready, the next camera that was coming up. On this particular day we go on the air, and at a certain point, I realized that Kingman Moore, the director, was not functioning any more. In point of fact, he was slumped down on the console. So I had to take over calling the shots, which I did because I knew the show, and meantime there are people coming in and out of the control room and they took him away in an ambulance. It turned out that he had a bleeding ulcer and had hemorrhaged. There were young guys who would either crack up or have a heart attack or smoke themselves into oblivion, literally because the pressure was so great. This was great training for the movies years later. By the time I hit a movie set at Warner Bros., it seemed like a piece of cake!"

One of the ways TV people relieved the tension was relaxing at Hurley's Bar in Rockefeller Center on Sixth Avenue, an easy stumble from NBC. "It was fun," Penn recalls with pleasure. "We all hung out together Sunday night. If you wanted a drink, you knew to go to Hurley's. Everybody would be there."

The camaraderie began to break apart on September 4, 1951, when the transcontinental coaxial cable went into service, making simultaneous nationwide television transmission possible.[2] Martin & Lewis—who, by this time, had signed to make movies for Paramount—were needed in Hollywood, so NBC decided to ship *The Colgate Comedy Hour* out after them in time for Christmas. For Lear and Simmons LA was home. But Yorkin and Penn found themselves in a strange land. Housed at the venerable Hollywood Roosevelt Hotel—a block away from the El Capitan, where *Colgate* would originate—the two easterners stepped out into the warm December daylight and squinted. It wasn't that the sun was that bright, but that it was reflecting off the metal Christmas trees that lined Hollywood Boulevard. "We became hysterical," Yorkin says. "We looked at each other and said, 'This city is not for me.'"

Having learned the show's routine in New York, Penn and

Yorkin were tasked by the network with training their LA floor-directing replacements. "It was really the first time the LA crew had done a show this complicated," says Yorkin. "They hadn't had enough experience to do a show that turned out to be kind of a *Hellzapoppin'*."

Nevertheless, *Colgate* settled quickly into sameness. Rehearsals took all week, but not until Saturday and Sunday did they come together (if then). One weekday Penn happened to run into actor Harold Gordon, who had just appeared in Elia Kazan's latest film, *Viva Zapata* (1952). "What are you doing now?" Penn asked.

"I'm studying with a fascinating guy," Gordon said.

"Who?"

"Michael Chekhov."

Chekhov, the nephew of Anton Chekhov, was a moderately busy character actor in Hollywood who was best known as Ingrid Bergman's mentor, Dr. Brulov, in Alfred Hitchcock's *Spellbound* (1945). He was known to theater cognoscenti, however, as a formidable acting teacher who offered his take on Stanislavski's Method to a cadre of malleable Hollywood performers. When *Colgate* went into hiatus in July and August of 1953, Penn arranged to audit Chekhov's classes. "He didn't require you to do any acting, which was just as well because I can't act at all," Penn reports. "But I got a terrific education. He would break down a scene, and then he would do something that was more than a little ingenuous. He used to talk about 'the *otmossphere,* the *otmossphere,*' by which he meant the emotional and physical *atmosphere* of a play. One time, I remember, he said, 'All right; we're in the basement and there's a broken pipe and the water is leaking, but don't worry about it, the plumber will be coming. So all right, let's talk acting.' While he's doing that, he was being conscious of the water and the water dripping, and everybody picked it up. It was one of the best lessons I've ever had in my life. Everybody had the same obstacle, which was, 'It's wet down here.' It changed how you walked, how you felt."

During this time, Penn also wrote and directed a play of

which he insists he has no memory other than that he staged it at the El Capitan while it was dark between *Colgate* shows. Both Eddie Cantor's and Jerry Lewis's representatives saw it, however, and each recommended that his client hire the thirty-one-year-old Penn as his permanent *Colgate* LA director. It turned into a tug-of-war. "Jerry came to me and said, 'I want you to direct the show next year' because I'd already been the AD [assistant director] and knew the cameras, and they knew I knew them," Penn says. "And then Cantor's manager came in and said, 'I want you to direct *his* shows.' So here I was, all of a sudden, staring Big Time in the face, when I get a call from New York."

"Hey, Pappy," the familiar southern voice said, "This is Fred Coe."

In the years since leaving the Town Theatre in June of 1944, Coe had held a succession of stage managing jobs, then arrived at NBC's New York City affiliate, WNBT-TV, where he was hired as a floor director. By 1947 Coe's talent had been recognized by the network, and he was searching for material to fill its rapidly expanding broadcast schedule. He also needed directors, and asked Vincent Donehue, who was helming *Philco Television Playhouse*, to recommend one. Donehue was familiar with Penn's aplomb and gave his name to Coe, who immediately recognized his former Fort Boy and called him in LA. "There's a fantastic treasure house of short stories—Faulkner, Hemingway," Coe pitched Penn, "except it's unavailable to dramatize because it's told in the first person. Why shouldn't we be able to dramatize it?" It was his notion that the stories would work on television if the camera itself became a character. His idea was *First Person Playhouse*, and it debuted as a summer replacement for *Gulf Playhouse* in 1953. Almost immediately, Coe abandoned Faulkner and Hemingway in favor of original works commissioned from a growing stable of young writers, including Horton Foote, Tad Mosel, Robert Alan Aurthur, Stewart Stern, and Paddy Chayefsky.

"I dropped the Martin & Lewis show and the Cantor show and took off for New York," Penn recalls with relief. "I figured that, if I wanted to be in TV, I had to be in New York. So I came east."

On the first day of rehearsal, however, Penn realized something he'd been rising too fast to notice: he had never directed professional actors. That would be solved in a battlefield promotion by the tragically brilliant Kim Stanley.

5

The Edge of Chaos

It will come as a shock to those who wax nostalgic about the golden age of television to learn that the golden age of television was never meant to last. It was a marketing ploy, a loss leader contrived by television networks to first, entice people to buy TV sets and second, to confer prestige upon the new medium. Between roughly 1948 and 1961 various anthology series would come and go, but the remarkable fact is that, for much of this time, the public could see a live, original dramatic presentation every night of the week.

Fred Coe became the most celebrated producer of these shows, and when he and Penn joined forces on *First Person* it was the beginning of a productive thirteen-year collaboration that started on television and expanded to stage and screen.

Working with Coe, Penn knew he was at a threshold. Telling trained actors how to act in an original drama was something that he hadn't perfected. Even Michael Chekhov's immersive acting classes didn't prepare him for the one performer who dominated the stage without ever being seen: the camera.

First Person turned out to be clever in the abstract but awkward in the application. The idea of making the camera not just an observer but a participant meant that people would talk directly to it, breaking the sacred theatrical "fourth wall" and creating subtle but insurmountable problems: main characters would be heard but never seen (except in mirror shots); it would be hard to cut to different points of view; handling props was awkward.

First Person was cheeky and its results varied. Penn and Bob Costello, whom Coe also engaged to direct (although Penn helmed the majority of the shows), gamely found ways to visualize such stage directions as "An old man, THE CAMERA, opens his eyes slowly" or "The girl, Cecilia, THE CAMERA, is seated on the front porch" that were thrown at them by writers Robert Alan Aurthur, Paddy Chayefsky, Horton Foote, Tad Mosel, Harry Muheim, and David Shaw. They wrote the eleven *First Person* episodes that aired Friday nights between July 3 and September 11, 1953, and went on to create even greater works for the mentoring Coe.

"When he would get a glint of talent in a writer, he'd bring that writer in and he'd give him a deal," Penn reports. "He'd say, 'I'm gonna pay you, now go off and write the script.' Sometimes we'd end up throwing it away, and sometimes it would be *Marty.* We were a very good, pretty tight group."

Not everyone had TV ambitions. "Of all the playwrights in Fred's stable," says Horton Foote, "I was the least interested in film, so I was surprised at how I took to something which you couldn't repeat in the theater."[1]

Once written and cast, each show would spend seven or eight hours around a table being read aloud and then be blocked on a marked-off rehearsal floor. It would then move to the studio for a day of camera blocking, another day of dress rehearsal, and, finally, broadcast. The next day it all began again. "We were never out of rehearsal," Penn sighs.

Each piece presented a separate challenge. "If the story said, 'It was a hot day and nothing was moving,' what was the viewer looking at?" Penn asks rhetorically. "If you say, 'it was a hot day and my dress was sticking to me,' there's something for the camera to capture. We developed a kind of visual language designed to create the atmosphere, the climate, and the given circumstance."[2]

Breaking the fourth wall didn't always work, but it was often intriguing. In *Desert Cafe,* the formidable Rod Steiger was cast, voice-over only, playing a disagreeable vagrant who decides to settle down and open a garage after finding comfort with cafe owner James Westerfield, a boy, and the boy's father, Frank

Overton. Penn directed it admirably, but it was the series premiere, and he was still finding his way.

In *The Death of the Old Man*,[3] Will Mayfield lies on his deathbed recounting his life story while his family hovers, waiting for the end. What he fears is not death but the interruption of tradition, a continuity respected less by his own children than by Sealey, the family's black servant who, Will comes to realize, has been the true force binding the white Mayfields together. More confined physically than other *First Person* efforts, *The Death of the Old Man* is a chamber piece of carefully orchestrated emotion in which despair gradually turns into release.

First Person's contrivance was not always successful. In *The Comeback*, written by David Shaw, the camera plays a theatrical agent, Jack Warden, tasked with breaking the news to his ageing female client, Jesse Royce Landis, that the part she's up for is not the ingénue but the ingénue's mother. Warden's voice-over narrative intercuts with his spoken dialogue, and at times "his" hands reach from behind the camera to fumble with props. Penn was trying everything. "Nothing was a lark in *First Person*," he admits. "We were always making it up, and it was maddening."

The more he directed, the more something else was becoming clear to him: "I didn't know what to say to the actors. With *Tears of My Sister*, I thought, 'You have to bite the bullet. You've got Kim Stanley and you better give it your best shot.' I worked with her, saying, 'Kim, I don't know anything. You're gonna tell me what you want to do here.'"

Penn's "best shot" turned out to be a bull's-eye. *Tears of My Sister* is one of the series' finest efforts. Stanley is Cecilia Monroe, a young girl who comes to realize, though not fully understand, that her older sister is being married off to a man she doesn't love in order to save her family from penury. The mercurial Stanley, who is never seen, captures Cecilia's innocence within Foote's delicate writing. "Kim Stanley was just wonderful," pronounces Foote, "and Arthur created a kind of magical sense that permeated everything."

The device was even more fully realized in the eighth installment, *Crip*. Penn's camera becomes a brain-damaged boy, Alan, who, deprived of speech and mobility, is hidden away by his family. But his parents don't realize that the "accident" he suffered when he was eight took his speech and movement but not his mind, and it is the compassion of a new neighbor, played by Kathy (Kathleen) Nolan, that rescues him from a life of seclusion. Penn locks his camera in place, panning and tilting but otherwise immobile, until the moving ending when Alan miraculously rises to speak his own name and thus liberates himself.

The final show in the series was written by Paddy Chayefsky and includes Kim Hunter, Mildred Dunnock, and Joseph Anthony. *A Gift from Cotton Mather* refers to an antique hourglass that's been in Beedee's (Dunnock's) family since her ancestors arrived on the *Mayflower,* and it's a constant reminder to her browbeaten husband, Max (Anthony), that she married beneath her, a theme she has raised their daughter to encore and that will continue to reverberate in the family unless Max breaks the chain of snobbery. Chayefsky's bravura script is matched by Penn's direction, which is intricate and muscular.

By the time of *A Gift from Cotton Mather,* both *First Person* and Arthur Penn were chafing at their restraints. Fortunately, *Philco Television Playhouse*[4] was coming into its own, and Coe needed to expand his directing roster. He favored Penn but wanted affirmation, so he asked Kim Stanley. Recalls Penn, "Fred, who loved her, came to Kim and said, 'Is Penn the guy?' She said, 'Yeah.' Fred said to me, 'Hey, Pappy, I want to talk to you.' We had a suite of offices in NBC where we all hung out—writers, directors, everybody. He told me in his office that I had the job. That's when I got to *Philco,* which was a shock."

"I was happy to see him pick Arthur," notes Bud Yorkin, who had taken over *Colgate.* "I knew he'd be perfect for Fred. They were so different. Arthur was wonderfully calm, if that's the word, with a good sense of humor. You had to have it to exist with Fred because he was a very tough producer, always looking for perfection."

Coe's cheekiness is the stuff of legend, as Yorkin relates: "The one that he's famous for is a scene where the camera comes around the bend and dollies down to a fountain, and in the fountain you see somebody's head in the water, a nun. The finish to act 2 was this nun, her face head-down in the water. Fred had obviously said, 'When you come around the bend with the camera you gotta cue her to take a deep breath and get her face in the water.' He says, 'Cue the nun' and the stage manager, who's behind a pole, waves frantically at this elderly nun. Fred says again, 'Cue the nun!' Then one beat later, '*Cue the nun!!*' and finally he screams, '*Will you cue that goddamn nun?*' and his voice leaked out of the stage manager's headset into the boom microphone, and it went right out over the air. Everybody who was watching *Philco* heard it. It made one of the biggest stories the *New York Times* had in years."

Philco had an advantage over other live network dramas: it aired on Sunday nights, when Broadway theaters were dark. This gave the show the pick of stage performers, especially those in hit plays who treasured relief from the monotony of a long run. It wasn't easy, but at least it wasn't boring. "You had to get on the air and go live," Penn says.[5] "The technology wasn't up to the medium. We'd have extra cameras standing by in the hall ready to go, boom, condition red, get in there and fix the fucking thing, and let's go on. There were no zoom lenses, which meant you had to get off that camera to another camera to be able to change lenses. You carried that sort of thing in your head. You're figuring, 'Okay, now, I'm going to go to a neutral lens here and stay there. The guys are going to release the next camera to get to the next set because we're going to fade up there, and we'll only have one camera.'"

"In point of fact," Penn added during a panel at New York's Museum of Television and Radio, "we had all the shots laid out and we had a cue in our script where the shot was going to go. But we would be watching those monitors like we were hovering over a newborn baby, watching somebody develop a piece of emotion that had not been there, or had only been there inchoately, and then slowly expanded. So it was [to the technical director]: 'Don't take it . . . don't take it . . . I know that's your cue, but don't take it . . . hold it, hold it, she's great! Oh, NOW!' It was that kind of empathy that the really, frankly, good directors were able to practice in the control room rather than the mechanical thing of [just taking shots].[6]

Writer Tad Mosel puts it another way: "Nobody in his right mind would ever do live television." Yet he did, famously (*The Waiting Place, The Lawn Party*). "You only had opening nights, no second nights. That was its virtue and its defeat. It generated an excitement among the audiences because they knew that the actors were doing it then, for them, in their living room, and if the actor flubbed a line, the audience was with him: 'Oh, thank heaven, he got it, finally!'"

"All you could do was once, one time," adds Horton Foote, sounding relieved. "There was the live, and then there was the kinnie." Foote wrote the first script Penn directed for *Philco*, *John Turner Davis*, and says, "It was something that Fred Coe commissioned me to write and I asked for Arthur. I loved working with him. He had a real sense of poetry—and he probably wasn't even aware of that—but he had a very poetic vision. Arthur understood my material better than anybody who's ever done it before or since. He had a wonderful understanding of acting and people."

Actors were also beginning to find Penn exciting to work with, even if he was still learning how to work with them. "Typical experience," he says. "Early on in *Philco* I was doing a show with Julie Harris. Julie Harris is one of the major figures of the American theater, and we rehearsed this thing and I said, 'Gee, Julie, I don't know.' So we try it again. I think we did about five rehearsals on this spot and I finally said, 'There's something wrong here, something wrong.' And we went over what I had said to her at the outset. Either I had said it backwards or she had understood it backwards. Finally she said, 'Oh, you mean *this!* The opposite!' This is a disciplined, major actress who was trying to do what some techie is asking her to do. And that's what gave me [impetus to] learn the actor's language. And I did. I learned it very quickly."

Penn's preference for Actors Studio performers led the Studio's Paula Strasberg personally to invite him to join. The Actors Studio and television drama developed in tandem. Unlike

Hollywood actors, Studio actors didn't scorn TV; to them, acting was acting.

But if Hollywood wasn't knocking at television's door, Madison Avenue was. The prestige of *Colgate, Philco, Gulf, Goodyear, U.S. Steel,* and other drama series emboldened the agencies to try to control program content. This did not sit well with the creative people, who resented the intrusion of sales department dilettantes attempting to bend and censor content to better show off their products. The interference bred frustration and dissent among Coe and his staff, and defections—primarily by writers who sought the money and relative freedom of Hollywood—began. Chayefsky sold his *Goodyear Playhouse* script *Marty* to the movies in 1954 and followed it to Hollywood. Its 1955 release and subsequent Oscar shattered the demarcation between TV and film. In short order Horton Foote adapted *Storm Fear* (1955) and Robert Alan Aurthur wrote *Edge of the City* (1957). Directors John Frankenheimer, Franklin Schaffner, Robert Mulligan, and Delbert Mann also headed west, abandoning television when films offered more opportunity.

Penn, however, resisted, staying in New York to direct a remarkable range of material. *The Lawn Party* has Geraldine Fitzgerald as a midwestern woman who wants to raise her social status by throwing a soiree but alienates her own family as she decides which of her neighbors is worthy of setting foot in her backyard. Writer Tad Mosel recalls, "That was the first time that I was working with Arthur on the set. That was such a delicate play. You almost couldn't feel it; it would slip away from you, and he caught that, he caught that beautifully. He was not a cut-and-dried television director. He would do different things, try different things, which in those days was quite unusual because so much was at stake."

Paul Newman was becoming a fixture on live television drama by the time he was cast in Mosel's powerful *Guilty Is the Stranger* as an anguished young GI freshly back from the Korean War who visits the home of a dead army buddy in an attempt to bond with the boy's parents. His own emotional needs become his ruination, however, when it turns out that he barely knew the young man, if at all, and may, in fact, have been responsible for his death. Newman's intense acting style is clearly from a different universe than that of his costars Fay Bainter and Patricia Crowley.

Another Newman-Penn collaboration—this time for *Playwrights '56*—hit a tragic snag. *The Battler* was adapted by both Sidney Carroll and A. E. Hotchner[7] from one of Ernest Hemingway's Nick Adams stories. "It was to star James Dean as a punch-drunk prizefighter and Paul Newman as Nick Adams," says Penn. "Dean was to play a forty-five-year-old punch-drunk fighter. I hadn't worked with Dean but I knew him from the Actors Studio. Ten days before we were to do it, Dean was killed. Despite our shock, we asked Newman to do that part and we got Dewey Martin to take Newman's role. Paul played it extremely well. Mind you, this is a play going out live that starts out with Paul Newman as a busted-up prize fighter; his face is totally distorted, he can barely talk, he's sitting by a hobo campfire, and then it flashes back to his youth when he is a beautiful young boxer in a love affair with Phyllis Kirk. At the end, he has to be the punch-drunk prizefighter again.[8] We did that live. Robert Wise saw his performance and asked him to do *Somebody Up There Likes Me* which, essentially, was the beginning of Paul's movie career. Perhaps James Dean was the more logical choice, but James Dean was dead and Paul inherited, to some degree, that part of the role."

Penn, eager to break rules and explore new techniques, found Actors Studio students simpatico. That weighed against him, however, when he tackled *State of the Union* on NBC's *Producers Showcase*. An early experiment in color broadcasting, *State of the Union* was adapted from their 1945 Broadway hit by Howard Lindsay and Russel Crouse. Cut by two-thirds, the show told of an idealistic industrialist (Joseph Cotten) enticed by powerful business interests (John Cromwell) to run for the presidency who learns he must compromise his ethics along the way. The production transcends its muffled material thanks to the crackling interplay between Cotten and Margaret Sullavan, who give subtle and personable performances, and Penn's multilayered staging. Their acting style contrasts with Cromwell's, who blusters his way through his role of the intimidating corrupter Conover. There were reasons for this, as Penn learned during rocky rehearsals. "We started work and it was going badly," he says. "I thought, 'Jesus, am I out of my depth here?' So I told Joe Cotten and Maggie Sullavan, 'I'm sorry, I may not have expressed myself well; this is what I intended.' They'd say, 'Yeah, oh yeah, we got it, okay' and the next day do something different. We were into it about ten days when Joe Cotten came to me and said, 'We want to go to lunch.' So we went to Dinty Moore's—Maggie and Joe and I—and he said, 'Order a martini.' I said, 'Hey, Joe, I can't drink, not in the middle of the day.'

"He said, '*Order a martini!*'

"So I order a martini. He said, 'You don't know what the hell's been going on, do you?' I said, 'No, but if I can't get you guys to either understand me or get it across . . . ' He said, 'No. What's happening is that we're working with you all day and Cromwell takes us over to his apartment and has us redo the scene his way, so we're coming in the next day with half yours, half his, and we don't know what to do about it. We just wanted to tell you what's been going on and we're going to stop it. We're not going to see Cromwell any more. We'll go with you— you seem to know what you're doing' which, of course, in the medium, I did. And from then on, everything went smoothly."

State of the Union was a rare established hit, but scripts written specifically for the format also achieved greatness. Four that Penn directed stand out. *My Lost Saints* (written by Tad Mosel) is a delicate entry in the "kitchen sink" school of drama with an outstanding cast. Mosel's favorite actress, Eileen Heckart, and Lili Darvas make it memorable. Heckart is the domestic in the Hallet household who has come to feel like a bona fide member of the family. When her simple farm woman mother (Darvis) visits and falls ill, Heckart finds her loyalties torn between her true and her adopted families. It is a pure character piece in a confined setting that never feels limited thanks to firm direction, focused performances, and attentive camera cutting.

Parent-child reconciliation is also the theme of *The Heart's a Forgotten Hotel* (written by Arnold Schulman) on *Playwrights '56*. Set in a failing Miami hotel managed by Edmond O'Brien, who is also failing in a sea of debt, it follows the realization by O'Brien's son, Allie, that he is a more responsible man than his father, yet he vows to stick by his father's side and, in effect, raise him.

Star in the Summer Night, written by Tad Mosel, of whom it was fast becoming apparent that Arthur Penn was his best interpreter, is a wistfully elegant fable. A once-famous stage star, Adeline Gerard (Lili Darvas), has outlived the public's memory of her and is reduced to singing in a small nightclub. Though she must compromise in life, she retains her honor, and this enables her to persevere. Despite flirting with bathos, *Star in the Summer Night* is a sure-handed work, written with a hard center to its gentle edge and directed with a sense of firm delicacy.

Mosel's haunting *The Waiting Place* was the Christmas production for *Playwrights '56*, and it remains one of his favorite works as well as a refreshingly bold piece for television. Kim Stanley plays Abby, a fourteen-year-old girl on the brink of puberty. She dotes on her widowed father, Malcolm (Frank Overton), and invents a boyfriend in the hopes that this will make her father pay her more attention. Dramas about fathers and daughters tormented by their feelings for each other were not standard fare in American television in the 1950s, but *The Waiting Place* avoids luridness by its forthright performances and delicate direction. It was, nevertheless, a troubled production. Although Mosel crafted it especially for Stanley, the actress, then nearly thirty-one, doubted her ability to pass for fourteen. She became simultaneously demanding and passive-aggressive, but it worked. At a Christmas party that Fred Coe threw while the show was in rehearsal, Stanley ran into actor Frank Overton, whom she preferred to the man who had been cast as her father. Stanley threw her arms around Overton and said, loud enough for Coe and Penn to hear, "Oh, I wish *you* were playing my father!"[9] The next day he was.

Despite his success, Penn was becoming dissatisfied with the medium. "There's a promise in live TV which we could never fulfill," he told writer Richard Schickel, "which is the promise to be exactly at the right place at the right time dramatically. We did the best we could, but there was no possibility to explode time, to open time out so that you could perceive stuff. And clearly this is something that I became more than a little fixated on."[10]

As an in-demand television director, he sailed from project to project with comforting regularity, all of them in New York. But change was in the airwaves. Although the creators of anthology dramas plied their craft with little network oversight, when sponsors began to pay attention to content, so did TV executives. "I wanted to stay in live television," Penn says, "until a certain point, which was when *Philco* and *Goodyear* suddenly discovered that there was a sizeable enough audience for them to take as much time with the commercials as we were taking with the shows."

But rescue was near. CBS producer Martin Manulis, eager to mine the Hollywood talent the way Fred Coe had utilized Broadway, was overseeing the development of *Playhouse 90* in Los Angeles. The series was to be driven by stars as well as writers, and would become the emblem of television's golden age even as it hastened the end of it.

6

Built for Television

Hollywood hated television. At first the studios simply closed their eyes and wished the glowing new toy would go away. Then it was "It's only a fad," as they had said of the talkies. At minimum, the Founding Moguls agreed that they would never allow their precious product on the tube. That posturing ended in 1956 when Columbia, Warner Bros., Fox, and MGM all sold their pre-1948 libraries to the enemy, which had been subsisting on titles from independent companies like Republic, Monogram, and others that were more concerned with cash flow than prestige. By then several of the majors had also, with varying degrees of prescience, set up in-house TV production and syndication arms. If there was any resistance, it came from agents who resented the lower fees and possible stigmatizing of their clients by home-screen appearances.

The new breed of New York stage actors, however, had no qualms about appearing in the live dramas emanating from the East Coast. Acting was acting, and when the industry moved west in the middle 1950s, these stage-trained performers followed. The migration favored CBS, which had begun building a sprawling studio near the Farmer's Market in Los Angeles that would be called CBS Television City. "That was a facility built for television," Penn says. "It was like heaven because we were not confined to three cameras. We were up to four, five, six, seven cameras if you wanted. [They] were real movie stages."[1]

To occupy the premises, the network planned an ambitious

show known only as *Program X*. By the time it hit the air on October 4, 1956, it was called *Playhouse 90*. The story of *Playhouse 90*—which, half a century after its disappearance, remains the emblematic live television anthology—belongs to Martin Manulis. As Fred Coe was to live drama in New York, Manulis was to its Hollywood counterpart. Manulis's mandate from the network was to cast movie stars, but he had his choice of directors and writers.

Martin Elliot Manulis had been producing, directing, and sometimes acting in plays—not student productions, but professional plays—even before graduating from Columbia University in 1935 with a degree in English lit. He had enrolled early, at sixteen, with hopes of getting into Columbia's famed graduate school of journalism, but fell into theater when a friend dropped out of an acting role and the desperate director handed it to him. Forsaking journalism, he mounted a succession of productions with famous people in unusual roles, a tradition later to be known as "stunt casting." Accordingly, writer Thornton Wilder, hostess Elsa Maxwell, and critic Lucius Bebe became actors; producers Antoinette Perry and John C. Wilson directed, and so on. The affable Manulis worked his way up within New York's tight-knit Broadway community, married stage actress Katharine Bard, served in the navy in World War II, and returned to resume his stage career. By 1951 it was clear that his career was at a standstill, so his wife suggested he try the medium that was keeping her busy between plays, live television. As producer over the next four years, he rose through such series as *Studio One, Suspense, The Best of Broadway,* and *Climax*. Manulis brought not only showmanship but a sense of order to CBS's amorphous producing system. For all the prestige that the Tiffany Network enjoyed with its news division and radio shows, its television operation lacked cohesion.[2] By the time *Program X* became *Playhouse 90,* Manulis had a firm grip.

"The search was on for original scripts and source material or adaptations of plays and novels," he said, "everything of quality that could make varied, stimulating, and exciting programming. The directors saw, in the new format, a creative opportunity to use their talents well and to expand them."[3] John Frankenheimer and Franklin J. Schaffner directed shows in rotation with such other young talents as Arthur Hiller, Daniel Petrie, George Roy Hill, Robert Mulligan, and Arthur Penn. Each production took three weeks from table read to air and paid its director $15,000. "I signed on to do four *Playhouse 90s*," Penn says. "*The Miracle Worker*[4] was first, *Invitation to a Gunfighter* second, *Charley's Aunt* third, and *The Dark Side of the Earth* fourth. By the time I got done doing *The Miracle Worker* I was already a little bit sick of Hollywood actors. They were good, but I was getting people who were not getting jobs in movies."

For his second *Playhouse 90*, Penn was given a script that Leslie Stevens had written from a story by Hal Goodman and Larry Klein. *Invitation to a Gunfighter* was a psychological western at a time when the psychological western was only just coming into being, notably in the films of Anthony Mann, and later of Penn himself. The story is a variation on the warning "Be careful what you wish for"; gunfighter Hugh O'Brian terrorizes a small western town, so the people hire another gunfighter, Gilbert Roland, to chase him away. When Roland becomes more despotic than O'Brian, the townspeople rehire O'Brian to get rid of Roland. "It was non-horse western because you couldn't get a horse on the stage without the horse going to the bathroom every four seconds," recalls Del Reisman, *Playhouse 90*'s story editor. "Martin gave it to Arthur; it was kind of like, 'It's your turn, Arthur, this is the script.' He brought excitement to it and brought some psychology into the characters. I always admired Arthur for that because it was just a routine story, and by plunging into it the way he did, he gave it some substance.

"Gilbert Roland came into the rehearsal hall," continues Reisman, "and he had some kind of Mexican sombrero with spangles, shirt open down to here, and big leather wristbands. He was a delightful person, but he was an old-fashioned movie star, and he was letting everybody know it. He would be at one end of the rehearsal hall, and Arthur would call him, and Gilbert would turn around like he was posing, like he was looking for his close-up. It was a crazy show, but Arthur really brought something to it."

The most important thing Penn brought to it was Anne Bancroft as Julie Bickford, the sheriff's daughter. He knew her as a B-movie actress but wasn't aware of the depths of her talent until a dialogue exchange in which he tested her with some indirect direction. "There was some obvious line like 'Come here to me,'" he says, "and she said it, I think to Hugh O'Brian. And I said to him, 'Don't go to her.' And she said, 'Then I can't say that; I can't say that because if he doesn't come, what's the point?' I said, 'There are other meanings to that.' And *this thing* happened in her eyes. She suddenly could *see* it. And she said, 'Oh, yeah! I'm not talking about physically coming over here where I am, I'm talking about "Join me."' And I think it was the moment where Annie suddenly realized that the literalness of the lines was not what we were talking about. We're talking about human behavior and human interaction over and above our speech level, and far more meaningful. *Subtext*. Annie said later, 'That was the moment I understood acting for the first time.'"

"Something in me always knew it," Bancroft confirmed.[5] "But I think the person that brought it out of me was Arthur Penn. It was during that show that I really had an awakening. Whatever it was in me that was lying dormant and waiting for someone to make me aware, Arthur did it."

Del Reisman, who later became one of television's most successful writers and served as president of the Writers Guild, watched the Penn-Bancroft collaboration take shape. "Arthur turned Anne Bancroft from a rising young actress into a major actress," he notes. "He was so skillful at that, and I don't remember ever hearing Arthur launch into lengthy Stanislavski speeches. He was very basic but very skilled."

Although Manulis favored originals, he wasn't averse to reviving a theatrical warhorse when deadlines pressed. "His brilliance," Penn commends, "was that he was just indomitable. The show was going to go on no matter what. When, out of my four shows, I still didn't have one of them, he said, 'Let's do *Charley's Aunt* with Art Carney.'[6] Putting the endlessly inventive Carney in drag was the kind of perfect star casting that CBS wanted Manulis to pursue. Art was a funny man; my God, he was funny!"

Also effective was Rod Serling's timely and disturbing *The Dark Side of the Earth*, set in Hungary during that country's uprising against Soviet occupation the previous year. Taking the side of the freedom fighters, it focused on the tense relationship between Russian colonel Sten (Van Heflin) and a Hungarian collaborator (Jerry Paris). The relationship was equally tense between Penn and Heflin, whom the director recalls as "a guy who used to be a good actor and became a Hollywood star and didn't really want to work any more."

"There was a moment in it where he felt he had to weep, and I said that was lovely if you could do it; whatever's there is fine. We started rehearsing and, bing, there were tears. What I didn't realize was that he was popping a little capsule of ammonia. Until we got into the camera rehearsal and I heard the pop, I didn't know what was going on at all. I said, 'Van, you can't do that' and he said, 'You won't hear it. I'll cover with a cough.' And he did. But these tears that were apparently coming out of deep feeling were induced by ammonia."[7]

The Dark Side of the Earth wrapped Penn's four-show commitment to CBS, but he returned a year later to direct a program that remains controversial. *Portrait of a Murderer* was constructed from taped interviews with real-life murderer Donald Bashor that had been conducted by his prison cell mate prior to Bashor's recent October 1957 execution in California's gas chamber. (Released from prison after serving time for robbery, Bashor started robbing again, then turned to killing.) Penn and Leslie Stevens devised the script, and Manulis had the inspired idea to cast the immensely likable teen heartthrob Tab Hunter (*Damn Yankees, The Girl He Left Behind,* and others) wildly against type as Bashor.[8] Hunter's studio, Warner Bros., where he was under contract, was amenable, but Hunter, even though he yearned to stretch his image, wasn't sure. "I was in the East with [agent] Dick Clayton and I had just finished working with Sidney Lumet on a *Hallmark Hall of Fame* called *Hans Brinker and the Silver Skates*," Hunter says. "Dick told me that Arthur Penn would be calling me about a television show. Well, I was frightened of TV. I read the script and I absolutely loved it. Arthur called me in my hotel room and I said to Dick, 'I don't want to talk to him, I don't want to talk to him.' I was scared to death! And Dick said to Arthur, 'Oh, Tab's right here,' and he handed me the phone. I could've killed Clayton. And Arthur said, 'Hi . . .' and he was so nice."

"'What do you think of the script?'

"I said, 'Well, you know—' and everything I tried to find fault with, he agreed with me, so I had no argument. He's really bright. I said, 'But this bothers me . . .' and he said, 'I couldn't agree with you more . . .' and he was, 'You're right about that, we can work on that' and before the end of the conversation I had agreed to do the show."

"I think it's one of Tab's best performances," Penn commended. "There was a kind of improvisatory aspect to it. You live 'in the moment,' which is something you'll hear again and again at the Actors Studio. You're 'in the moment,' which means you use what is there at present. You don't go back and imitate a piece of your own behavior in the past in order to satisfy that moment. You do what is there. And what is there is going to be all right, I promise you. Tab Hunter was seeing it for the first time and it liberated him from this rather rigid pretty boy thing. I remember, after killing a woman, [he] runs down in the basement to escape and knocks over a basket with some clothes. He stopped and meticulously put it back. It was a piece of inspiration and he was so into it that he did it. If there is a legacy out of live television, it was that: we could see a body of behavior that we don't see in television and we certainly don't see it in films."[9]

Shortly before it aired on February 27, 1958, *Portrait of a Murderer* raised sponsor concerns not because of its crime but because of its punishment. "We get right near to the end [of run-through]," Manulis recalled, "and the [Southern California] Gas Company is right there [saying], 'You can't have him killed in the gas chamber,' which was how California executed people. There was no way. This was a famous case. I said, 'Stand by us in this. For one thing, we're almost to air, and second, we'll be a laughingstock and it certainly isn't going to do the network any good.'" Manulis won the day and the show aired with the scene intact: Hunter is led into the gas chamber, strapped to its chair, and the door is sealed shut. As the camera pulls back, Bashor laments, in voice-over, "Such a shame that doctors or judges can't just kill the bad part and return the good part."[10]

Given the violence inherent in the story, Penn achieves extraordinary power by not showing it. An offscreen murder is heard only as a distant scream followed by Hunter's hurried exit from the victim's house as he drops the crowbar murder weapon and runs off, barefoot, into the night.

"Luckily," says Hunter, "when shows like that came along, I was able to finally make the right decision to do them. I wanted to make Bashor very meticulous about things. Arthur's feed to the actor is the fuel so you can really go with your imagination and your concentration."

As one of the busier television directors, Penn had not given much thought to getting married and having children, but by the end of 1958 he had done both. Peggy Maurer had been studying with Lee Strasberg at the Actors Studio almost from the moment she arrived in New York at the age of twenty-one, bent on becoming an actress. Fine-featured, regal, and brashly intelligent, she had been born on February 26, 1931, in McKeesport, Pennsylvania, to John Frederick Maurer, a doctor, and his wife, Dorothy Christine Elizabeth Long Maurer. Almost as soon as they had Peggy, the Maurers moved to Acosta, Pennsylvania, a mining town, where they settled in and he opened his medical practice.

Love had drawn John Frederick and Dorothy to each other, but it was Dorothy's mother, Euphamia Eton Long, who made them tie the knot. "He got my mother pregnant," Peggy declares many years later. "I guess Famie came after them with a gun or something, but they got pregnant and he married her." No one messed with Famie. "An old Scotch name," Peggy says. "I think she would rather have been called Dorothy, Christine, or Elizabeth, but she got Euphamia and became Famie." Whatever the reason for her obstinacy, Grandmother Famie was one determined woman. "She was nasty," her granddaughter corrects. "She would chase me out of the house, but I could run fast, so I would run out of the house and over the fence and literally disappear. I was four or five years old. And she would have to give up. Of course, I would have to come home, and she would finally get me. But for a long time I was on the run." Peggy's mother could not intercede. "She couldn't fight my grandmother, who was four foot nine and could give you a short rib punch that would bring you to the ground in no time."

Famie had similar disdain for her husband, Albert, who ran a delicatessen and operated a kind of Depression-era lottery known as a "suit club." "For a quarter you could buy a ticket on a suit and there would be a raffle and you would win a suit or not win a suit," says Peggy. "He would have a pocket full of quarters which he would jingle, but we still felt very poor. And my grandmother just killed him. She was so disappointed in him for not being better. He would do things like go to the store, which was up an enormous hill, and he had a heart condition. She didn't care. I would scream and carry on and lie down on the floor and kick my heels and yell, 'You're killing him! If he dies, I'll kill you.' That was our conversation." Years later Peggy learned a possible source of Famie's acrimony: Albert had a mistress over that hill.

The Maurers were a collection of hidden tensions. Early in his life, Frederick had set his sights on becoming a doctor, which amused his Swiss-German immigrant family, who mocked his dreams. "You know how he did it?" Peggy recalls with pride. "He did it by staying up after school, walking across the Monongahela Bridge that joined McKeesport and Pittsburgh, and working in the steel mills shoveling iron ore every night until he couldn't breathe and he could hardly walk. Then he took his shoes in his hand—this is his story—walked back across the bridge and into bed. When he did his homework, I have no idea. It was a hard life. But he did go to medical school."

Her mother, too, faced obstacles. Beautiful but possessed of a terrible stutter, Dorothy worked quietly as a secretary in the Jones and Laughlin Steel Mills under a boss who was attracted to her. The man's infatuation persisted even after Dorothy wed Frederick. Peggy remembers, "For years he sent her sealed birthday cards that she hid in her underwear drawer. I am sure she never forgot him. He also bestowed on her a beautiful large ring of lavender cut stone in briolette fashion and held in a delicate filigree setting of white and yellow gold. I still have it and I occasionally wear it. Once, after giving it to me, she asked for it back and, like the adamant teenager I was, I refused. I needed one thing from my mother that was beautiful."[11]

As the only physician in a coal-mining town, Dr. Maurer held a position of prestige. He also owned the town's only car, and young Peggy would ride with him on house calls and emergencies. By the age of five she had witnessed the range of injuries, illnesses, and degradations suffered by the miners and their families. She later remarked, "In time all the men who lived there died, then the women. It was as though they all sank back into that same earth they dug."

Like her father, Peggy was torn between the things she had to do and the things she wanted to do. They both loved the arts, yet had to attend to matters in their working-class town.

After living in Acosta for five years the Maurers relocated yet again, to Greensboro, Pennsylvania, where the doctor became the head of the X-ray department at the local hospital. In 1941 his wife presented him with a son, John Albert, named after her father. The ten years between the siblings gave Peggy perspective. She noted that Johnny grew emotionally dependent upon their father, and their father, in turn, made demands on the boy that might also be construed as dependence. This became a problem by the time John entered medical school, yearning to follow in his father's footsteps. His father would phone him before every test and demanded the boy call him afterwards. "He had terrible test anxiety," Peggy reports. "A lot of kids do, and I kept saying to my father, 'Listen, that can be handled, but you have to do it through a psychologist.' And he said, 'Nonsense!' He made life so hard for my brother than he flunked out. So he tried dentistry and that didn't work. He graduated from college and he ended up with a friend running a medical lab. He did it very well because

he knew a lot about medicine, but he was sad. He would have been a wonderful doctor. He was kind, endearing, and he needed some lift, some strengths, some belief. But he wasn't gonna get it from my father." Ultimately, John Maurer would die of throat cancer brought on by smoking.

A fascination with words[12] and an uncommon sensitivity in observing others led Peggy to enroll in Carnegie Tech to become an actress. When she was graduated and moved to New York, her acceptance at the Actors Studio coincided with Arthur Penn's ascendance, and given his regard for Studio students, it was inevitable that their paths would cross at a casting session. "She auditioned for me on *Philco*,"[13] Arthur Penn says. "I asked, 'What are you doing?' and she said *The Three Sisters*. I'd read about it. I got a ticket and went down to see it, and she was plenty good, so I hired her. And that's when we started going out—right away.

"This was a new time in the theater, the beginning of off-Broadway. There was a guy named David Ross, an Israeli, who came here and made a lot of money in the stock market. But he was theater-stricken, so he rented a space downtown and—the Blacklist was already in place—he got a lot of the top Group Theatre actors, or actors who were either not in the Group but in that same crowd, to be in *The Dybbuk*. And then he said, 'I'm going to do the Chekhov plays,' and the first one was *The Three Sisters*. One sister was Sean Penn's mother.[14] Phil Loeb was in that, and killed himself shortly after.[15] David Ross had the good sense to do these and, boy, they were getting *some* reviews, too!"[16]

"It was quite an experience for me," Peggy enthuses, recalling not only her big break but the acting lessons. "I mean, I had read Clurman's book[17] and I knew about the Group Theatre, but these seemed like old-timers and here I was in their midst. And every now and then Giggy Young[18] would come up to me and say, 'Honey, play the objects.' And at first I thought, 'What? Play the objects?' And then I got it: this clock was my mother's clock, she used to wind it up for me in order to please me, et cetera. The imagination goes. It was wonderful. I was so grateful to them, I really was."

If Arthur and Peggy were in step as far as dating, she fell behind as a performer on their first day of *Philco* rehearsal. "I started a television show by sleeping in," she says. "I worked a Friday night show, Saturday matinee, Saturday night show, Sunday matinee, Sunday show, and four hours of Chekhov all those times in a row. It's a wonder I didn't turn into my character. I slept in and [associate director] Gordon Rigsby called me and said, 'Miss Maurer, what time do you think we begin?' I said, 'Ten o'clock.' He said, 'Well, do you know that it's now ten twenty?' I said, 'I'll be there before ten thirty.' Did nothing, just slipped into my jeans and off I went. I arrived at the place, heart beating, and here's this well-known television director. He greets me at the door, hand on my shoulder: 'Just relax. Here, take my coffee.' I said to myself, 'That man I'll marry!' And we just fell in love—*bang*—like that."

At the time, Penn was linked socially with two other women: writer Jay Presson and actress Gaby Rodgers.[19] But he soon turned his attentions exclusively to Maurer. He even spent some of his $300 weekly salary on a winter coat to replace the one she had to borrow from her *Three Sisters* costar Eileen Ryan for their first date.

Courtship had to be fitted around their respective work schedules. Penn was involved with *The Battler, The Heart's a Forgotten Hotel, The Waiting Place,* and *Lost*[20] on television, while Peggy was appearing in *The Three Sisters* onstage and on TV in *The Pardon-Me Boy* and *Incident in July.* He also directed and helped shape, in 1955, an early version of the teen drama *Blue Denim,* written by William Noble and James Leo Herlihy, a former Black Mountain College classmate.

Then they both got Hollywood offers. Peggy costarred with Richard Boone and Theodore Bikel in a grisly thriller called *The Spot on the Wall,*[21] and Arthur was given *The Left Handed Gun,* which was a visionary western. That's not what it was supposed to be, but thanks to the foresight and electricity generated by the people involved in making it, that's what it became.

7

Kid's Play

"I'm the most creative editor in Hollywood, and I'm going to edit your movie," the stranger announced, extending his hand. "My name is Folmar Blangsted."[1]

The pronouncement took Penn by surprise as he was pushing to finish his first feature film within its twenty-three-day shooting schedule and minimal $400,000 budget. But not as surprised as he would be on the twenty-fourth day when he drove to the studio expecting to work with the editor. "When I arrived on the Warner lot," he says, shaking his head, "my parking place bore another name." A further check let him know that his services were no longer required, and that the studio machine would take over. "I had to acknowledge," he admits, "that Hollywood had mastered at least one aspect of human interaction: termination. At that point I felt that the movies were not for me."

That was the way Hollywood worked: the director directed, the editor edited, and the studio ruled. The policy frustrated Penn, who was, by any definition, a de facto editor. "I was doing live TV drama, which meant we were using sometimes three, four, five cameras," he explains. "There was no tape. I was editing on the air between shots to tell the story and had every expectation that I would edit this film. I didn't know that even big directors like Ford would have their films cut by contract editors, contract cutters. Cutting me off like that from my movie was stunning. I thought, 'That's the end of movies for me. I'll never do this again.'"

Flash back two years. *The Left Handed Gun* was originally a *Philco Television Playhouse* written by Gore Vidal and directed by Robert Mulligan under the title *The Death of Billy the Kid*.[2] Its star was a relatively unknown Paul Newman, and it related the legend of the friendship between youthful outlaw William Bonney[3] and Pat Garrett, the lawman who ultimately killed him. It had been Vidal's intention to show how an iconoclast (Billy) is ultimately co-opted by the very forces he is rebelling against (society). "My decision," Vidal told his biographer, Fred Kaplan, "was to show not so much Billy himself as the people who created the myth of Billy the Kid."[4]

Newman and Vidal had tried setting up the project at Warner Bros. in 1956, but Jack Warner, aware of Newman's contempt for his debut in the studio's 1954 biblical epic *The Silver Chalice*,[5] was not about to agree. When Fred Coe offered to produce, Warner mellowed. Coe first offered it to Delbert Mann, who was otherwise committed, then to Robert Mulligan. When Mulligan departed (or was fired; sources disagree), Coe asked the loyal Penn to take the reins.

"It was not a script that I was particularly fond of," Penn says. "I said that I would do it, but that I would like to have the script considerably altered. Fred asked me who I would like to have work on it, and I said Leslie Stevens. He then took all those facts to Warner Bros., who acceded with several cutoff conditions. That is, they had to approve of the script, the cast, and the budget. All of those conditions were met and we made the picture."[6]

The welcoming ritual to the studio included a tour of the lot by Jack L. Warner himself that Coe and Penn dutifully endured. "Naturally, he was very proud of the place," Penn recalls. "There were four or five big pictures in the works. In the course of the walk-around—which was intimidating, to say the least—we went onto one stage where they were painting the world. *The Old Man and the Sea* was going to be a little boat in this vast sea—I think it was two stages put together to make it go on forever. It was extraordinary. Jack is going on in his charming English: everything is fuckin' this and fuckin' that. Then we go by a small office and he turned to us and said, 'You guys are from television, right?'

"Fred said, 'We are. That's where we came from.'

"Warner said, "That's my son-in-law. He's got this goddamn television. He doesn't know what the fuck he's doing. You want to take that over?'"

Coe and Penn waved off J. L.'s offer, insisting that they were there to make movies. Within a year, the son-in-law, William T. Orr, would make Warner Bros. the most successful provider in television.[7]

As their tour ended, Penn casually asked if he might see the processing lab to get a sense of how film was developed and handled. Warner ignored him, so Penn phoned the lab himself to arrange a visit. "I arrived the next day and out front are all the technicians in white smocks, like troops being reviewed," he marvels. "The lab supervisor said, 'Nobody who is doing a movie here has ever asked to see the lab!'"

Although its roots are in history, *The Left Handed Gun* takes Vidal's theme of media exploitation and applies modern psychology to Billy's motivation. The Bonney/Billy legend comes out of the Lincoln County cattle wars. In 1877, Englishman John Tunstall bought his way into the American cattle industry bent on putting his competitors out of business. The competitors had different ideas, of course, and in consort with the local sheriff, murdered Tunstall. Tunstall's partner, Alexander McSween, and fifteen-year-old ranch hand William Bonney sought revenge. After political machinations led to Bonney's capture and escape, Sheriff Pat Garrett tracked him down and killed him in July of 1881.

"This is a completely fanciful version of Billy the Kid," Penn admits, "but I was determined to have . . . this kind of story which skirted between fanciful play and the violence of the West, and the reason for Billy the Kid to have become the national figure." Billy entered myth, Penn explains, because "there was, somewhere close at hand, somebody who was a news reporter, or made the news, whether it was true or not. The news that they sent back to the eastern journals became like comic books, and they developed the tale of Billy the Kid, almost all of it totally fanciful."[8]

Once ensconced at the studio, Penn and Stevens started rewriting Vidal's 128-page script.[9] They had just tried saving Stevens's play *The Lovers*[10] on the road, and now they set about rewriting *The Death of Billy the Kid*. This irked the fractious Vidal, who had assumed that the same team that had been successful on television would make the movie. "In principle," Vidal told Coe, "there is certainly nothing wrong with you calling in another writer and probing him with my script, but I believe you should have done me the courtesy of telling me *before* you made this arrangement rather than after."[11]

But Penn and Stevens were on a roll. "We thought it would be interesting to take the story of a western juvenile delinquent, which is how Billy was always regarded, and find a basis to authenticate that existence," Penn says, positing, "Why did a juvenile delinquent spring up out of the West, and why did he remain so legendary and so much a part of the national consciousness? Taking that as a departure point, we decided we would give him a distinct family, and if we give him a distinct family we thought we would have to go back to his infancy, and the childhood of the Kid is relatively unknown except that he is supposed to have come from New York. No, it would be better if we chose a surrogate parent as we all do in our later life—an uncle or a friend. And that's what we did. We chose a man, Mr. Tunstall, who became a sort of idealized parent, before whom Billy solicited attention. Then, when Mr. Tunstall is killed, Billy takes up the cause as if it had been his lifelong mission. It was a need for revenge that antedated his relationship with Mr. Tunstall, a psychological requisite that was formed in his early, early childhood."

In the film, a parched and exhausted William Bonney (Paul Newman) wanders into Tunstall's cattle drive and becomes entangled in the Lincoln County cattle wars. When the pacifist Tunstall is assassinated by an opposition gang that includes the local sheriff, Billy kills the sheriff, precipitating a violent pursuit that chases Billy and his cohorts Tom Folliard and Charlie

Boudre to Mexico. There Billy encounters Pat Garrett (John Dehner), whom he'd met briefly in New Mexico. Billy's hothead-edness and single-minded pursuit of Tunstall's killers lead him to break other rules. He sleeps with Celsa, who is the wife of the town gunsmith, Saval, and kills one of Tunstall's remaining assassins during Garrett's wedding. It is this breach of manners, more than Billy's breaking the law, that makes Garrett put on a sheriff's star and track him down. When all Billy's friends are either alienated or killed, Billy loses control in front of the syco-phantic pulp writer Moultrie (Hurt Hatfield). Seeing this display, Moultrie's whole construct collapses, and he turns against his "creation." Betrayed and adrift, the unarmed Billy goads Garrett into killing him.

Because Warner refused to pay actors to rehearse, the cast members gathered on their own at the Penns' rented house in one of Hollywood's canyons not far from the studio (though New-man was seeing Joanne Woodward, he was not yet divorced from Jacqueline Witte). Newman flourished under Penn's guidance. "I would encourage things," Penn notes, "but Paul was a very trained actor by now and filled in Billy's inner life, so we saw contradictory things that only very good actors can do where they're playing two things at the same time."

Penn's first day on a movie set was "astonishing," he reports. "The first shot is a wide-open countryside. It's ostensibly one character, Paul Newman, carrying his saddle, so that you know he's lost his horse, and he's walking poorly. Russ Saunders, who was my AD, had gone around the countryside and we picked a beautiful location. Day One I get driven there and get out of the car and, my God, there's a herd of cattle, there are tables laid out for the crew, there's cook wagons and dressing rooms and I was just astounded. I knew that those existed on other pictures. I just hadn't put it together with *me*."

The veteran Saunders had begun as a stuntman and later became a successful assistant director. There was little about filmmaking that he didn't know, and he would become a main-stay in Penn's creative coterie. "Russ was my best teacher," Penn apprises. "What I remember was his saying to me, when Paul passed the camera on that first shot, 'Say "cut." Say *"cut!"'* And that's the title sequence of the film. I really had had no time on a movie set. After that, he became my buddy. I remember saying to Russ, 'Look, I can stage this so that this comes into this, and this, and then you follow this and go here.' He said, 'No, no, break it up. Break it into pieces because you'll never be able to cut it.'

"I liked the single camera because you were responsible for a single frame. On multiple cameras you knew the guys that were operating them and you knew that they would come on or about what you were asking, but not exactly. So this was a pleasant experience. Then you could turn around and cut to, say, Jimmy Best, which is a flexibility you never had in live TV."

Penn learned filmmaking quickly. Studio politics came later. "I was shooting the scene where Billy fires on and kills Denver Pyle," he describes. "It's ever-so-slightly slow motion, and then ever-so-slightly fast motion as he hits the ground. Well, I get a note from Steve Trilling:[12] 'Absolutely no slow motion.' The next day: 'No speeded-up motion.' I got notes later on: 'Too many close-ups,' and the next day was the same scene with the wide shots: 'Too many wide shots.' It was the same scene which we had already covered long and close. The lack of knowledge—not of the old buccaneers like Jack Warner and Harry Cohn—but of the people they brought in, was astonishing."[13]

Penn immediately encountered crew intransigence. "Our schedule was so tight, and I had had experience only in TV so in preparation for shooting, I'd gone around with little Dixie cups, nailed them into the ground, with the lens: this is a 35, this is a 50, et cetera. The cameraman, J. Peverell Marley, comes on the set and whoa! Furious! Just furious. And it was that way all through the shoot. I saw this when another crew went by us while he was practicing his golf swing, and one of them said, 'How's it going, Pev?' and he said, shaking his head, 'I got one a them *TV guys.'*"

Today Penn puts this resistance into perspective. "We were bringing the fragility and audacity of live TV to films," he says. "We had the audacity that came with the new medium. We didn't know boundaries. We would make demands on the crews—with great resentment—but that resulted in a change of movies. By the time I got good enough to know what I was doing, I made *The Miracle Worker*. The arrogance of a cameraman shaking his head was meaningless to me by that point, but it was paralyzing when I started out. No, it wasn't paralyzing. It was briefly stunning. And then it was, 'Go fuck yourself.'"

The resistance continued when the director tried applying innovative storytelling to what the crew assumed was a meat-and-potatoes horse opera. "There are the two famous sequences," Penn recalls. "One is where Denver Pyle gets shot, and he's blown out of his boots, and a little girl starts laughing at the boot, and her mother slaps her.[14] That's a very often cited sequence. Another one—and this is where the crew thought I was crazy—is in a steaming room where they're having a bath, and Billy goes to the window and, in the steam on the glass, sketches the configuration of the future scene.[15] They kept saying, 'But that hasn't happened yet, boss,' and I'd say, 'Yeah, but it's *gonna* happen.' I couldn't get it through to them. They just finally said, 'He wants it? Do it!' That was a sheer violation of what they had been taught. 'The line' was sacrosanct. You practically had to kneel every time you crossed it. The idea that you could cross the line!"[16]

Expert in the multiple cameras of live TV, Penn felt hamstrung by Hollywood's single-camera tradition. One day he quizzed Pev Marley, "Why don't we have a second camera?"

"Because I'm only lit for one camera," the DP (director of photography) growled back.

Nevertheless, Penn ordered a second camera to be slaved (synchronized) a few degrees off from the main one to save time as well as capture the action from another angle. Marley's response? "I refuse to be responsible for anything but the one camera I'm lighting for." Penn was aghast. "My God," he thought, "he refuses to be responsible!" When Marley finally acceded, Penn noticed that the DP had written on the slate, *Slave camera unlighted. Arthur Penn, director*—code to studio bosses watching the rushes that it was the director's fault, not his, if the footage was ruined. It wasn't.

Despite pressure to produce a standardized film, *The Left*

Handed Gun is awash in Freudian symbolism: the death of Tunstall deprives Billy of a father figure; Billy and his chums live a prolonged, id-driven adolescence in which killing is a game; and the women Billy encounters—all of them married—assume Oedipal roles. In what would become a Penn trademark, glass is used as both a window (access) and a lens (insight).

"I thought it was important to inject these kinds of personal pieces of material into it," Penn told interviewer Richard Schickel. "I now see in it certain references between me and my father. The relationship with Mr. Tunstall is based on a kind of desire to engage more closely with a kind of father figure, and that's terminated rather quickly and vividly in a killing. Conceivably, that launches Billy on his career. That's the story of it from the psychological standpoint, and that reflects something of my own personality, I think."[17]

Hinting at such interpretations, Penn warned the *Los Angeles Times* before the film's release, "This isn't a typical western. You remember the old controversy over whether Billy was left-handed or whether the most famous photograph of him was printed in reverse?[18] We believe that, spiritually and psychologically, he was left-handed. He saw everything 'through a glass darkly'[19] and we are using glass symbolically throughout the film."[20]

And then there was the character of Moultrie. Invented by Penn and Stevens to personify Vidal's theme, he's reminiscent of pulp novelists like Ned Buntline and publisher Beadle and Adams who embellished the Old West for profit. But Moultrie is in it for something else: he is drawn to Billy, who doesn't grasp that the man's interests are sexual as well as commercial. The emotions surface in a scene where Moultrie, who has idolized Billy, realizes that the attractive youth has feet of clay. Moultrie decides to betray Billy as much to purge himself of his obsession as to rid society of a menace. The scene, daringly played by Hatfield, was cut by the studio after censorship threats.

"What a scene that was!" Penn recalls. "We went in Pat Garrett's bar, and Moultrie is a kind of alcoholic, but he's more than an alcoholic, he's a bit of a hysteric, too. He's at an acute anxiety state. He is profoundly rejected by this figure that he had had a large hand in elevating to an almost godlike capability. He came in and said, 'Something has to be done' in that faintly southern prissy way, and Garrett said, 'Yes,' and put a bottle of whiskey and a glass on the bar. Moultrie started to betray Billy, and slowly Garrett gave him the whiskey, and at that point Garrett went out of the room. [Hatfield's] tears were just coming out. He was drinking his booze and weeping like a baby at betraying Billy and getting his whole sense of pride and order. It was an insane episode of a man in a profound, prototypically Judas experience that was supposed to touch a cultural nerve. It was a very crucial scene. But I guess people don't cry in westerns—certainly not men."

Hatfield's portrayal caused immediate reaction. On May 3, 1957, Geoffrey Shurlock, president of the Production Code Administration, wrote Jack Warner (more accurately, the studio's Finlay McDermid), "[We] regret to report that, while a basically acceptable story might be derived from this material, the present version seems to us to be unacceptable under the Code." The "Code" was Hollywood's official censorship office. Formed in 1930 and bolstered in 1934 by the industry trade group MPPDA (Motion Picture Producers and Distributors Association, now the Motion Picture Association of America), it was the censorship office's job to vet scripts prior to production to indicate elements that might run afoul of local censorship boards were they to make it to the screen.

In *The Left Handed Gun,* Shurlock's watchdogs cited:

A great number of personalized and quite brutal killings;
Clear suggestion that Billy has an adulterous affair with
   Celsa without any sense of sin whatsoever or any
   awareness of wrongdoing;
Moultrie's reactions to Billy "sometimes seem erotic and
   possibly effeminate."

Shurlock ended this first appraisal by saying, in effect, "Why discuss other, minor details when you've got these three big ones," triggering a back-and-forth that lasted until the film was released.

In light of Penn's and the studio's experience ten years later with *Bonnie and Clyde, The Left Handed Gun* presages the moral upheaval about to hit Hollywood. The film's conflicting themes of fact, fame, and alienation will become more pronounced by the time of *Bonnie and Clyde*, but *The Left Handed Gun* is a shot fired across the bow of America's growing fascination with celebrity. As Penn told writers Eric Sherman and Martin Rubin, "The need to have heroes be genuinely heroic seems to be an absurdity and a foolish intention, and when somebody like the Hatfield character is let down, his revenge knows no limit."[21]

Deliberately paced and atypically histrionic for a western, *The Left Handed Gun* showcases Paul Newman's early acting style: moody, brooding over some private event, and visibly tormented. The film ranges from playful (when Billy and Celsa embrace during a village fiesta, the scene dissolves to fireworks going off) to shockingly violent (as when Billy shoots Pyle out of his boot). Although the film's requisite gunfights are of the bloodless variety dictated by the Code—particularly the rule that a firing gun and its victim cannot be in the same frame—Penn pushes the envelope by having Billy's friend Folliard scream as his gunshot wound is treated, and his other friend Boudre whimper pitifully after his spinal cord is severed. Billy himself is badly burned during his escape from McSween's house fire. Finally, both Billy and Moultrie derive sexual thrill from death: Billy by causing it, Moultrie by fluttering near it.

Using the full size of the movie screen, Penn stages action in long and medium shots, allowing characters to relate to one another within the frame. This choice would frustrate Blangsted when he tried to alter Penn's rhythms, so the studio called in composer Alexander Courage[22] to underscore dialogue in a manner that tries to change the pace of the performances. The picture's violence caused Shurlock to demand, "Remove kick in face in fight with soldiers," "Reduce shot of Moon's face flattened against the glass as he slides down dying," and "Reduce Tom's screams as Billy pours whiskey into his wound."

Stevens's script had already been denuded of most of its religious content. Although Billy becomes the recipient of Tunstall's

Bible, from which he first hears the words "through a glass darkly," and somehow intuits that God wants him to avenge his mentor's death, the filmmakers were forced to cut Billy's questioning of why God wanted the man to die. As later with *Bonnie and Clyde,* however, it was the film's moral ambivalence that piqued the censors: "Does story tend to enlist sympathy of the audience for the criminal?" asked Shurlock before self-answering, "Both yes and no." Of course, that was the very point that Gore Vidal had been trying to make, not only about Billy but about the society that created and venerated him.

For Penn, the film was about "how a boy of no particular history emerges as a figure in American life.[23] The more subtle part of it is a beginning of the substantial awareness of the press and how they choose heroes and then, in the case of Moultrie, turn on them."

But the debate never happened. Warner Bros. dumped *The Left Handed Gun* despite supportive (if dispassionate) trade reviews. It would, however, be noticed in Europe by the emerging nouvelle vague although, as Penn observed, "Jack Warner wouldn't know what *Cahiers du cinéma* was if it bit him in the ass."

Penn's dismissal from postproduction irritates him to this day, not only for imposing a factory-like sameness on films that studios insist on calling "product" but for thwarting the very process that could create art as well as commerce. "The shots [in *The Left Handed Gun*] have a kind of mathematical continuity," he explains. "They follow the script, but that doesn't nearly produce the film. There may be two hundred shots in the script and maybe eight or nine hundred shots in the final movie. A film, after all, is *rhythm,* and that's what bothered me about having *The Left Handed Gun* recut. When directors complain, 'Somebody recut my film,' it's not as if somebody has totally desecrated it. It is that you have a rhythm in mind, a certain way that you're going to tell your story so that slowly, slowly it picks up velocity and then, *boom!* it reveals itself. If somebody comes in in the middle of that velocity, while you're building it, and says, 'That's too long, let's speed it up here,' well, if you speed it up here, you're robbing it from the end. Everybody thinks that film is made up of little pieces. Actually, film is one piece—one experience—and if you change that experience here, you change it, inevitably, there."

Not content to banish its director, the studio shot a new ending. In Penn's version, he says, after Billy is killed, "We stayed on Moultrie and then from some of the houses women came out with little candles, but they were dressed in black. And that was it. In the extant version, Garrett's wife suddenly appears and tells her husband, 'You can come home now.' It doesn't make any sense at all, but that was typical Warner Bros. ending for a movie."

As a final affront, Penn wound up catching his own film by buying a ticket to Loew's Eighty-sixth Street Theatre, where it was playing on the bottom half of a double bill.[24] Although he was upset at the time, he kept in mind that his goal all along had been theater, not movies and, in fact, he already had a play that he wanted to direct, one that was being written by William Gibson. "The play wasn't really finished and there was no absolute guarantee that we were going to be able to do it. When Bill Gibson couldn't get it produced, I took it to Fred Coe."

The two-character play that nobody wanted to produce would soon bring great success despite a fair amount of birthing pains. It was *Two for the Seesaw.*

8

Four for the Seesaw

William Gibson was twenty when he realized he'd married the wrong woman. It was 1934, he had dropped out of City College of New York, and he was trying to be a writer. Instead, he'd gotten married. "I was headlong, maddeningly in love with her," he admits, "but a year or so later I just wanted to get out of it." Then he met Margaret Brenman, a Brooklyn College psychology major who was reading Freud's introductory lectures and was as stable as he was adrift. Gibson became enamored both of her and of what she was studying, and they started seeing each other.

In 1939, after selling a story to *Esquire,* he felt confident enough to submit a play to the socially aware Group Theatre. Their reader, Molly Day Thatcher, Elia Kazan's wife, saw promise in Gibson but not in his play, and suggested he take a job with another theater to learn how to write for the stage. His agent, Leah Salisbury, secured him a position at the Barter Theatre in Virginia that summer, where he wrote five additional works, none of which got produced.

On December 6, 1940, Brenman and Gibson married and moved to Topeka, Kansas, where she interned at the Menninger Clinic while taking her doctorate at the University of Kansas. Her stipend supported both her and her husband, and when she earned her doctorate, Dr. Karl Menninger himself offered her a position. William joined the board of the Topeka Civic Theatre but caused a minor scandal when, to avoid the organization's conflict-of-interest rules, he submitted a play he had written under his brother-in-law's name and it was accepted for production. (The work, *A Cry of Players*, about young William Shakespeare, would not see a production until 1968.)[1] The Gibsons had lived in Topeka for eight years when Dr. Brenman-Gibson got a job offer from the Riggs Center in Massachusetts,[2] and the couple relocated. She continued to be the breadwinner of the couple, an arrangement with which her husband became increasingly uneasy. He left her for a year to live in New York, but Margaret was not alone for long. "Bill was in love with his work as well as with Margaret," Peggy Penn, a friend to them both, clarifies. "I think she wanted all his attention on her, and when she didn't get it, she had an affair with [psychoanalyst] Merton Gill."

Penn and Gibson connected fatefully during Gibson's New York sojourn, when Penn was visiting the city from Black Mountain College. They both turned up at the boardinghouse where two actresses they were dating happened to be staying (this was before Arthur met Peggy). "It was out of that context that Arthur and I kept in touch," says Gibson. "He wrote me a letter or two from Europe and I replied." During that year, Gibson studied with Clifford Odets at the Actors Studio, then reconciled with his wife and took a job at Riggs teaching piano to the patients and staging occasional plays.

"Much to my surprise," Gibson says, "I found myself—while Margaret was pregnant with our son—writing a novel[3] about Riggs. It not only was published and was sold to MGM, but I suddenly was making money. I talked myself into going out [to LA] and doing some rewriting for [producer John] Houseman and [director Vincente] Minnelli, and at the end they offered me a job on the next movie, and I said no because we had just bought, with MGM's money, this house,[4] and I had one act of a play that I wanted to get back to. The play was *Two for the Seesaw*, and Arthur and I were in touch all the time."

The road from page to stage was not smooth for *Two for the Seesaw*, and Gibson traced it with painful acuity in his 1968 chronicle, *The Seesaw Log*.[5] The play is a reluctant romance between two people who are lonely but don't want to admit it. Gittel Mosca (Anne Bancroft) is a struggling dancer living in New

York. She meets Jerry Ryan (Henry Fonda), a Nebraska lawyer who has separated from his wife and has ventured to the city to reclaim his independence. He is alternately needy and giving, and so is Gittel, but it takes awhile for them to get in sync. Gittel senses before Jerry does that his wife wants him back and, frustrated at his inability to commit, has a fling with an old flame. Torn by guilt, Gittel also tries to hide from Jerry the fact that her bleeding ulcer has erupted, and as act 2 ends so, very nearly, does her life. The moment is a riveting curtain.

"The audience is aware that she's bleeding before Jerry is," Penn says, "so they're more in touch with her feelings. The scene is a very hostile scene from him until she finally cannot sustain herself as an antagonist and says, 'I'm bleeding, Jerry.' And it was wonderful! Anne had this funny little false fur black jacket and I had her put it on backwards so she was able to keep her stomach warm. She was a beat-up soul, and then [the hemorrhage] came. It was a pretty explosive moment in the theater, damn dramatic." Eventually Jerry returns to his wife, even though he and Gittel are still in love. She has become stronger and more secure despite losing him, and he will doubtlessly ruminate on this affair for the rest of his life. Thus both souls have a future, but not with each other.

Gibson was wrestling with act 1 in 1955 when Arthur and Peggy visited Stockbridge to announce their impending marriage. "He brought me to see the Gibsons, to meet them and spend the weekend," Peggy says. "I liked them enormously, but I thought, I'm so young compared to them, and they're so knowledgeable compared to me. Margaret used to say mean things to me like, 'So what's wrong with your identity that you have to be an actress?' And I would always say something like, 'I thought I was enormously imaginative to be able to do this and to also be in love with Arthur.'"

Margaret was a challenge Peggy was ready to meet. "Sometimes they [the Gibsons] would fight, but she would always win," Peggy says. "Margaret was tough, and Arthur got sick on his stomach every time we went down there in the old days because she was on him all the time. Although we had a lot of fun down there, we also had a lot of *strum,* a lot of stress."

After they had been dating for eight months, Arthur proposed to Peggy, not by asking but by stating, "I think we should make plans." "It seemed like such a natural progression," he says. "We were totally together by that point, although not a lot of time had elapsed."

Early the next year they came back to Stockbridge, stayed at the Gibsons' home, and "published banns," a New England legal tradition that gives two weeks for anyone to object to the union. No one did, and on January 27, 1956, they were married in the Congregationalist Church. Says Gibson, "Although Arthur's Jewish and Peggy is I-don't-know-what, they wanted to get married in that church." Brother Irving took the wedding pictures. But it was not all happy.

"My parents did not wish us luck," Peggy says. "They couldn't care less. My mother wouldn't even discuss it. Not my father; he came up and dropped $1,000 on [Arthur's] shoe."

"He handed it to me," Penn corrects gently. "It fell."

Part of the Maurers' coldness was Penn's Judaism, even though he didn't practice it. The rest, Peggy says, flowed from her parents' alcoholism.

Peggy Maurer had not been the first woman that Penn brought to Stockbridge. "Before he got married," Gibson says, "he would bring ladies up here for a weekend. There were a couple of pleasant ladies. He said something to Margaret and me: 'I always knew, when I got married, that I would be monogamous.' That was a question which everybody I know, including me, has found very intriguing: 'Is Arthur fucking around with these beautiful actresses or not?' and the answer was 'Not.' And nobody could believe it. That's an unusual fact in Arthur's life. How did he know he was going to be monogamous when he got married? *How did he know that?* I didn't know that about myself."

Before long, the Penns bought the house up the road from the Gibsons as a getaway from their New York City primary residence. It was a house with a history. Built by William Black, who ran the Chock Full o' Nuts coffee company, it was later purchased by famed developmental psychologist Erik Erikson[6] and his wife, Joan, when he became affiliated with Riggs in 1951.

When marriage and motherhood drew Peggy increasingly away from acting, she began pursuing psychology, studying at the New School in New York and benefiting from the mentoring of Brenman and Erikson. It might be said that buying the Erikson home completed the transformation, or was at least a significant omen, for today Peggy Penn, PhD, is a supervising faculty member of the Ackerman Institute for Family Therapy with a specialty in the effects of combining writing with therapeutic conversations.[7]

Meanwhile, Gibson was mired in *Seesaw* and facing a real-life drama: survival. Between Margaret's pittance from Riggs and the last of his MGM money, he was courting penury. He called Penn in New York, where he was going from one live TV show to another, and admitted flat out, "I need money."

"What do you have?" asked Penn, aware that television was constantly foraging for material. Responded the writer, "I did this dance narration."

"Tell it to me."

And with that, William Gibson spun Arthur Penn the story of *The Miracle Worker* (see chapter 9).

As the Penns were settling into married life, *Seesaw* was adrift. Clifford Odets, Gibson's mentor, urged him to abandon it. Penn insisted that Odets was wrong and gave it to Fred Coe, who embraced it. Then everyone spent the better part of a year looking for actors to say yes. Not just any actors, but names sufficient to attract investors. Among the women who were approached to play Gittel were Gwen Verdon (no), Kim Stanley (never replied), Barbara Baxley (no), Gaby Rodgers (no), and Julie Harris (couldn't see herself as a Jewish girl from the Bronx). Men asked to play Jerry included Paul Newman (movie commitments), Fritz Weaver (had just signed for another show), Van Heflin (no), Jack Palance (no), Barry Nelson (no), Eli Wallach (no), Don Murray (no), Robert Preston (no), and Jack Lemmon (no, twice). Richard Basehart was interested yet elusive, but recommended for Gittel an actress that Gibson and Fonda had never heard of, but that Penn had worked with and forgotten: Anne Bancroft.

Although the Bronx-born, twenty-six-year-old Anna Maria

Louisa Italiano had not yet appeared on the New York stage, she had acted in several TV shows (as Ann Marno) and a handful of movies that exploited her aesthetic rather than thespic talents. In person she was far more impressive, radiating a life force that galvanized Coe, and he urged Gibson to hurry east after he finished his *Miracle Worker* commitment to meet her.

Gibson liked her immediately, but he also realized that "she was an unknown; we couldn't raise any money on her. We were in New York for two hours together in Fred Coe's office, and from there she was going out to the coast. Arthur talked to her out there and sent a message back to Coe, which was, 'She's Gittel on the hoof.'" In other words, cast her.

With the unknown Bancroft on board it became essential to sign a male star who could open the play. Coe approached Henry Fonda who, although a Hollywood legend, regularly renewed his theatrical roots, having just ended a year's run in *The Caine Mutiny Court-Martial*. He consented to host a reading in his New York apartment. Before they went, Coe and Penn urged Bancroft to leave as soon as it was over to allow them to confab with Fonda. According to Gibson, Fonda "read seldom" and Bancroft "read interminably," the upshot of which was that Fonda felt the man's role was underwritten and asked for changes, preferably before he went off to Europe the next week with his wife, Afdera, to visit her family in Villefranche. Gibson returned to Massachusetts, hurriedly rewrote Fonda's part, and sent it to him. In August of 1957, Coe received a telegram from Fonda in Europe: "I'm yours." The show was quickly capitalized at $80,000 (some of which Fonda himself put up). By September, Penn and Coe had wrapped *The Left Handed Gun*, Penn had directed *The Dark Side of the Earth* on *Playhouse 90*, and on November 4 everybody was back in New York to start rehearsing *Seesaw*.

"Arthur and I would have discussions in his apartment when we were in rehearsal in New York, before we went out on the road," Gibson relates, "and Arthur would say, 'But does he have a right to say that?' and I said, 'What do you mean, "Does he have a right"? He *says* it!' What's implicit in 'Does he have a right?' was that the audience isn't going to like it. At one point I said, 'I don't know where this play is going,' and he said, 'The girl will lead you. Wherever she wants to go, that's where the play will be.' It was a big learning experience, and painful for me, but both Arthur and Fred—and Hank Fonda, too—were all concerned that they wanted this character to be sympathetic, and he's not really a sympathetic man. He's trying to survive, and he's using the girl to survive on. That was the kind of discussion that kept happening every day. We were all riddled with anxiety. Arthur and Fred's anxiety took the form of being at my mercy, because if I didn't deliver the lines, they couldn't solve what they saw had to be solved. It was a baptism in fire. I don't know how Arthur and Fred put up with me. I was trying to be obedient, but all the time I thought, 'I wish these two guys would drop dead.'

"There was a basic flaw in the play itself," Gibson now admits. "I don't think they were wrong, by the way. I was not trying to justify the man, and they felt he had to be justified. I was writing the play out of personal guilt out of such a relationship I had had where I just dumped the girl. Now, the play has to say—and I wanted this—that they each get something valuable from each other. I don't know if the girl got anything from me, but I got *Two for the Seesaw*."

By Thanksgiving, *Seesaw* was in previews in Philadelphia. Early December brought it to Washington, DC. Meanwhile, Peggy remained in New York, where she was about to deliver their first child, and stayed with the Arnold Schulmans. "They insisted I live in their house," Peggy says, "and Arnold slept every night in his clothes in case I called out in the middle of the night. Isn't that adorable? When I did, he leapt out of bed, and I said, 'You're dressed!' He said, 'Well, are we going somewhere?' And I said, 'Yes, I think, to the hospital.' My water broke. I called Arthur to tell him."

"Yeah," Arthur adds. "At four o'clock in the morning! [Still in Washington, DC], I had taken a sleeping pill. Bill and I had had an argument about rewriting; he had said to me, 'You have no soul.' So when Peggy called and said she was in labor, I told her, 'Will you make sure and call me back?' and hung up.

Peggy: "So I thought, 'That's the end of my conversation with that man.'"

"And then I called back," Penn hurriedly adds. "Got on the train—'cause there were no flights in those days from Washington—and up to New York."

Peggy: "You must have thought the baby would be born by the time you got there."

Arthur: "It was iffy. You know, there were no cell phones, I had no way of knowing. Fortunately, I got here midday, midafternoon, and Matt wasn't born till eight o'clock (on December 13, 1957). As for the play, the reviews were coolish in Philadelphia, warmer by a lot in Washington, and then we came into New York to the Booth Theatre, and we started playing previews."

With the Penns as newly minted parents, Gibson was left in Washington to birth his play. This did not please Fonda, who had been growing increasingly uneasy. Fonda was a complicated man whose affable screen image was at odds with his aloof, moody private personality. Once he started peeling the layers off Jerry Ryan, he found him an unsure, distant, even deceitful man who abandons Gittel emotionally long before he deserts her physically. He also knew that the production was depending on him, what with a novice costar and a first-time Broadway director and playwright.

"We went into production and then Fonda found out that it was the girl's play," says Gibson. "It wasn't his play, and he was the big star, and it was a couple of months of constant humiliation for him. He didn't take it, perhaps, with maximum grace.[8] It was complicated by the fact that Annie was such a talented performer and Hank wasn't. I mean, Hank had a marvelous quality on stage—everybody said 'star quality' and it's true—when he got onstage and walked, you looked at him. But when he said my lines, you didn't listen to him. I would write jokes for Fonda, and Annie would feed him the line and get the laugh on the feed, and Fonda would be left with the limp jokes. This happened a dozen times." Fonda felt left in the lurch. Where he liked to freeze a play several days before opening, Gibson and Penn's constant rewrites threw him off his process.

Bancroft's process was also in conflict. Although Gibson feels that "her performance was what really made that play sing," Peggy saw that "that didn't please Henry Fonda either. He used to say to Arthur, 'Look at her, look what she's doing. Blubbering all over the place, has to blow her nose.'"

Gibson shakes his head. "I never understood, really, why [Hank] wired Fred from Europe. I asked Fred while we were on the road, 'What did he see in this play?' and Fred said, 'He fell in love with the girl.'"

Says Penn, "Hank said, 'I thought this was a play about two charming people.'"

Adds Gibson drolly, "I think he misread the play somehow."

"It was a very emotional play for that period," Penn says. "There hadn't been a Gittel. This was not all that long, particularly for women, after the World War. It was '57. Women were not portrayed that way in theater until then. She was a real New York dancer—a lousy dancer; you knew she was lousy, but she was doing the thing."

Bancroft, of course, well understood Gittel and impressed Penn more with each preview. "She's just going day by day increasing in strength and power. I kept saying to her, 'You're a street fighter, Gittel, you're a street fighter, don't let him [Fonda] get away with it,' and she would rise to it. And then came the call from New York and I left, stayed there through the birth of Matthew, then went back to Washington, and Annie had been growing during those three days. Bill was directing it. Sort of. He makes no pretensions about it."

Without Penn as buffer, enmity developed between playwright and star. Alternately crabby and seductive, Fonda finally turned on Gibson when the playwright poked his head into his dressing room at the Booth Theatre on opening night to wish him well. "Fonda excluded me from his dressing room," Gibson explains, quoting the actor as saying, 'I don't want to see that prick anymore,' or something like that, to the stage manager. I didn't mind that. I felt he was a pain in the ass, which he was; other directors from other shows who worked with Hank always complained about him. He was, in part, what he seemed to be on the screen—candid, straightforward—but he was a lot of other things besides."

The rewriting continued during New York previews, baffling the production team because no two audiences reacted the same way. "When we'd have just an ordinary preview with just a New York audience, the play would rock," reports Penn. "When we'd have a theater party: cool, chilly. Some nights we're a big hit and some nights we were not. The night before opening night, there was one of those Hank Fonda crowds. Black tie. Prep school. And here's Gittel Mosca! Just chilly in the house—to die. And Hank said, 'See? I told you'—he was mean that night—'Now you know.'"

The night before opening, January 15, 1958, Penn and Coe took Gibson to dinner. Over cocktails Penn told him he wanted another scene rewritten. Gibson was stunned. "I said, 'You want me to go home and rewrite this page *tonight* and you'll put it in?' He said, 'I'll put it in tomorrow.' So I went back to [the] friends' house where I was staying—Margaret was there—and I sat up till two or three o'clock in the morning writing, doing this final act of rewriting. In the morning I got up early enough to call Arthur, and I dictated it to him. It was like six new lines or something. There was a long silence and he said, 'It seems enormous.' I said, 'I think you're right.' We'd had trouble enough with Fonda to give him this stuff the night he was opening. So Arthur said, 'I'll do it directorially.' He did it in an afternoon—I wasn't present for it—and then the show went on and was very successful. In fact, that evening is when Fred said to me, 'You're the most creative prick I know.' I guess he was referring to the difficulty they had of getting ideas into my head when they were on the road. But, anyway, I never forgot that compliment."

Sulking in a theater party at Sardi's on opening night (January 16) while Penn, Gibson, Coe, et al. were waiting elsewhere for the reviews, Fonda was flabbergasted when the papers declared *Two for the Seesaw* a hit. Still irritated with the product, however, he declined to extend his performance contract once it ended and was replaced by Dana Andrews.

With *Seesaw,* reflects Gibson, "Arthur was now a 'big

Broadway director' overnight, like I was a 'big Broadway play-wright' overnight. That's a conspicuous position that you don't get into by being a steady worker. I don't think success in any way ruined us. I think it was good, if it's good to have money and solve problems that are not solved in other ways. Money is not an unmixed blessing, but it was nevertheless great for it to come in.[9] This is the change in Arthur's life: he suddenly became, instead of an obscure success in television, a highly desirable property. Those are big changes."

Penn regarded the changes objectively. "I just thought that was how it was," he said. "This was the first of five shows that I did and they all hit. And I thought, 'Boy, this is a great life. You don't have to worry about working in movies.'"[10]

Seesaw's Broadway success did not block another rebuff from Hollywood. The screen rights were bought by producer Ray Stark, who announced that he was going to shoot and release the film while the play was still running. By this time Lee Grant had replaced Anne Bancroft (who had gone on to *The Miracle Worker*), and Dana Andrews had been replaced by Jeffrey Lane. Stark's ideal casting was Elizabeth Taylor and Paul Newman (earlier paired in *Cat on a Hot Tin Roof*), but Taylor was delayed by the eternal *Cleopatra,* so the producer engaged the effervescent Shirley MacLaine and the laconic Robert Mitchum. The results, directed by Robert Wise,[11] were predictably bland.

"Ray rejected me as a possible director and Bill as a possible screenwriter," Penn now chuckles, "and they start rehearsal in California. Finally, we get a call saying, 'We can't find the jokes.' Fred Coe said, 'So what?' Ray said, 'I'd like to pay you for one whole performance and have them play the play and we'll photograph it.' And Fred said, 'Go fuck yourself.' Of course, the film had nothing. Because they're not jokes, they're *behavior* jokes. And if you're not Annie, with a certain style, it's not funny."

Additionally, *Two for the Seesaw* defied the stagecraft of the time. With the setting in two separate New York apartments—Gittel's downscale dancer's flat and Jerry's Spartan bachelor single—the telephone connecting them becomes, in effect, a third character. In order to keep the story moving, Penn and scenic

designer/lighting designer George Jenkins devised a technolog-
ically advanced (for its time) staging: twin turntables. "I was
always worried that it was going to be visually uninteresting
after awhile," Penn shares. "George and I discussed this problem
again and again, and we came up with this solution of two wagons, each with a turntable on it, so that every scene was a different perspective. It was almost like a movie in that respect. By
the time we opened in New York I had so integrated the behavior and movement of stuff around the set that it went from one
to the next to the next to the next and the curtain never came
down."

Anne Bancroft won the 1958 Tony for her lead role, and
Penn, Gibson, and Coe were nominated for their work. In 1973
a musical adaptation, *Seesaw* (book by Michael Bennett, music
by Cy Coleman, lyrics by Dorothy Fields), ran just over three
hundred performances. Ken Howard and Michelle Lee played
Jerry and Gittel with, somehow, thirty-three supporting cast and
chorus members.

Over the next few years Penn and Gibson would collaborate
on *The Miracle Worker, Golden Boy, Monday After the Miracle, Golda,* and other adventures. Their families became even
closer friends, and their lives and careers would intertwine on
multiple levels. "It has to be stated," notes Gibson proudly, "that
Arthur and I, it's like two organisms with one brain. I never met
anybody or worked with anybody where he understands what
I'm about to say and think and I understand what he's about to
say and think, and the communication is very quick because of
mutual understanding."

The enduring essence of their friendship may be found in the
inscription that Gibson wrote in the published edition of *Two
for the Seesaw* that Penn keeps in his Stockbridge home: "For
Arthur—friend and midwife—with love, Bill."

9

Three Miracles

"Whenever I get into this story," says the author of *The Miracle Worker,* "I feel I'm in the presence of something supernatural." For half a century William Gibson's play has been celebrated as a timeless tale of love, devotion, and understanding. It began on television, was a triumph on the stage, and became a classic on film before retiring to the repertoire of high school drama departments. What is not generally known is that the story of Annie Sullivan and Helen Keller started life as a ballet.

It began when Gibson was staging plays with patients at the Riggs Center in Stockbridge, Massachusetts, where his wife, psychiatrist Margaret Brenman-Gibson, was on staff. "We had, at that time, a folk minstrel whose name was Richard Dyer-Bennett," Gibson states. "He and his wife, Mel, came up—she was a dancer, except she'd had some kind of accident with her leg so she was retired. She was a very smart cookie. Margaret said she was a witch because she could look at how people moved and would have a psychological portrait of that person. Margaret got Riggs to hire Mel as a physical action therapist as part of the activities program. I had this drama group, and I thought we might do an original evening of one-acts. I thought I could provide a script for the dance."

Years earlier, Gibson had come across a collection of the letters that Anne Sullivan had written home to Boston almost every day when she was in Tuscumbia, Alabama, trying to teach young Helen Keller. Keller had become world famous for overcoming the deafness and blindness that had struck her in infancy. But few knew that it was Annie Sullivan, a twenty-year-old graduate of the Perkins Institute for the Blind in Boston, herself partially sighted, who became Keller's teacher.

Gibson first read Helen Keller's *The Story of My Life*[1] in grammar school, not knowing that most of the manuscript had been suppressed. "The real book," he later discovered, "consisted of three large sections: the first was Helen's *Story of My Life;* the middle part was a long essay by John Macy[2] on the pedagogical techniques of Annie Sullivan teaching Helen Keller; the third section was all the letters that Annie had written back to Perkins Institute. I don't know whether anybody would have the materials to disprove this, but this was edited by John Macy, who was a literary man, so the book must have been his idea. And that means that these letters, which are perpetuated in this book, had passed through his hands. Now, you may remember a scandal in which the Sacco-Vanzetti letters turned out maybe to have been written by a Boston reporter. It's not likely to me that the [Sullivan] letters are pure. John must've 'helped.' But they portray an extraordinary girl in an extraordinary story."

Here Gibson—a lanky black Irishman who favors directness—softens. "I've often thought," he says, almost reluctantly, "that the only evidence in my life that persuades me there's a God is this story. Here you've got this crippled child down in Tuscumbia—here you've got this crippled young woman, twenty years old, up in Boston—and it takes these two half-lives to make one life. This cannot have happened except by Jehovah's intersession, right? All of this came out of those letters, whether they're Annie's or not. And the facts of her life are extraordinary, so I'll believe the letters. That was what set me off."

Without *The Miracle Worker,* few would know of Sullivan's contribution, yet Keller's triumph over adversity still made hers the better story. Indeed, as Annie caustically remarked when she accepted an honorary degree from Temple University in 1932 and the press huddled around Helen, "Even at my coronation, Helen is queen."[3]

Helen Adams Keller was born June 17, 1880, on her father's

estate in Tuscumbia. Her father, Captain Arthur Keller, was late of the army of the Confederacy, and her mother, Kate Adams, was related to Robert E. Lee. The exact malady that robbed the girl of her sight and hearing at nineteen months is unknown—sources suggest meningitis, scarlet fever, or diphtheria—but her father was half a step away from committing her to an institution when her mother took charge. The Kellers—thanks to the intervention of a Baltimore physician and later of Alexander Graham Bell—reached out to the Perkins School in Boston. The school's director, Michael Anagnos, suggested recent graduate Annie Sullivan as a suitable teacher for Helen, who was just shy of seven.

At twenty, Annie Sullivan was already a survivor. When she was five she caught trachoma, a chronic infection that progressively scars the cornea with each painful recurrence. By the time she was eight her mother had died, and when her father, Thomas, could not support her and her brother, Jimmie, he consigned them both to a workhouse in Tewksbury, Massachusetts. Within three months Jimmie died, leaving Annie not only distraught but helpless, for he had been her eyes.

When she was fourteen, Annie took charge of her own fate. Members of a state commission had heard about conditions at the Tewksbury Almshouse, and during their visit, Annie followed them around. As they were about to leave, she pushed her way through to the head inspector and announced—some say demanded—"I want to go to school!" In a rare sympathetic response to a public ward's request, the Bay State enrolled her at Perkins. There she had eye surgery that improved her vision to the point that she was able to see text. When the inquiry arrived from the Kellers, Anagnos knew that the feisty Sullivan would be just the person to help Helen. In March 1887, he dispatched her to Tuscumbia and the rendezvous that would change countless lives.

Gibson became fascinated with the letters that Sullivan wrote to Anagnos during her period with Helen. Deems the playwright, "It was like falling off a log; the action was all laid out in Annie's letters." The rights to Annie's letters, however, were controlled by her biographer, Nella Braddy Henney, an editor at

Doubleday publishers. Gibson sent *Seesaw* to Henney, and Henney, impressed, cleared the rights.

The timing was fortunate; the Gibsons' combined income from Riggs was proving insufficient, so the writer placed a hurried phone call to Arthur Penn in New York, where he was directing *Philco Playhouse,* to ask if NBC needed material. When Penn said yes, Gibson sent the dozen pages of notes he had written for the unproduced Dyer-Bennett ballet. Intrigued, Penn joined Gibson, and together they sketched out a structure. Penn: "I'd say, 'Here we'll break for commercial' and 'Here we'll break for commercial' and inevitably, as a result of fitting it to the requirements of television, a form emerged that was essentially a three-act play, only it was in five or six acts for television." The men devised two narrative devices that, while facile, are appropriate: using Annie's letters to Anagnos, and having Annie talk to herself with the assurance that the deaf child cannot hear her.

Penn got Gibson a $500 advance and proudly handed the pages to NBC. "And then," Penn sighs, "they said, 'Nah; who's gonna watch a piece about a blind, deaf girl?' So I said, 'Well, fuck you—I'll go to CBS.' Same response! It wasn't until Martin Manulis had *Playhouse 90* and was a much brighter, more responsive intelligence and said, 'What have you got?' that I sent it to him and he grabbed it."

The $500 option turned into $10,000 once Manulis greenlighted the project, and Gibson traveled to the coast to revise the script, consistent with Penn's collaborative process and Manulis's writer-friendly policy. The impending production forced Penn and Gibson to finally focus on what the piece was truly about. Above and beyond the obvious—that "her business in life was to redeem a life lost," as Gibson put it—it was also, more importantly, he realized, about the power that comes from language. Denied it, Helen was isolated; taught it by Annie, she emerged. For that reason it is essential to see (as many do not) that *The Miracle Worker* is about Annie Sullivan, not Helen Keller. "Otherwise," jokes Gibson, "it would be called *The Miracle Workee.*"

Gibson quickly learned the tricks of live television, such as extending a scene among supporting players so the main character can run across the studio for the next scene to begin, sometimes allowing for a costume change en route. "Like putting on a stage play," he compares, "the rehearsal period was very familiar to me, but the actual physical mechanics of getting it photographed were quite new. Arthur was sitting in the control room talking to the camera guys. I remember once that somebody was supposed to go up a flight of stairs and Arthur said, 'Missed it!' The camera hadn't gotten there in time. That was live television; it was very exciting."

Mindful of the symbiosis between *Playhouse 90* and Hollywood, Manulis cast Teresa Wright in the role of Annie Sullivan and Patricia (Patty) McCormack, who had memorably played the title character in the 1956 film *The Bad Seed,* as Helen. "I was eleven," says McCormack, who has continued acting, "which was the outside of my still looking like a child. The very next year, everything changed on me, and I looked like a young lady. Patty [Duke, who would play Helen onstage and in the film] is actually a year younger than I, but she's teeny-tiny, so, in those days, she could play a baby forever." (Duke was fifteen when she did the movie.)

McCormack notes that this *Playhouse 90* was different from others in which she appeared. "We started before the normal rehearsal period because we learned sign language. We also shot [on film] chicks hatching at a farm." Airing on February 7, 1957, the program also starred Katharine Bard (Mrs. Manulis) as Mrs. Keller; Burl Ives as Captain Keller; John Barrymore Jr. as Helen's brother, James; and Akim Tamiroff as Anagnos. Right from the start, Penn places the viewer at Helen's point of view as her parents and the doctor lean over her crib marveling at how she has pulled through her mysterious brain fever. But no; the Kellers soon discover that their daughter can neither hear their shouts nor see a lamp waved before her eyes. "She can't hear you!" Mrs. Keller wails. Combined with an iris-down effect that strangles the shot, it is an economical and horrifying beginning that never lets up.

It isn't often that a television show, now seen only on crude kinescope in museums, retains its power half a century after it was aired, just once, on February 7, 1957, but *The Miracle Worker* holds its own. "It was a huge success," Penn notes. "For one of the very, very first times they got this volume of phone calls from all over the country at CBS about the show."

It's instructive to realize that the highly skillful production was not unusual, but rather the normal level of professionalism for network television shows of the era. To the people who worked on it, *The Miracle Worker* was just another job.

But not for long. Six months after *Two for the Seesaw* opened and Henry Fonda left the show, Penn and Gibson were elated when they saw that their discovery, Anne Bancroft, was able to carry the play on her own. She had become a star. This pleased Gibson who, while *Seesaw* was on the road in tryouts, had taken Penn aside and announced to him that he was going to turn *The Miracle Worker* into a stage play. Penn's skeptical response was "You're out of your fucking mind. The climax of your play is two hands on a big stage, and how are we going to get the meaning of that to project to the audience?" Gibson assured him, "Trust me."

Another reason for Gibson's enthusiasm surfaced when Penn discovered that the playwright had already offered the role of Annie to Bancroft: he had become smitten with her. "I was sort of in love with Annie [Bancroft]," he admits. "We never had any affair, but we had some kind of an intellectual rapport that was like an affair, but intellectual—and I digested that."

Coe was brought in as producer, and the *Seesaw* team was complete. Then another problem arose. Gibson recounted: "When Anne left *Seesaw* and went directly into rehearsals for *The Miracle Worker*, she played Annie Sullivan as though she were Gittel, and I said to Arthur, 'I've made a terrible mistake.' And he said, 'I'll fix it.' He gave her an Irish accent, a brogue, which Annie Sullivan did not have. But now all over the world Annie Sullivan has a brogue because Arthur was trying to get rid of Gittel in Anne Bancroft."[4]

Casting Patty Duke, who would rise to fame in the play, started with a pro forma meeting in Penn's office. "We sat down and he wanted to know what I knew about Helen Keller," Duke wrote in her autobiography. "Well, the poor man, I just told him everything there was to know. I seemed to be this extraordinarily articulate child who knew all about frustrations and psyches and everything. He had no idea how intensively I'd been preparing for that question for a year and a half. He'd ask me, 'What would you say if you were Helen Keller' and I'd come back with 'I wouldn't say anything.' Penn was probably thinking, 'This kid's been well programmed.' He was warm and charming and I already had a crush on him.

"After an audition and two callbacks, the phone call came: 'Okay, but if she grows another two inches she's out.'"

Duke admitted her schoolgirl crush. "I just thought he was the most handsome, the most sexy man ever. I even loved the clothes he wore: khaki pants and a white shirt, and the way he stood in his white tennis shoes with one foot turned a little bit.[5] He'd walk by and my little heart would absolutely flutter. I used to screw things up just so he'd come and talk to me and give me a little more direction."[6]

Duke remarked that Penn used whispers and gentle humor ("Duke, you're all right for a girl") to help her find her character and gain confidence. By the October 19, 1959, opening at the independently owned Playhouse Theatre (like NBC, the dominant Shubert brothers didn't think a play about a deaf and blind girl would sell), Duke and Bancroft were fast friends and perfectly matched. *The Miracle Worker* enjoyed a twenty-one-month, 719-performance run.

The stage play powerfully turns the television drama into an immediate, intimate experience. After its harrowing prologue the story jumps forward six years to find Helen a feral child indulged by her family. In a last move to forestall commitment to an asylum, her mother recruits Annie Sullivan, whose sight has recently been restored, as Helen's teacher. Annie takes over, much to the irritation of Helen's father, and demands full control over the highly resistant girl. At a family dinner celebrating Helen's achievement of eating with a spoon and folding her napkin—something Annie suspects is learned but not understood—Helen stubbornly reverts, and Annie clears the dining room. The "table scene" showdown became a celebrated nightly event between two committed actresses, Bancroft and Duke.

"It takes nine minutes—most evenings it took nine, maybe sometimes ten, sometimes eleven—which was the full willpower of opposition," the director recalls. "That's where you really go to the heart of it. The choreography follows from the depth of intention and intensity, and the placement on the stage is interesting. In that scene, Annie chases the entire family out. She's left with herself and Helen. I had this big table which had accommodated six or seven or eight people, now with just two people. I started it with Anne facing the audience, and it just seemed flaccid, you know. And I thought, 'Wait a minute, wait a minute, I'm talking about the audience here. Let me talk about the two of them.' So I put Anne with her back to the audience. Helen started alongside her. Helen would refuse to eat properly and crawl away under the table, and Annie would run around, pick her up, bring her back, and that gave us a kind of spring-like energy that kept that scene going. If we were able to see all the expressions from the outset, it would reveal too much. We had to be in that 'How do I solve this one?' mode, and the best way was *not* seeing Annie make solutions. She would just watch that child, and if she threw the napkin down she would grab it and put it back. Bill wrote that scene very carefully. The full credit for that scene goes to him. On top of that, we had the blessing of these two really great actresses, and they would spare nothing. They were black and blue a good part of the time. They never did the same thing twice—never! That subtle little napkin drop. That's a little insurrection. How's it gonna be responded to? And that's the beginning of the end of the play."

It is in the penultimate moment when, in Gibson's words, "the miracle happens." Once again testing Annie's mettle, Helen defiantly empties a water pitcher. In response, Annie drags her to the pump on the lawn to refill it. As Helen waits for the liquid to flow, she suddenly recalls from deep in her memory a word she spoke before sickness claimed her hearing: "waa-waa." Miraculously, she connects the concept of the alphabet that Annie has been spelling into her hand with the reality of the world around her. Soon she is dragging Annie across the yard absorbing language with lightning speed: *Ground. Pump. Step. Trellis.*

"Mrs. Keller! Mrs. Keller!" Annie cries out, summoning Helen's parents, "SHE KNOWS!" Helen runs into her mother's arms while reaching to Annie for the word: "M-O-T-H-E-R." Then to her father for Annie to spell "P-A-P-A." Finally Helen points to Annie, who spells, "T-E-A-C-H-E-R."

Audiences responded with tears and applause, and *The Miracle Worker* was a Broadway triumph. At the 1960 Tonys at the Hotel Astor on April 24, sitting at Helen Hayes's table, Arthur Penn won the award for Best Direction. He accepted, saying briefly, "Without embellishment, thank you all very much." He also accepted William Gibson's award for Best Play with a gracious "I wish this truly were my award. It's for William Gibson who couldn't be here tonight, but he did ask me to express one thought, which was that certainly he couldn't accept this award without first expressing his great indebtedness to the two people who truly lived the drama: Annie Sullivan and Helen Keller."

Anne Bancroft won Best Performance by an Actress in a Drama, saying, "There are three reasons why I think I deserve this, and that's Fred Coe, Bill Gibson, and Arthur Penn." John Walters also won Best Stage Technician, and Patty Duke received a Tony as Helen. George Jenkins was nominated as scenic designer.

It is as a film, however, that *The Miracle Worker* survives most memorably. As Penn's measured reentry into movies, its production provides a clue as to how he asserted his power upon a system he would forever keep at arm's length.

It is also the only instance in which the same director guided the same material through three different mediums, adjusting his vision to accommodate each of them and ultimately achieving success in all. This is possible, Penn breezily told *Variety* as the film was shooting, "if you have a good property and have time off between the various versions to work on other projects."[7]

The movie was not a foregone conclusion. The good news was that United Artists was interested. UA enjoyed the respect of filmmakers because it allowed them to make their films their own way once management had given the production a green light. The bad news was that UA's green light specified that Anne Sullivan should be played by either Elizabeth Taylor or Audrey Hepburn.

"At that point," says Penn, "Bill and Fred and I said, 'We go with Bancroft.' UA said, 'Oh, no, that's impossible.' We held out. Bill was solid as a rock. He took less money—considerably less—and we held out for her." Gibson's loyalty to Bancroft was equaled by his loyalty to Sullivan and Keller, who was still alive (she died in 1968 at age eighty-seven). To make the film their own way, the trio set up Playfilm Productions and spurned UA's choice of Taylor or Hepburn, for whom the studio would have guaranteed $2 million. With Bancroft, the offer dropped to $500,000.[8] The modest financing was to become an issue, as Penn would later reveal in an American Film Institute seminar: "When we did, in fact, exceed the very modest budget by even a slight margin, the first monies came out of our salaries so that Annie, Fred Coe, and Bill Gibson and I, each of us, I think, ended up with half-salary for making the film. The salaries were not bad to begin with—they were $75,000 apiece—we ended up with $37,500."[9]

The film was shot in Middleton, New Jersey, and at Big Sky Ranch in Simi Valley, California, the combination of which doubled for Tuscumbia, with interiors at the Hyde-Brown Studio at Twenty-third Street in lower Manhattan. The shoot was not without tension, most of it within the director, who still carried the scars from having *The Left Handed Gun* wrenched from his hands. In the three years since, however, that film had earned recognition in Europe and he had enjoyed five Broadway hits, so he felt confident in pushing the cinematic envelope with *The Miracle Worker.*

"Where we had voices on the stage out of Annie's past," he describes, "now I wanted something visually equivalent. It was done by a very complicated process. We blew the image up to the point where the emulsion broke down to where you could just barely discern a figure. We had to blow it up thirty-two times so, in order to shoot a close-up, we used a very wide lens from all the way across the studio and cut a dot in a matte in front of our viewfinder, and that dot is what we used. We knew that that dot would eventually fill the screen when we blew it up to that point. We built a series of mattes to get this shot or that shot, and blew it up to where the image was just disappearing."[10]

As was the case at Warner, the Playfilm crew also needed occasional persuading. "I'd come up to a shot, say, 'We're gonna be on a dolly here but I want a swinging arm . . . '

"'Oh, you can't do that, sir.'

"'Why?'

"'It's just not done; it would drive the audience crazy.'

"'Let's drive them crazy. Let's do it.'"

As a result, *The Miracle Worker* becomes Penn's most affecting work. Yet committing the cathartic "pump scene" to film initially vexed the director. "I'd seen it a hundred times in the theatre," he explains, "and every time it just killed me seeing that the entire audience was in tears. When I came to shoot it, I thought, 'don't piss in the mustard. Get your camera back just the way it was. Show us the full action and it'll be distant—like it was in the theatre.'

"So we do it, and I got to see the dailies, and it's terrible. *Absolutely terrible*. Something that I was about as familiar with as anybody can be. And I thought, 'Why is it terrible?' Because it stressed us back into a *spectator's* role rather than a *participant's* role. What I realized then, for the first time, was that I had to go in and fragment that event. Helen's mind, Helen's face, Annie's face, Annie's responses, seeing something in Helen's face, water dripping onto the child's hand, another motion on her, et cetera—to make it sort of 'exploded drawings.'[11]

"So I came back the next day and said, 'Fellas, back we go. We're gonna break this down into every sensory moment and we're gonna photograph that by itself.' We had originally shot it in a master where she threw the pitcher away and said, 'Waa-waa.' Then they went right down to the ground. Essentially, that was the film experience that really taught me something about movies."

Penn and director of photography Ernesto Caparrós resolved

that the audience should stay with Annie and Helen by moving the camera with them as they discover the world through Helen's newly piqued senses. "When I came back to re-shoot it the crew was standing around and they started crying," Penn says. "This tough crew. There were tears, and at that point Caparrós realized that, maybe, this was gonna be something. I mean, there were grown men standing there weeping. Suddenly Ernie, a rather cynical Cuban, got the idea—Academy Award!—and from that moment on it was, 'Oh, I have to light the *chadows*—chiaroscuro."[12]

Film editor Aram Avakian made it a point not only to read the script but to attend the table reading to gain a more organic feel for the project. He recalled, "Patty, then 14 years old, as Helen Keller, has but one line of dialogue, 'Wa-wa . . . ' but she is present anyway. She fills in the bit parts, of older people, sometimes in heavy accents, a great mimic, and in between lying or sitting on the floor, going through incredible exercises, never idle, occupying herself with difficult physical tasks, her legs twisted under her haunch, lacing her high boots literally behind her back, her unseeing eyes staring off into a black corner, accomplishing all, her blank eyes never wavering from that black corner. Meanwhile, the others read, everyone literally, except Anne Bancroft, having created and played the part for more than a year, sits knitting, no script before her, barely audible but firmly articulated as Annie Sullivan." He adds, "At the end of the reading: tears in my eyes."[13]

Avakian, who had previously edited news and documentaries, approached *The Miracle Worker* with a journalist's cynicism. "He said, 'What's this film about?'" Penn recalls, "and I went into a long talk about how it's essentially language, and language is the essence of civilization where you can then express experience that occurred to you that you can convey to somebody else who wasn't there, and that's the way civilization was able to build . . . ' et cetera. And he said, 'Oh, you want to make a *good* movie!' That was Aram!"

Penn used the film to rediscover the motion picture medium. "In a play, almost everything has to be articulated orally," he points out. "When I came to shoot the movie it never occurred to me that we didn't need all of that stuff; all we needed was to *show* it."

The film's musical score increases the emotional experience. Composer Laurence Rosenthal had been asked to create incidental music for the stage version, but Penn deemed that the play didn't need it and took it out during Philadelphia previews. "They unhired me," Rosenthal jokes, quickly adding, "when they decided to make the movie, Fred and Arthur felt that, while you can do a stage play without music, you can't really do a film like this without music." Rosenthal returned to score the film: "Arthur was absolutely determined never to yield to any impulse that would produce a feeling of sentimentality. He didn't want to tear-jerk; he wanted to keep it objective and true on the completely correct assumption that the story itself is so loaded with emotional impact that you don't have to indulge that."

Instructively, Rosenthal's score symbolizes the Helen-Annie story arc. "What I was really trying to do was, in some way, capture the feeling of living in a world of darkness and silence," he says, representing the two women by "the hollowness of those two clarinets and the weaving, falling series of progressions which is part of the theme." Notably, as teacher and pupil come together at the end of the film, their two themes merge. "When she leaves her parents and comes back to Annie and points at her and wants to know, 'Who are you?' 'Teacher,' at that moment you can see just a glimmer of a tear coming out of Helen's eye. I remember Aram Avakian saying, 'That is a 1 million dollar tear.' It's the first time you feel this kind of emotion coming from the child. The audience is always absolutely completely shattered by that whole scene."

Which is exactly what Penn wanted to avoid, according to Rosenthal. "I did feel that Arthur was so intent on the idea that the film should not get sentimental that he kept holding the reins back on the music," he says, "and even in the pump scene, I did it the way he wanted; we spotted it, and I didn't entirely agree with the spotting. He said, 'Let's take the music out here.'" They did, and the scene—as it had the first time Penn shot it—went dead.

Realizing this, the filmmakers scheduled another scoring session and recorded a musical bridge. The results, despite Penn's ascetic vow, have moved audiences for decades. But first United Artists had to be moved.

"UA was dubious," Penn says. "When we finished the cut, the ceremony was that we would show it to Arthur Krim and Robert Benjamin and David Picker. So we did, and they said, 'Give us about five minutes.' They went out in the hall and they came back and said, 'Okay, we'll distribute it.' Not long after this, Penn and Gibson arranged a screening for their star, who brought with her the man who would become her husband after a two-year courtship: Mel Brooks.

The Miracle Worker was sold on the platform manner of the day: a New York opening on May 23, 1962, followed by key cities, and then wider suburban theater release on July 28, 1962.

Academy Award talk began almost immediately and continued through the end of the year. Duke and Bancroft did, indeed, win Oscars, and Penn, Gibson, and costume designer Ruth Morley received nominations. Bancroft, however, couldn't accept hers in person. She was appearing onstage in New York in *Mother Courage* and watched the ceremony on television with her fiancé, Mel Brooks. Bancroft's statuette was accepted in her absence by Joan Crawford.

There is, however, an ignominious footnote to *The Miracle Worker*'s triple crown. In 1979 NBC and Melissa Gilbert's company, Half-Pint Productions, remade the property as a TV movie. This time Patty Duke, thirty-two, played Annie, and Gilbert, of TV's popular series *Little House on the Prairie,* played Helen. It was directed by Paul Aaron and nominally produced by Fred Coe, although it soon became apparent that Coe had been hired for his name, not his expertise. "They brought Fred out and they humiliated him," Penn says flatly. "Fred would say, 'No, that's not the scene,' and they'd say, 'Come on, what the hell's he doing here?' He was a very proud man and a wonderful producer, and they broke his spirit."

On April 29, with less than a week left to shoot the TV film, Coe was taken to the hospital with an aortic aneurysm. He died the next day, after deputizing executive producer Raymond Katz to take over for him. He was sixty-four.

It's Penn's belief that Coe's treatment by the TV people led to his death. But in sad truth, he was already dead, broken by alcohol, a failing heart, and being consigned to the shadows by an industry he had helped create that no longer recognized the debt it owed him. Indeed, when Cecil Smith of the *Los Angeles Times* interviewed Coe on the Simi Valley location of *The Miracle Worker,* the once-dominant producer ventured that the medium had changed to the point where "I don't recognize it much any more."[14]

10

The King of Broadway

In 1960 Arthur Penn had the kind of year that people sell their souls for. Between February 25 and November 30 he scored five hit plays, one film, and a brush with American political history. Best of all, none of it had anything to do with Hollywood.

"I didn't have a continuing ambition in film," he insists. "I thought it was a bizarre medium: you do these things, then somebody else puts it together, and it comes out on the bottom half of a double bill in New York. That's where I saw *The Left Handed Gun*. And that was the end of it. Until the reviews began to come in from Europe."

In this period he and Peggy made their Upper West Side apartment into the city home they wanted. They dug in, raised Matt, and took full advantage of Manhattan. In July of 1958 *I Bury the Living*, which Peggy had filmed as *The Spot on the Wall* while Arthur was making *The Left Handed Gun*, was released to theaters. She would take only a handful of additional acting jobs before entering the New School to begin studying to practice family psychology.

As for Arthur, he made no secret that he preferred theater to movies, and after winning the directing Tony for *The Miracle Worker*, he had his pick of projects. *Toys in the Attic* came to him via Kermit Bloomgarden, playwright Lillian Hellman's perennial producer, who showed Penn the first two acts. Penn instantly committed to direct it and then worked with Hellman to shape the rest.

Hellman was a test of patience. A New Orleans Jew warped by her family's obsession with money, she compensated for the social ostracism she had endured as a girl with a sharp tongue and exceptional intellect. Her first marriage, to New York press agent Arthur Kober, ended in divorce, but through him she made literary contacts. She didn't become a playwright, however, until falling under the charm, tutelage, and ultimately, the codependency of writer Dashiell Hammett. Hammett guided and goaded her through her first play, *The Children's Hour,* which led to a successful screenwriting career in the 1930s. "Dash" and "Lilly" nobly weathered the Red Scare in the early 1950s, he by serving prison time,[1] she by refusing to cut her conscience to fit that year's fashions. Hammett would die, broke and broken, on January 10, 1961, during the run of *Toys,* but Hellman never lost her fire.[2]

"She was tough," Penn appraises. "She was not always justified in being tough, but she was—" (he pauses thoughtfully) "—an unattractive woman who compensated for it with a good intellect and talent and a certain generosity. She said, 'I'll be the godmother for your daughter' when Molly was being born during that period.[3] She did generous things, but she expected generous things in return: she gave presents; she wanted presents."

The gift she gave Penn and Bloomgarden was a play about love. Yet, as she later qualified to the *New York Times,* "Not all kinds of love—so-called love—are noble and good, that there's much in love that's destructive, including the love that holds up the false notions of success, of the acquisition of money."

Equating money, power, and family had been a recurring theme in Hellman's plays, particularly *The Little Foxes* (1939) and its prequel, *Another Part of the Forest* (1946). *Toys in the Attic* follows the internecine intrigues of the Berniers sisters, Carrie and Anna, when their lovable scoundrel of a younger brother, Julian, shows up with a new wife and a scheme to get rich. Things go awry when sister Carrie, for reasons tinged with incestuous feelings for Julian, meddles in the marriage and muddies the business deal, with violent results. They all live unhappily—but with their eyes open—ever after.

Penn, Hellman, and Bloomgarden assembled a cast that included Jason Robards Jr. as Julian, Maureen Stapleton as Carrie, and Anne Revere as Anna, as well as Irene Worth, Rochelle Oliver, and Percy Rodrigues. Rehearsals began in early 1960 with the playwright at the director's elbow and at the cast's throats. As he had from *Philco* to *Miracle Worker,* Penn put *Toys* on its feet well before its cast was familiar with the material. They explored it together as a group endeavor, frequently sacrificing Hellman's precise dialogue in favor of subtext. It drove the playwright nuts.

"Lillian you don't mess with," Penn cautions, as if she still hovers. "She was marvelously unreasonable. She would sit there and cough, registering her disapproval. I finally said, 'Lillian, go home. Let me have a few days without your presence. Come back and, if you don't like what we're doing, fire us and start over. But we can't go anywhere this way. Everybody's in terror of you.' She did, and when she came back we were better."

From the start, Penn realized that his two biggest stars, Robards and Stapleton, were having an offstage affair, not with each other but with the bottle. "They would finish rehearsal and go next door and have a glass of vodka that was *that big,*" he indicates, holding his finger and thumb wide apart. "They were terrified of Lillian. I don't know what their feeling about me was, but they would spend themselves at night afterwards—hang out with actors, get drunk—and then come in the next day not able to work. Certain days, Maureen would stretch out on a bench and just go to sleep in the middle of rehearsal. The other actors knew, so they were all very pessimistic." This was not news to anyone on Broadway; Stapleton's and Robards's drinking, jointly and severally, was legendary, but so was their talent, which is why Penn persevered. "People said to me, 'You're crazy to have them both in a play.' Which was true: I *was* crazy. They *were* wonderful—*eventually* they were wonderful—we got some real steps forward. And then we went to Boston."

The Hub in those days had three things no other tryout town could claim: it was far enough away from New York to discourage Broadway gossip-hunters; preview audiences were sophisticated but not jaded; and critic Elliot Norton. When *Toys* hit

Beantown, the city also had something else: another play in the same throes, only with less success.

"Laurence Olivier was directing a play with Charlton Heston in Boston," Penn recalls.[4] "Apparently a lousy play. Lillian and Olivier knew each other from the Goldwyn days.[5] We would meet every night after the show at the Ritz-Carlton Hotel, up in the mezzanine, and have some supper, a drink, and talk. I would sit there just listening; they were wonderful stories. One night Olivier came in and asked Lillian and me, 'Do you know anybody in your cast named Mo?' That's Maureen's nickname. I said, 'Yeah, we do.'

"Lillian said, 'Why?'

"He said, 'Well, I got awakened last night by a call put through to me from inside the hotel saying, "Sir Laurence? Would you like to fuck?" and I said, "No, not particularly," and hung up. Then I come down this morning and there's this note saying, "I'm so terribly sorry," signed 'Mo.'" Penn grins at the memory. "She was that out-front. We laughed about that for a long time."

Hellman could be just as forward as Stapleton, not about sex but about politics. Though she was intolerant of those whom she suspected had betrayed her and Hammett during the witch hunts, she held others to a moral compass based not on their politics but on how they applied them. "There was this little girl in her that was very much there," Penn reports. "She was able to attract a wonderful circle, intellectually, mostly men. During that period there would be Dwight McDonald, [Norman] Podhoretz, [William] Styron, in Lillian's place—right-wing, left-wing. She would always give dinner parties. She thought she was a wonderful cook; she was just okay. During this period, Dash was essentially dying upstairs; he had emphysema very bad. He liked beautiful women. His favorites were Patricia Neal and Peggy Penn. They would go up and read to him and spend time with him. That was all right with Lillian as long as they were occupied elsewhere: Patricia was safely married to Roald Dahl at that point.

"But she was an unforgiving woman. I once made the mistake of trusting an interviewer who then printed something I never said: that I accepted *Toys in the Attic* because Lillian had been blacklisted. The reverse was utterly true. The fact that it was in the newspaper enraged her and embarrassed her, and it embarrassed me, and we had a falling-out and never spoke again. Lillian's skin was very thin, very thin.

"Lillian was clearly of the Left. She made no bones about it. But she was denying that she had been in the Party. I don't know whether she was or not; she never said anything to me about it. But she hated Kazan, she was furious with so many people who had testified. I mean, Odets. Odets![6] I said to Kazan years later, 'Apparently the night before, Lillian was somewhere where Odets was, and Odets was saying, 'I am a man of the Left!' and Kazan said to me, '*I'm* a man of the Left. You get your *own* Left!'"

Toys in the Attic was nominated for Tonys for Best Play and Best Actor (Robards) and Actress (Stapleton and Worth), and won for Featured Actress (Revere) and Scenic Design (Howard Bay). Despite its success, it would be Lillian Hellman's last original play produced, and when it was bought for the movies, Penn declined to become involved. Instead, he was set to direct the two hottest performers in the country, who not only worked without a script, they worked without a net: Mike Nichols and Elaine May.

Nichols and May had met at the University of Chicago in the 1950s while each was studying drama, he with Lee Strasberg and she with Maria Ouspenskaya. By all accounts it was creative kismet for, however incisive or brutal either might be toward third parties, they gave each other safe harbor. They decided to form a comedy duo and migrated to Chicago's improvisational Compass Players (forerunner to Second City), developed routines, and eventually acquired as manager Jack Rollins, who began securing club bookings. Along the way they did guest spots on Steve Allen's influential network TV variety show, were hired by NBC Radio to create skits for the network's *Monitor* broadcast magazine, and finally performed a routine on the January 14, 1958, edition of NBC-TV's remarkable eclectic arts series, *Omnibus*.[7] In a rare programming move, the episode ran on a Tuesday instead of the show's usual Sunday afternoon slot, and people saw it. A lot of them. And, in showbiz parlance, Nichols and May killed.

They were erudite and yet not esoteric; even their most arcane skits—their classic "Pirandello," for example—worked because general audiences in those days were more broadly educated than today's TV-bred comedy-club crowd. "However smart it got, it always stayed funny," praised Steve Martin, who shares those traits. "It never got smug."[8]

The pair was performing at the Blue Angel in 1960 when Broadway producer Alexander H. Cohen was inveigled by actor Alfred Drake to see them. Cohen was duly impressed, invited them to return to the legitimate stage, and booked the John Golden Theatre for an October 8, 1960, premiere of *An Evening with Mike Nichols and Elaine May*. Nichols realized that performing for a club audience was one thing, but a New York theater crowd was another. The show needed shaping, and Nichols knew that Penn, whose *Miracle Worker* and *Toys in the Attic* were still running, was the man to bring it from nightclubs to Broadway. "Because you're gonna go out there, just two people for two hours, in front of a tough New York crowd, there needs to be a system," Penn insisted to them. "We went on the road that summer, toured up through New England, Martha's Vineyard, Nantucket, just playing it and finding the style of it."

To add perspective, Penn asked a new friend to accompany him. He had met Gene Lasko over dinner at the home of Carol Johnson, a friend of Lasko's wife, Joyce, and Peggy Penn. As the dinner conversation turned to New York theater, particularly how bad it had become (notably excepting Penn's), Lasko and Penn bonded creatively and personally. Lasko joined Penn, Nichols, and May on the shakedown tour. Although the core of *An Evening with . . .* was to be the pair's polished routines about life and relationships, the most celebrated part was an improv segment in which they took suggestions from the audience and built a scene around them. "Give us the first line, the second, the closing line, and in what style," Penn describes them as saying. "Opening night somebody said, 'Shakespeare,' and Mike kicked it one notch higher and said something like, 'How about a *Jewish* Shakespeare?' and doubled the task. It was sweaty time."

As for the staging, "We used minimalist stuff. We didn't

really have a designer to design the set. So we tried a variety of
sets 'cause each little theater that you go to puts up its own set.
At a certain point, I remember that Mike, when we were already
heading into New York, thought that Dick Avedon, who was
a good friend of his, would design the set, and Dick did, but it
was the goddamnedest, most complicated set you have ever seen.
Finally, we're in the Golden Theatre[9] in New York, and there's
no set. I was passionate about Bentwood chairs.[10] I said, 'You
know what we need? We need chairs that you don't really see.
A little couch that you don't really see. Just a pretty shape. Let's
get Bentwood furniture.' There was a beautiful two-seater where
they did the necking scene of the adolescents, and a chair here
and chair there, and that was it."

The show's content was nowhere near as simple. The sketch
that closed the first act, "Pirandello," purposely made the audience confuse the actor with the role, as befits its namesake. "It's
brilliant," Penn says, "and it scares the audience. They start out
as characters, then something clearly goes awry, but they are
going to carry on, and they carry on, but something is bothering
them, and slowly they begin—you can feel the hostility emerging between them—and then, at a point, they drop the characters and they become Nichols and May and Mike says, 'Elaine!
You can't,' and they get to the point where you swear you're in
the midst of an absolute breakup, and just at that point they turn
and say, 'Pirandello!' Curtain. It was stunning. It was so stunning
that, even with a sophisticated New York audience, people were
walking out on it. They didn't get it. Fortunately, enough got it
that it was a big hit. But it scared these theatergoers."

Nichols and May had no idea how good they were. "They
had all the panics," Penn smiles. "We went to dinner at Frankie
& Johnnie's, which was right across the street from the Golden
Theatre, and I said, 'You know, in a week you're gonna be big
stars in that theater,' and Mike said, 'What if we flop?' Dead
serious. I said, 'Mike, you're *not* gonna flop.' 'But how do you
know?'" The next day's reviews proved Penn correct.

With *An Evening with Mike Nichols and Elaine May* up and
rolling, *Toys* on the way to running 456 performances, and Tad

Mosel adapting James Agee's *A Death in the Family* (see chapter 11), Penn and Fred Coe got a call in September of 1960 from a man who had nothing to do with Broadway. His name was Chuck Spaulding.

Charles Spaulding had been John F. Kennedy's Harvard classmate. Now involved in Kennedy's presidential campaign, he had a proposition for the two TV titans that would change history. The three television networks (ABC, NBC, and CBS) had persuaded Congress to suspend the FCC's equal-time rule to allow the major party candidates to have face-to-face televised debates. Kennedy, the junior senator from Massachusetts and a virtual unknown, was to appear opposite Vice President Richard M. Nixon, each trying to win the White House in the national election less than six weeks hence. Representatives of the candidates had already agreed on the color of the set (neutral gray for the black-and-white broadcast), which man would stand where, and how high each podium was to be.

"They didn't know what to do on television," Penn explains. "So each of the camps said, 'Well, we'll hire advertising agencies who know this business.' The advertising agencies didn't know diddly. They knew about a product, but they didn't know what would happen in a debate. So Chuck and Fred and I went to Sardi's for lunch one day and said, 'They're gonna have their camp and we're gonna have our camp, and we have agreed that the lengths of time on camera for one would be the equivalent of the time on camera for the other.' It didn't take Fred and me three minutes before we said, 'Close-ups! That's the only thing. Let them do whatever they want, but we stay with close-ups on Kennedy. Close-ups and shoot from slightly below eye level.' Which, essentially, is what we did."

The producer of the first debate, on September 29, 1960, was thirty-seven-year-old CBS staffer Don Hewitt. Hewitt, later to run CBS's flagship *60 Minutes*, deftly balanced the egos invading his CBS Chicago studio. "I had a meeting with [Kennedy advisor] Ted Sorenson and Jack Kennedy one week before the debate in a hangar at Midway Airport in Chicago," Hewitt says, "in which he asked all the right questions: 'Do I stand? Do I sit? How much time do I have to answer?' He was very curious. I never saw Nixon before that night. Kennedy spent that afternoon boning up. Nixon spoke to the Carpenters [union] and treated the debate like it was just another appearance. Kennedy knew how important it was and rested that afternoon to get ready for it. To Nixon it was just another campaign experience."

Hewitt denies acceding to either set of advisors. "I was asked by the Nixon people not to take cutaways of Nixon while Kennedy was talking," he reports, "and I said, 'I'm sorry, I can't do that. If you're gonna have a debate, you want to see the other guy's reactions to his questions.' Their reason was that he'd been ill and he tended to sweat and he'd be mopping his brow and it would look like he was overly concerned or overwrought, and I said, 'I'm sorry.'"[11]

The Kennedy camp, Hewitt says, "didn't need that. First of all, extreme close-ups are overdone, anyway. Kennedy looked spectacular. He walked in that studio looking like a Harvard undergrad—perfectly tailored, fit, tan, all together. Nixon had had a staphylococcus infection, banged his knee on the car when he got out, looked liked death warmed over, had a lousy makeup man, and looked terrible. There was absolutely no reason for anybody to look for an advantage for Kennedy."[12]

Penn explains the chicanery of which Hewitt may not be aware: "John Kennedy in close-up is going to be very much more appealing than Richard Nixon. And that's what we did. Nobody knew. They made these rules: 'If you go in for a close-up of your candidate, we're going to do the same thing for ours, and for the same amount of time, too.' Every time we went in, they went in. We wrecked him. When I told this to Warren [Beatty, while making *Mickey One;* see chapter 12], he said, 'You guys elected Kennedy!'"

By the time Kennedy narrowly beat Nixon on Election Day, 1960, Penn and Coe weren't watching television. They were rehearsing another play that would become a genuine phenomenon. It was Tad Mosel's adaptation of James Agee's Pulitzer Prize–winning novel *A Death in the Family.* Coe, aware that he needed a more upbeat title if he was ever going to get anyone to consider financing it, let alone pay to see it, renamed it *All the Way Home.*

11

The Little Play That Could

When James Rufus Agee was seven, in 1916, his father died in a car accident. In 1955, when he was forty-six, Agee himself died in the back of a taxicab. On his desk lay an unfinished semiautobiographical manuscript about his father that he had titled *A Death in the Family*. It tells how the Follets of Knoxville, Tennessee, deal with the loss of their young patriarch, Jay, who, like Agee's father, is killed on the road. These ordinary people's lives become extraordinary under Agee's observation, among them Mary, Jay's wife; her religious zealot sister, Hannah; Ralph, Jay's boastful brother; Andrew, Mary's artistic brother; everyone's aged grandparents; and Jay and Mary's six-year-old son, Rufus, who has to process it all.

Agee, whose sharp-edged film criticism and character-driven screenplays were literate without being stuffy, brought a gentle simplicity to his novel. But because he died before he could finish it, it remains open to speculation as to what changes he might have made during the editing and refining process. When it was published in 1957, CBS acquired it as a possible *Playhouse 90*, with Fred Coe in mind to produce. Even after it won the Pulitzer Prize in 1958, however, the network shelved it, giving no reasons, and that was supposedly that. But not for Coe, who had lost his own father too early to know him and undoubtedly felt a kinship with young Rufus.[1] Coe bought the property from CBS but rather than try to pitch it to another network, called his *Philco* writing stalwart, Tad Mosel.

"I thought, 'He's going to invite me to do the teleplay for that beautiful novel, and I'm not going to do it,'" Mosel recounts, "because on *Playhouse 90* you had to have six commercials, and that would have been a disaster." Instead, Coe leaned across the luncheon table and asked Mosel, "How would you like to do *A Death in the Family* for the stage?"

Because the novel was unfinished, Mosel faced an unusual challenge. "I had a terrible time," he says. "There was no form, and I have to have a form, I just have to. I finally found a little excerpt—it's only a few pages—of Rufus remembering when his mother was pregnant, and I thought, that's it, it's in the book, I just have to shift in time so that she's pregnant in the play. And that meant that we did not have to have [Rufus's gestating sister]." It also meant that the company only had to hire one six-year-old principal actor and not worry about also finding a four-year-old who could act. "So I got rid of little Catherine, put her inside Mother, and I had the theme of the play!" Mosel smiles. "Nobody who ever saw that play has ever remembered that Mary isn't pregnant in the book."

While Mosel struggled with the script, Coe struggled with fund-raising. Unable to fully capitalize the production through his regular angels, he approached producer Arthur Cantor[2] and the play limped, still financially short, toward a New York opening.

Set design and casting proceeded with equal invention. The play's episodic structure that had so challenged Mosel inspired designer David Hays[3] to create a multilayered, visually open set. This allowed Penn, through lighting cues, to "cut" from one scene to the next, making changes as swiftly as he did on television, a device that is still in practice today.

Colleen Dewhurst won the role of wife Mary Follet, and Arthur Hill became Jay. Jay's brother, Ralph, was played by Clifton James, and Lenka Peterson was sister Sally. Lillian Gish was Catherine Lynch, and Aline MacMahon was her über-religious sister, Aunt Hannah. A strange old woman named Lylah Tiffany, a street musician whom Coe discovered playing accordion outside Carnegie Hall, became a character called Great-Great-Granmaw.

Dewhurst served both as a powerful mother Mary and as the glue that, Mosel feels, bound the play together. "A lot of actresses could have done it," he says. "But it needed the extra 'thing' that Colleen gave to it, which is star quality. That's all I can put it down to. See, it was a disjointed play. It needed a strong actress, and Colleen was it." When Dewhurst got pregnant during the run[4] (says Mosel, "George Scott came up, banged her, and went back"), Lenka Peterson replaced her.

During this period several people became a part of Penn's behind-the-scenes stock company. Gene Lasko would serve as an advisor and would rehearse replacements for his plays, keep them fine-tuned, and assist the director closely on his films. Their association grew into an unshakable trust. Another regular was Porter van Zandt, an eccentric stage manager who was primed for anything. "This is kind of a rap on him," says Lasko cheerfully, "but it's relevant to stage managers and production managers in general. One day, backstage, he opened his jacket and was wearing a coin changer. That was so that, if an actor had to go out to make a phone call, he wouldn't have to run around looking for change and get back late. He did have a sense of humor about himself. I once asked him if I could borrow a pen or a pencil and he opened his jacket—like a man exposing himself—and the pocket on the right side of the jacket was lined with about ten or fifteen pencils of different kinds, and he said, 'Which one would you like?'"

Despite the drama *behind* the scenes, Penn and Mosel became aware during the New Haven tryouts that there was not enough drama *in* the scenes of *All the Way Home,* which became the play's new, less morbid-sounding title. "There were things we thought worked in the script that just didn't work," Penn reflects. "Tad is a very good writer, but it didn't have drama."

Agrees Mosel, "The third act was an endless parade of people in black clothes. It ran to almost midnight. I looked for Arthur at the end of the performance and I couldn't find him. I finally found him upstairs in the balcony of the empty theater, off in a corner. I said, 'Arthur, what is the matter?' He said, 'It was god-awful.'"

The New Haven preview was the first time all the elements of *All the Way Home* were brought together in one place, and Penn was acutely, even painfully, aware that the whole was not yet close to the sum of its parts. "I don't know how it happens," he reflects, groping for an explanation. "I don't know what it is. It is a moment when, somehow, you stand there saying, 'I'm hearing words but I'm not hearing real talk. How can we restructure this?' and then you start digging. And that's what we did." His Manhattan friends offered him little comfort. "All the smarts of New York came up to see it," he steams. "The real 'in' crowd. They all said, 'Close it. Close it. You can't open this.' That was the wisdom. And we said, 'No! We're gonna work on it and bring it in.'"

"In fact," Peggy Penn adds to her husband, "you came home that night, sat on the steps, and cried. Matt woke up and came down and put his arms around you, asking me, 'Why is Daddy crying?' I explained that he loved this work and didn't want it to close. I put Matt to bed, assuring him that his father would do everything he could to keep it open. Then I went back to where Arthur was still sitting on the step. I said, 'I agree with Matt—you can't close it, you can't. Tell Cantor you'll do everything possible to keep it open.' He thought a bit longer, put his raincoat back on, and went back to the theater."

There were still problems by the time the play moved from New Haven to Boston, where the Hub's leading critic, Elliot Norton, who had been so helpful in the past, gave them an unenthusiastic review. Mosel, still rewriting under Coe and Penn's guidance, began to realize that the problem lay in the prickly relationship between Mary and Aunt Hannah. In the story, Mary begs God's forgiveness for being unworthy, and her spinster sister, Hannah, tries to trump her by spouting Gospel instead of giving sympathy. The way Mosel had written it, Mary stoically ignored her. At one particular Boston run-through, Mosel had an epiphany, not only from the scene but because actresses Dewhurst and MacMahon hated each other.

"Miss MacMahon was used to taking center stage," Mosel recounts. "She was the kind of person who, when you're talking, would pick lint off [to draw attention]. So when she said to Colleen Dewhurst, 'Our Lord's on the Cross, what did He say?' Mary originally gave her a minor response and we moved on to the next moment. I was sitting with Arthur in the auditorium when Miss MacMahon went, 'Our Lord's on the Cross. What did He say? "Father, into Thy hands I commend my spirit,"' and I said to Arthur, 'If I were Mary, I'd hit her.' He turned to me—those eyes, they gleamed—and he said, 'You go back to the hotel and write *that*.' I went back to the hotel, and I sat with my pencil and my paper and I said, '*What did I say?*' When I said, 'hit her,' I didn't mean a wallop. He meant I should find a few *words* that hit her. I puzzled for a long time and I came up with the line that went, 'You've never had anything *but* God, Aunt Hannah. I had a *husband*. I was married to a *man. I won't have God in his place!*'[5]

"Well, the first time Colleen said that line on the stage, *you knew that a line had been said!* It was to her own archenemy, for one thing, but it was the perfect line for Mary to say. Miss MacMahon's nose was out of joint because her moment had been ruined, and we *knew* it had been ruined, but the second act had been *made.*"

Elliot Norton, whose love of theater included uncredited consulting with troubled plays, came back and rereviewed *All the Way Home,* and this time he sent it to Broadway with his blessing. The premiere was set for November 30, 1960, at the Belasco Theatre.

The New York critics were respectful but not enthusiastic, and with $400 in the till and only $3,500 in advance sales against a $23,000 weekly breakeven, Cantor leaned on Coe to close the play. Coe agreed, planning to shut down on Saturday, December 3, and no protests from Penn could change his mind.

And then it happened. A friend called Mosel on Saturday afternoon, hours before what was to be the last show, and said, "There's a run on the theatre!"[5] Word of mouth had begun. Arthur Cantor rushed to the Belasco and breathlessly asked the matinee crowd to tell their friends that, if they came, he would extend the run another week.

Penn picks up the story. "The newspapers wrote about it rather coolly, but Ed Sullivan had seen it and got on the air on Sunday, December 4, and said, 'Listen, this play must not close. It's a wonderful play,' and *bing!* That was the power of television."[6]

"Thank God for Ed Sullivan," Lasko adds. "It was very gracious of him to recognize the importance of that play. Nothing else like that ever appeared on his show to my knowledge. It was usually scenes from comedies or musicals." All Sullivan did was acknowledge two cast members seated in the audience, the TV equivalent of a column item in a newspaper. But it was an extraordinary gesture among a remarkable number of good deeds, if not outright miracles, that the play enjoyed:

Mike Nichols bought a newspaper ad with his own money urging the public not to come see *An Evening with Mike Nichols and Elaine May,* which was still running, but to attend *All the Way Home* instead.

Despite the posting of the closing notice, says Mosel, "the cast was loyal to the teeth. I think that, if that play does have a moral, it's Life Goes On."

Gels on stage lights fade over time and have to be replaced, but Union contracts demand that the entire production staff be on hand for it. One Sunday the lighting manager sneaked into the theater and replaced them on his own. At the next performance, someone marveled, "Funny, the play seems brighter," and the lighting manager smiled back, "Gels sometimes renew themselves."

Tad Mosel: "There were little boys in the play and one of them couldn't tie his shoes. No one could touch his uniform except his mother, and we had to hire a dresser to come in at seven o'clock every night to tie the boy's shoes. So Porter van Zandt had a children's party one Sunday afternoon and somehow, in the course of that afternoon, that little boy learned to tie his shoes!"

For four months, the play stayed alive with barely enough advance to open its doors for each show. At the 1961 Tony Awards, Colleen Dewhurst won for Best Featured Actress in a Play, but Penn, scenic designer Hays, costume designer Raymond Sovey, and the play itself, though nominated, all lost. Then, on May 1, 1961 (which also happened to be Tad Mosel's birthday), *All the Way Home*, like James Agee's *A Death in the Family*, won the Pulitzer Prize.[7] That's when the carriage trade—the swells who had urged closing the play back in New Haven—started showing up.

For Penn, however, the Pulitzer was second to a more rewarding prize: on March 10, 1962, he and Peggy became the parents of a daughter, Molly. Unlike Matt, who leapt out, Molly was reluctant to emerge, and the doctor had to bring on labor. "It was a very tough birth because of the inducement," Peggy has no trouble remembering. "But she was perfect at birth and had Arthur's hands, and they fluttered like fans. I kept wanting to photograph them. She was a divine baby; a *divine* baby, but as time went on, she had a divine heart as well! 'Course I also knew something by then about babies, so maybe that is what helped her be so divine."

Adds Arthur with equal pride, "That's Matt's favorite line: when Peggy showed up at the door carrying Molly, he said, 'What is this? Aren't I doing a good enough job?'"

With *All the Way Home* a hit, Mosel, Penn, and Coe acquiesced to an offer from England's ITV to create *Three Roads to Rome* for the network's *Play of the Week* series. It was a ninety-minute show made of a trio of one-acters, something at which the creators were past masters. Mosel adapted the playlets from works by Aldous Huxley (*The Rest Cure*), Edith Wharton (*Roman Fever*), and Martha Gellhorn (*Venus Ascendant*). All of them starred Deborah Kerr.

Success. It all seemed so comfortable, so right. Although Penn was vastly successful, he paid it little mind. Fame "sort of snuck up on me. I was not 'of the street,' of the showbiz gang. There are a lot of showbiz actors who hang out at the bar at Sardi's till all hours and get to know everybody, and that's their life. That was not my life because during this period I had my kids. I would get home at night and try to see them before they were asleep.

"I had a sense, during the period of these plays, that 'This is right; I *should* be doing this; I know how to do this; I'm at home.' I can't properly estimate what years in live television had done for my nerves. It was tough to make me scared. I'd had a couple of plays and I said, 'We're gonna work on these up till opening night. I don't give a shit if we do a completely new act, but we're not gonna give in to failure.' In some cases, I couldn't avoid it and they flopped,[8] but I fought for them all the way."

Broadway success, the Tony, the Pulitzer, and the solid commercial performance brought renewed movie offers. This time, Penn felt sure, he would take Hollywood on his own terms.

He was wrong.

12

Train Wrecks

When Penn returned to Hollywood, Hollywood was dying. The Founding Moguls were buried, retired, or forgotten, and their decades-old studios were poised to be absorbed into conglomerates that saw them as "leisure time activities" rather than entertainment kingdoms. Only United Artists, which had been sold and restructured after two rudderless decades, had the right idea: function solely as a financier and distributor. UA was proud of two things: not owning production facilities and never taking a picture away from a director.

"After *The Miracle Worker,* I had this very nice reputation," Penn notes, "but I hadn't made any money in movies. My salary on *Left Handed Gun* was $17,500 for the whole movie. *The Miracle Worker,* because we had held out for Anne Bancroft, was very close to the vest all the way. Here I am, the picture's nominated, the two women were going to be nominated and would win, UA said to me, 'We have all these goddamn shelved scripts in our library and nobody's doing anything with them.'"

The script that Penn found most intriguing was drawn from a 1961 book by Rose Valland called *Le front de l'art.* Adapted as *The Train* by Franklin Coen and Frank Davis, it dramatized a daring scheme by the French Underground to save 148 packing cases of priceless art from the Nazis in the waning days of the occupation by delaying the train on which they were being taken from the country. Moved by the idea that the French would risk their lives for art—as well as the chance to reconnect

with the European friends who'd fêted *The Left Handed Gun*—
Penn told UA he would make *The Train*. He asked his agent,
Howard Hausman, to suggest actors to play the leading role of
Paul Labiche, a laborer who saves the art "without really genu-
inely understanding it himself,"[1] and Hausman proposed Burt
Lancaster.

Lancaster, who had taken ill after dubbing and truncating
Luchino Visconti's *The Leopard*,[2] accepted, based on Penn directing, and on July 23, 1963, the *New York Times* dutifully reported
that he would star in *The Train*. UA green-lighted the $5.8 mil-
lion project, and Penn was off to Paris to start preproduction.

What Penn did not know, however, was that Lancaster's production company owed approximately $2 million to United Art-
ists for past films and that both UA and Lancaster saw *The Train*
as a way to settle accounts. The results of this arrangement, Penn
says wryly, were "an experience. Off I went to Paris where I had
had a lot of friends and, because of my theater background, I
had met a lot of English actors. I had met Paul Scofield. I knew
Jeanne Moreau through the *Cahiers du cinéma* guys because
they had said, 'Penn is an American nouvelle vague director,' and
had sort of absorbed me into their ranks. I asked Jeanne; she
asked Truffaut if she should do it; he said, 'Yeah, do it.' And I
cast Michel Simon, that wonderful, superb actor. I had all these
people and . . . I laid out a lot of the action where the partisans
would stop the train, and the places where that was to occur. I
had this wonderful crew, a crew of real friends. The production
designer, Willy Holt, was a very brave Partisan who was captured and tortured and knew this world. The cameraman was
Jean Tournier; Bernard Farrel was my assistant. It was family.
We were all thrilled to work together. So here we are. We have
certain scenes that would have to be shot on the Place de la Con-
corde of the Nazi occupation of Paris. They won't permit us to
do that when there's traffic around because the French will get
furious to see the Nazi uniforms; we had to shoot that just at the
crack of dawn. I started shooting the movie, and I hadn't yet met
the star. Finally Burt showed up."

The scene involved Simon, as the engineer of the train, and

Lancaster, as the Resistance worker who engages him. As was Penn's wont, he covered from multiple camera setups.

"I was shooting rather a lot," Penn admits. "And I heard Burt saying, 'Oh, Christ, not another angle, come on!' And I'd say, 'Yes, one more.' And then I remember saying something to him like, 'Look, this next take, I don't want to know what you're doing or what you're thinking, but I wish you'd have a private thought that you really wouldn't like to tell me.' And he gave me a kind of a fishy look."[3]

Screenwriter Walter Bernstein, whom Penn engaged to do rewrites, concurs: "I was there when they were shooting it, and Arthur was pushing him, as an actor, to go for certain things. Burt was resisting. At one point—I'll never forget this—Burt turned to Arthur and said, 'Here, I'll give it the grin.' He was saying, 'I'm not going to do what you want me to do.'"[4]

Continues Penn, "We had lunch. Pleasant lunch. Finished the day without Burt—he was not in the rest of it—and I went and saw some dailies, then I went home. That night, Walter came over to the house and said, 'You're off the picture.' I said, 'What are you talking about?' He said, 'You're off the picture.' I said, 'Well, who's gonna do it?' He said, 'Frankenheimer.'"[5]

John Frankenheimer was, like Penn, an eminent director of live TV drama but, unlike Penn, had aggressively pursued a film career, directing *All Fall Down, The Birdman of Alcatraz,* and *The Manchurian Candidate.* He had just wrapped the political thriller *Seven Days in May* starring Lancaster and Kirk Douglas, for Douglas's company. Lancaster was so taken with Frankenheimer's efficiency and willingness to listen to his ideas that he got Douglas to release him from postproduction duties on *Seven Days* to knock Penn off *The Train.*[6]

From the start, Penn had sensed that Lancaster was uncomfortable with his direction. Penn was unlike the malleable Frankenheimer;[7] Lancaster had encountered in Penn a director who wanted him to stretch. Coming off the disappointment of *The Leopard* and a failed Oscar bid for *The Birdman of Alcatraz,* the shaken actor preferred to retrench.

At first Penn was shocked by the firing, then livid. "It was a staggering blow to my ego," he reflects. "I'd never been fired off anything in my life.[8] It was also clearly a setup. Frankenheimer, who was a very active DGA member, knew the rules: if you're replacing somebody, you call the person who's in the guild and say, 'These are the circumstances.' I said to Walter, 'He's gotta call me,' because that's the obligation of the Directors Guild; if you replace somebody, you have to call them. Never. Nothing. Never."

Penn's anger rose when he was summoned to a hotel room meeting with Hausman, UA president Arthur Krim, and an inscrutable Burt Lancaster. "Krim was speaking for UA," Penn says, "and he said, 'Any discussion of this matter is academic. We're going to allege incompetence.' My agent said, 'Won't that be hard to do since he just got an Oscar nomination for *The Miracle Worker?*' Then, of course, Krim swiftly took that back. And Burt never said a word. That was it. I was off the picture.

"I was furious," Penn fumes, "It was beyond chutzpah. It was beyond rage. It was a recognition that Hollywood operates on a moral system totally alien to me, and totally on its own terms, in the sense that the Lancaster indebtedness to UA permitted a guy as decent as Krim to do this, to allege that he would do this to somebody whose reputation would have thereafter suffered immeasurably. This was venality at a very high level."

Daily Variety of August 19, 1963, carried the news that Frankenheimer had replaced Penn "because of differences with producer Jules Bricken over approach to the material." Bricken, with a long producing and directing history in TV, was taking the fall for his star. Thanklessly, Bricken later caught heat from Frankenheimer who, when the film went over budget, told *Newsweek* (April 20, 1964), "Jules Bricken was totally irresponsible" and added that he had never liked the script. Shooting back, Bricken said, "If Frankenheimer didn't like the script, he shouldn't have accepted the job." Finally, in March of 1964, United Artists asserted its completion rights (repudiating its "hands-off" credo) by taking the film away from both its producer *and* its director.

Not until years later did Penn put the pieces together when, of all things, he got a phone call from Frankenheimer asking him to lunch. "We hadn't spoken or seen each other in this period," Penn recounts. "At lunch he explained that he had been really pretty profoundly alcoholic through this period, which partly accounted for the fact that the picture, under their auspices, went way over budget. He said, 'I'm in AA now. I feel obliged to apologize to you. I should have—I mean, I'd known you for years, we were friends during live TV . . . ' and I said, 'Yeah, I understand.' By then it didn't matter to me any more."

Vowing to reform the terms under which Hollywood makes movies, in late 1963 Penn approached Leo Jaffe, president of Columbia Pictures, with an unprecedented offer: "I said, 'I'll make you two movies for practically no salary and they'll cost less than $1 million each. The only thing is that you can't read the script. I'm just gonna go off and make the movie.'" Columbia agreed, and the result, released in 1965, was *Mickey One*.

Alan M. Surgal's script had arrived years earlier on Penn's desk as a stage play titled *Comic*. It may have had its roots in a news story about a small-time entertainer's body being found in the trunk of a car in Chicago.[9] When Columbia acceded to Penn's stipulations, the director decided to turn *Comic* into not only a motion picture called *Mickey One* but into an independent shot fired across Hollywood's corporate bow. "I felt that I don't give a shit if anybody understands this or doesn't," he now says. "I'm just gonna do my own work. And I did."

Variously called "a fever dream," "American *nouvelle vague*" and "a paranoid nightmare," *Mickey One* is easily one of the most abstruse films ever made by a major studio. A brashly talented nightclub comic (Warren Beatty) awakens one morning to learn that he is deeply in debt to the Mob for reasons that he cannot explain, and he is unable to either quantify or repay the amount ("How do you turn yourself in?" he begs). So he escapes, assumes a new identity as "Mickey One," and tries to disappear but is inexorably drawn back to the spotlight to meet his fate.

On one level, says Penn, "It's a film about a man who feels trapped: how we can personally get locked in our own fear, in our own terror, in our own humiliation. The story goes in one direction, then goes again in the same direction, only now you have different information because you have already gone through that loop once before." On another, angrier, level, it's an essay on what Penn calls residual guilt. "It started out to be a McCarthy film," he says, "everybody going around being so afraid of Joe McCarthy. What the hell do we have to fear? We were all ducking, society was ducking, saying, 'I'm not a Communist!' We were trying to destroy the radical past of our youth. What's wrong with that? If youth is not gonna be radical, who's gonna be radical? And why that drunk from Wisconsin was able to bring this country to its psychological knees was one of the most irritating things I'd ever encountered. So I decided to make a film about a guy who burns his identity, tries to pick up another identity, trying to get rid of some ancient guilt. He doesn't know what he's done or why he's done it, but he feels guilty, he feels wrong. By the end of the film he says, 'Fuck it, I've had it. I'm going to stand up and take it and deal with it.' And, of course, the moment anybody does that—as did Lillian Hellman in front of the [House Un-American Activities] Committee and said 'I'm not going to cut my conscience to fit the fashion of the times'—it was a shot in the arm. People said, 'Wait!' That was the theme of it for me."

Mickey One was the first time Penn worked with Warren Beatty. The actor, then twenty-seven, was as driven as Penn. Acknowledged as one of Hollywood's most skillful power brokers, he can be seductive (in every sense of the word), incorrigible, sensitive, shrewd, cavalier, and—perhaps his most important weapon—patient. He also has the objectivity to play against his image as the all-American winner by invariably casting himself as a tragic loser. Though he denies this, a list of his characters' fates shows otherwise; they include insanity (*Lilith*), ennui (*Shampoo*), and an overwhelming number of screen deaths (*Bonnie and Clyde, McCabe & Mrs. Miller, The Parallax View, Heaven Can Wait* [twice], *Reds, Bugsy,* and *Bulworth*).

Explains Penn, "Warren—a very smart guy—said, 'If I'm gonna work in this craft, I want to work with the best. I want to work with Inge, I want to work with Tennessee, I want to work with Kazan, I want to work with Penn.'" The actor had been only partly successful in meeting his ambitious (some would say arrogant) goal. As many rising actors do today, but few did then, he decided to develop his own properties. Throughout 1963, he and his agent, Charles K. Feldman, nursed a sex comedy called *Lot's Wife* through rewrites by a new talent named Woody Allen (sans Beatty, it became *What's New, Pussycat?* in 1965). But his heart was invested in a project titled *Honeybear, I Think I Love You* by the brilliant but reclusive novelist-screenwriter Charles Eastman.[10] It was on that mission that Beatty cold-called Penn one October morning in New York.

"I had never met him," Beatty said. "I had a script I wanted to discuss with him,[11] hoping he would direct it. So I took the simplest measure: I called him on the telephone at his home and introduced [myself]. We met an hour later. I never did have the chance to discuss my story. Arthur told me of *Mickey One* and I accepted there and then."[12]

The ever-wary Beatty had been impressed by Penn's direction of *The Miracle Worker*, but that didn't mean he trusted him with his career. He had just survived *Lilith*, playing a confused asylum orderly bewitched by a seductive schizophrenic (Jean Seberg), and despite filmmaker Robert Rossen's prestigious credits, Beatty felt abused by the director's ham-fisted approach. That, plus his natural actor's caution, challenged Penn to break through. "We met and got along more or less well," Penn says. "Warren is a covert personality. There's a distinct quantity of him that's hidden. It took a whole film for him to trust that he could be bad on film and that I would take it out."

Mickey One was made as a Florin-Tatira partnership, *Florin* being Penn's company and *Tatira* combining the names of Beatty's mother, Tat (nickname for Kathlyn Corinne MacLean) and father, Ira Beaty [*sic*]. After agreeing to form their company, Penn and Beatty apparently agreed on little else, particularly the tone of their production. "We had a lot of trouble on that film," Beatty acknowledged, "because I didn't know what the hell Arthur was trying to do and I tried to find out. I'm not sure that he knew himself."[13] Counters Penn, "I wasn't going to entertain compromise no matter what Warren was asking for. It was really a struggle of wills."

After rehearsals in New York, the company moved to Chicago for a fifty-five-day shooting schedule (which eventually stretched to sixty) on sets built at the Niles Studio and nightclub interiors at the fabled, yet shuttered, Chez Paree. Ensconced in the Astor Tower hotel in a suite with a piano, the star was so unsure of his character that he spiked his dialogue with old Milton Berle jokes. Penn was describing the film to outsiders as a comedy,[14] and he and his star were aware of the cinematic challenge of differentiating the way a performer acts onstage and behaves off it.

Beatty himself was not always sure. "I'll tell you an anecdote," Penn offers seductively. "Warren Beatty is a very handsome guy, and somebody pointed out to me that every time he got in an elevator and there was a mirror, Warren would look at himself. So I said to him, before we shot, 'Why do you do that?' And he said, 'I dunno, I think the main reason I do it is to make sure I'm still there.' And I thought, 'That's very astute. That would be a good characteristic for Mickey.' And so we sort of borrowed it."

Rumors have persisted for years that actor and director were at odds during shooting. Penn dismisses them: "This is from journalists who come onto the set, and if an actor and a director are having an argument, they interpret that as temperamental bad behavior or 'they're not getting along.' That's not at all what it is. It's 'We'll fight things through because we're two volatile people and we have strong feelings.' The last thing in the world I would want an actor to do is suppress or mute his own attitude, nor would I want him to ask me to suppress mine. So we sort of go at it. He's stubborn, and I'm stubborn, and we do it again and again and again and again. We slowly got closer and closer to the same place. But I learned more quickly when I could say, 'I have it, I got it,' than I did at the very beginning. For me it was mystical; it was going into this box and nothing was coming out; I wasn't in the control room!"

Penn confesses to making a film that expects more from the audience and critics than they were able, at the time, to perceive. "I chose obscurity consciously," he says, "and my feeling was, *you* figure this out, you the audience figure this out. I wanted to get in there and do something utterly personal, utterly my own way."

The director not only concedes the film's excesses, he revels in them. "I went ape," he says. "I decided, 'Look, this is not going to be a popular film. I want to tell everything I know and I want to play with the camera and I want to use all this and I want to expand on certain ideas that I had been developing.' Well, they're all there, made undoubtedly in proper proportion to where I would perceive it to be now. But, nonetheless, I am proud of the film because it was an attempt to take purchase on the medium."[15]

Mickey's key line is, "How do you turn yourself in?" It's as Kafkaesque as *The Trial,* except Mickey knows he's done *something* wrong; he just doesn't know *what.* Call it original sin or existential dilemma, it's emblematic of a generation of Americans coming of age under the weight of their country's guilt while seeking ways to atone for it.

Although Penn has admitted, "the symbolism almost makes me queasy,"[16] he agrees that being more specific "would have destroyed the film. I give the audience a lot of credit, but I thought that it was a little more vivid and clearer than, indeed, it is." The reception—or lack of it—hit him hard: "I went personally into a deep tail-spin as a result of what I found was a befuddling experience for most of the people who saw that film. I don't mean to suggest that I was ahead of my time. I blew it in a couple of places."[17]

Hindsight may rate the film more highly than does its director. Its disorienting, fragmented style, its pervasive sense of impending doom, and the way it keeps the viewer off balance make *Mickey One* a creature of a way of American thinking—an awareness of collective guilt, really—that was years away from happening. Was Penn adrift in the freedom he was accorded by the studio? Was he intoxicated with his European reputation as the leader of an American New Wave? It might have been a little of both, as suggested by events during the shooting. "We had such a good time in Chicago," recalls Jill Jakes, Penn's assistant then and later in his New York office. "New Wave people were coming to see what Arthur was doing. Truffaut was there, Godard was there, and Leslie Caron was having an affair with Warren at the time, so she was there."[18]

Casting Jenny, the woman in Mickey's assaulted life, proved tricky. They first signed Yvette Mimieux, but four days before production, MGM, which had her under primary contract, pulled her off the picture to make one of their own. At this point Gene Lasko, whom the director calls his "good right hand," told him about a Louis Malle film called *Le feu follet* and its young costar, Alexandra Stewart. To find her, Penn called practically the entire *Cahier du cinéma* crowd seeking a reading on Stewart who, it turned out, was Canadian and bilingual. He tried Godard, Malle, and others until he finally reached Truffaut. Lasko: "Truffaut said, 'Oh, she's wonderful.' Well, it didn't turn out that way. It was a terrible strain. Later, Godard shows up on the set in Chicago and told Arthur, 'She can't act at all unless you want somebody who's dead inside' or some similar phrase. Arthur said, 'But Truffaut said she was wonderful!' and Godard said, 'Well, he's sleeping with her.'"

Continues Penn, "Truffaut shows up in Chicago. What the hell is this? *Of course!* They were a *couple!*" Then he adds wryly, "That didn't last very long." Meaning Beatty.

Other performers brought their stories to the film's eclectic mix. One of the more unusual was Teddy Hart. Marvels Penn, "Teddy Hart, who plays the agent, a funny man, was in musicals. He did *The Boys from Syracuse.* I wanted to find him, and he's got an address on Park Avenue, and I thought, 'Oh, Jesus, he's working as a janitor or something.' I finally track him down: he's Larry Hart's brother. *Lorenz Hart!* The only heir to Lorenz Hart!"

Adds Jakes, "He got a Kurosawa actor, Mr. Fujiwara,[19] to play the funny little junkman who kept turning up in mysterious places, haunting Warren as some kind of omen for Warren's fate."[20] As "the artist," Fujiwara builds machines that self-destruct, an obvious metaphor for Beatty's character as well as the overall message of the film. He was based on Swiss kinetic artist Jean Tinguely. "I thought Jean Tinguely was emblematic of where we were after the war," Penn says. "You start making art out of the detritus of the war. I was thinking of the Japanese as the ultimate survivors after the nuclear weapons. I felt that they had been through the human Apocalypse and that some figure out of the trash had come, stood, and made art out of disaster. It's not a frivolously thought-through film. It may not be lucid, it may not be clear, but the thought was clearly there."

Aram Avakian, who edited *The Miracle Worker,* was hired for *Mickey One.* He and Penn discovered that they shared a fondness for the Sauter-Finegan Orchestra and, in fact, used Eddie Sauter's recordings as a scratch track during editing. Then they decided to make it permanent. "Eddie Sauter and Bill Finegan were a very advanced couple of musicians," Penn says. "Real advanced jazz. Aram knew Stan Getz, and he got Stan Getz to come in and improvise to the movie—a very sophisticated soundtrack. Eddie Sauter was the musical genius of arrangers, and it was with Eddie that I dealt. I said, 'This is what I'd like here.' He said, 'You don't want that.' I said, 'Well, I think I do, but, you know . . .'" The result was a moody and intimate musical score.

Just before *Mickey One* went into production, Penn had been romanced by producer Sam Spiegel, the elegant rogue, to direct Spiegel's upcoming superproduction of *The Chase* for Columbia. When Columbia screened *Mickey One,* therefore, it was with the knowledge that Penn would be helming their next big picture. This complicated matters when the executives sat in their screening room watching *Mickey One.* When it was over, Mike Frankovich, the studio's newly appointed vice president of production, phoned Penn.

"You've never heard a phone call like this one," Penn reports. "Mike Frankovich and the Jaffes are on the phone. They were lying through their teeth; they could barely get their jaws open. They hated the film. Shortly after this, Frankovich took me to a football game when the Rams were still playing out there, and he said to me, 'I'm going to give you a piece of advice. You're gonna make maybe ten movies in your life. Don't piss it away on this kind of shit.' What he meant was, make blockbusters."

Then the Shurlock Office weighed in. Three years away from extinction, Hollywood's censors were still on the job. Before the film was shot, they'd read the script and warned the filmmakers, "There should be no erotic significance to the mirrored walls and ceilings of the bedroom" (there were none in the finished film) and cautioned against violence and sex in a film whose very existence depended on the presence of both. This time, unlike *Left Handed Gun,* they raised no flags against the possible effeminacy of Hurd Hatfield's character, so Hatfield went ahead and added it himself. The film got its Code seal anyway.

Concludes Penn, "My feelings about *Mickey One* change all the time. Although I have certain concerns about it, I believed it is an extraordinary film, not just as a film, but as an event in the history, or however you want to put it, of the American film. And I don't take enough pride in that: that I sort of stood the studio system on its ear to make a film which is still celebrated. I wish I could say it was drawing a line in the sand, but I had to capitulate after that because we were broke."

Although he had been paid out for *The Train,* the money from *The Left Handed Gun* and *The Miracle Worker* was long gone. "We were living on the theater, and that's not a handsome return," Penn recounts. "We were tightening our belts. I remember when we went out to do *Playhouse 90* I didn't have enough money to buy a shirt. Peggy was brilliant with two kids and a nanny, but we were scraping."

Needless to say, there was no *Mickey Two.* Everyone at Columbia was shifting attention to *The Chase.* "All that gets talked about," Penn recalls, "is, 'Are you okay? Are you comfortable? Because you're gonna be handling Brando.'"

13

Brandeux

Jane Fonda stopped in the middle of her close-up and told Marlon Brando, who was feeding her lines from offscreen, "You're just the best fucking actor in the world." Directing them, Arthur Penn nodded his head in agreement.

"We had already finished Brando's aspect of the scene," he recalls. "We now turn around. We're on Jane. Marlon was off camera. And they went over what they'd gone over with Marlon on Marlon's takes, three or four or five times, and *he was still inventing off camera!* Here he was, finished, but he couldn't *not* respond to that moment, and it just stopped Jane and stopped all of us."

Later Fonda enthused to the press about her costar, "He will not settle for anything less than the truth. He wants to get to the root of something and not in the way most actors do in terms of script. If he sees something is wrong he cannot agree to do it anyway, he just cannot."[1]

It was the summer of 1965 and Chico, California, was doubling for the fictitious town of Harrison, Texas. The movie was *The Chase*, a steamy drama about an inbred community's meltdown when an errant son, Bubber Reeves, escapes from prison and comes home to exact revenge on those who sent him up. But first he has to go through Sheriff Calder, played by Brando.

As might be expected from the volatile casting of Brando and Fonda—along with Robert Redford, Robert Duvall, Angie Dickinson, Janice Rule, James Fox, and E. G. Marshall, among a roster of other actors, both established and new—there were intrigues behind the scenes. Most of them were caused by producer Sam Spiegel, and all of them were lobbed at Penn in the course of the troubled superproduction.

The Chase began as a 1952 play by Horton Foote that focused as much on Anna Reeves, Bubber Reeves's young wife, as on Sheriff Hawes (not yet called Calder) and his wife, Ruby.[2] Reflecting Foote's writing gift, it slowly reveals the interrelationships of the townspeople and the layers of deceit that make them collectively guilty for Bubber's predicament. Featuring John Hodiak, Kim Hunter, Murray Hamilton, and Kim Stanley under José Ferrer's direction, the play ran a bare thirty-one Broadway performances, yet attracted the attention of producer Sam Spiegel.[3]

Spiegel, who could charm a snake out of its skin and then refuse to pay for it, had distinguished himself over the previous ten years by producing the highly successful films *On the Waterfront* (1954), *The Bridge on the River Kwai* (1957), and *Lawrence of Arabia* (1962), among others. Success brought him international acclaim, but what he truly craved was repatriation into Hollywood's inner circle. Spiegel saw *The Chase* as his entree, not just by producing a star-studded $5 million picture[4] but also by making one that addressed subjects dear to the industry's socially conscious heart: southern racism, mob violence, one man standing up for principle, greedy industrialists, and sex. Although those elements were not the dominating focus of Foote's play, Spiegel had screenwriter Michael Wilson add them in his unsigned first draft dated March 11, 1959. Wilson, who was still on the Blacklist, had made previous uncredited contributions to *Kwai* and *Lawrence*; it would be thirty years before his credits were restored. Spiegel hired him on the sly—and probably on the cheap—for *The Chase*.

Where, in Foote's play, Bubber returns bent on killing the sheriff—and the sheriff knows it—Wilson's script has Bubber escaping from jail alone, killing two motorists and orphaning their child, then returning to town, not to kill Sheriff Hawes but to reclaim his wife, Anna, who has taken up with the son of the town's business baron, Val Rogers. It then becomes the sheriff's job to catch Bubber, return him to jail, and protect Rogers *fils* because the sheriff owes his job and political future to the elder Rogers. A subplot has Sheriff Hawes and his barren wife adopting the boy that Bubber orphaned.

Penn describes the sheriff as "a character who essentially fails and what you get through the film, I think, is a growing sense of his displeasure and disapproval. Yet we didn't want him to seem judgmental—you know, 'I'm so liberal and you're all so hard-nosed.' It was a peculiar role Brando found himself in."[5]

Believing that greatness emerges from conflict, Spiegel replaced Wilson with Lillian Hellman to focus the story's misanthropy.[6] Hellman astutely gave Bubber a co-escapee named Simmons who kills the motorist, who now is alone and has no child, in her "final script" dated March 30, 1965.

It had been Hellman who, impressed by Penn's direction of *Toys in the Attic,* recommended him to Spiegel. "Lillian really was the screenwriter," Penn says, and, indeed, she gets sole screen credit. "But she kind of collapsed on us. Lillian and I had gone through it many times, over and over again, and she was smoking relentlessly. She wore herself out; she was drinking and became dispirited. She left and went to Palm Springs."

But first she had made the sheriff, by now called Calder, less corrupt and more disgusted with the town's collective moral turpitude. Hellman may have marked hers the "final script," but Spiegel felt otherwise. He dismissed Hellman, who carped, "Decision by democratic majority vote is fine as a form of government but it's a stinking way to create," and hired Ivan Moffat for a polish.[7]

"I met [Moffat] once and then didn't see him again," says Penn. "I think he was the source of the pages that came from Sam to me. I would look at these pages: 'Who's this?'" Moffat added enough dalliances to populate a soap opera ("All the younger ladies in it had three breasts," Hellman snarked),[8] further bloating Foote's intimate drama. Then, in an act of irony that could happen only in Hollywood, Spiegel hired Foote back to untangle everything. "Yep," confirms the gentle Foote, "he finally brought me in to do some work, but there was not much I could do because, by that time, I was so disheartened. [Hellman] said that she used my play as 'a departure' and she departed so from it that I didn't really recognize it."

Brando, who had risen to superstardom in 1954 in Spiegel's *On the Waterfront,* was Penn's ace in the hole as well as the joker. Before production, the director met him at his house for lunch. "We got talking about the American Indians," he says, "and he told me about this wonderful phenomenon of this tribe, the Fukawi Indians, and I bought into it. It's an old story about how, when the chief is aging, they replace him, but they bring him along on a travois, and finally they arrive at the next day's destination. Of course, he gets off the travois, looks around, and says, 'Where the Fukawi?' I bit into it completely because he told it with so many anthropological references that it was absolutely stunning. I just about lost my soup when the punch line came. We bonded and remained good friends through *The Missouri Breaks* years later."[9]

Brando's playfulness hid an intense devotion to his craft, but producers regarded him as a troublemaker and tried to control him. This, of course, only made it worse. For *The Chase,* the studio bound the rebellious actor to a contract that, among other things, prohibited him from driving his motorcycle during filming. Needless to say, with Penn's help, Brando got even. Recalls Penn, "Sam would call me about eleven o'clock in the morning: 'Arthur, darling, how's it going?'

"'Fine, Sam.'

"'Marlon's all right?'

"'Marlon's fine.'

"'Jane's all right?'

"'Yeah, Jane's all right.'

"He'd run down the whole cast, and I'd say, 'We're going fine.' And Sam would always say, 'And Marlon came in the car?' I would say, 'Yeah, I guess so. He's here.'

"Then one day he said, 'Marlon's there?'

"I said, 'He drove his truck down.'

"'Oh? Really? All right.'

"Brando, of course, a couple of days later, puts the motorcycle in the truck, drives the truck down, puts the truck away, and parks the motorcycle in his space. He knows the call's coming, so he's sort of cueing me silently.

"'Arthur?'

"'Yeah.'

"'Marlon's there?'

"'Yeah.'

"'What did he bring, the truck or the car?'

"'Gee, I don't know, Sam. All I see is a motorcycle.'

"The phone gets hung up. We go on for a while, and the doors fly open and in comes Sam in his pajamas and robe. Of course, the whole place broke up. That was how we went through the movie. There was a lot of merriment."

"We have had a good exchange of ideas," the director diplomatically told Peter Bart of the *New York Times*. "Marlon told me at the outset that he would present his ideas and that if I didn't like them I should tell him so. That's the way it has been. Most of his ideas have been excellent."[10]

Off the record, however, Penn found himself losing control. When illness pulled director of photography Robert Surtees off the show, Spiegel replaced him with Joseph LaShelle without consulting Penn.[11] "A nightmare," Penn says of LaShelle. "The slowest, the worst of the Hollywood bullshit. All those big scenes in the junkyard? He lit them until we were dead. We wouldn't get on the set till one o'clock in the morning. Marlon would be out, everybody would be tired. Trying to work like that, it was just terrible."

Despite this, Brando energized the entire cast, and vice versa. "If the other actor is really credible," Penn notes, "then Brando comes up with some stuff. It helps him slide in, away from the phoniness of a movie set, and when he can make that connection—as he did with Angie Dickinson, with Janice Rule, with Jane Fonda—it's a terrific connection. He was wonderful in scenes with Angie Dickinson—soft, wonderful little improvisations, but holding the line of the scenes so she never was at a loss. Angie, you know, is a wonderful girl but [was] not an advanced actress. But in the scenes with Marlon she was responding to the freedom that he was offering, and it was wonderful. A lot of that, unfortunately, never made it into the final cut."

The most startling aspect of *The Chase*, yet one that has paled by comparison over the years, is its unusual (for 1966) level of violence. In the story, Sheriff Calder refuses to reveal the whereabouts of Bubber Reeves, hoping to recapture him before the town vigilantes do. Calder is accosted in his office by a gang of rednecks who beat him to a graphic degree never before portrayed in a Production Code–approved film.[12] The beating was encouraged by Brando, and the expertise that Penn gained shooting it marked him, well before Sam Peckinpah, as the American director most adept at using violence for dramatic purposes. Recounts Penn, "When we came to the big fight scene in the office where Dick Bradford and Clifton James beat him up, he said, 'You know how to do this?' I said, 'I guess so. We'll get some stunt guys.' He said, 'No, no, no.' He said, 'Have you ever seen a fight?' I said, 'Come on, Marlon, I've been in the army; I've seen a barroom fight.' He said, 'Here's what we're gonna do.'

"We had these wonderful actors that we could trust, and they would wind up with a punch and go right up and stop [at the face], but move the flesh. We were turning at about twenty frames per second, so it really looked like they were just killing him, and the blood came, and it was absolutely fabulous."[13]

Then it came time for Brando to fall off the desk at his full weight. Brando insisted on doing it himself in a near-split that must have hurt. "It was Brando's idea," commends Penn, "because I didn't know that part of movies. I'd thought I would do what they conventionally did: the guy would turn his head [and the punch would miss], and that was it. Marlon was a great help to me throughout, not ever really saying anything directorial, but technical. He was very experienced; he had just directed a very interesting film, *One-Eyed Jacks* (1961)."

The film's most disturbing violence, however, was based on an image that had already burned into America's collective consciousness: as Sheriff Calder leads the handcuffed Bubber Reeves to jail through a gauntlet of townsfolk, a man springs from the crowd and shoots Bubber in the stomach. Penn purposely staged it in remembrance of Jack Ruby's November 25, 1963, assassination of Lee Harvey Oswald. Unlike in the Brando beating, not one drop of blood appears, but the moment is shocking. It was not in the script; Penn, Brando, and Redford devised it themselves as the perfect coda to the incipient anger rising throughout the film. When it happens, Sheriff Calder explodes and mercilessly, cathartically, beats the perpetrator.

But the real fight was to come when Penn prepared to edit the film in New York with his longtime editor, Aram Avakian. "The original arrangement I had with Sam was that we would cut in New York because I already had the rights to *Wait Until Dark* and I had to [stage] it by a certain date," Penn says. "But it took months on the road before we could get it to Broadway. While I was away, I got a call from Sam saying, 'Darling, where do you want to cut the picture, Los Angeles or London?'

"I said, 'Hey, Sam, do you remember? We had a deal.'

"'No, I don't remember that. I'm going to take it to London.'" By the time *Wait Until Dark* opened, became a hit, and Penn could get to London to screen Spiegel's work, *The Chase* was beyond rescue.

"What they did," he described in a 1971 interview with critic Elliot Norton, "was that, of the available material, they made selections that I never would have made. I would have used other takes or other emphases in a scene. It's really not so much a question of leaving material in or taking material out, it's a question of tonality. Given a certain number of takes on a given scene, for instance, as you can imagine, with Brando, it might start here and it might end up dramatically way up at the top. Well, for the most part, I think they used the less colorful material and the less original acting material and, in that sense, I think they deprived the picture and Brando of what was potentially one of the more extraordinary performances he'd given in his life."[14]

"There's a rhythm," Penn elaborates. "You see things accumulating and gaining velocity, and if they don't have that, it's flaccid. And that's my feeling about that film: it's stately and flaccid. I just was speechless. I didn't know what to say. I knew I had a stillborn film on my hands," Penn reflects. "What it was, was a pure inundation into the practices of Hollywood. And those practices are both remarkable, intoxicating, and odious, so that the film is all of those things for me."[15]

Even though Penn and Brando couldn't get the fire they wanted onscreen, it was happening for real all around them: While *The Chase* was shooting, so was Los Angeles. "Watts went up during this period," Penn says. "It was a very interesting time."[16] The Penns were living in Sammy Davis's house on Sunset Plaza Drive, above the Sunset Strip. "Sammy said, 'You're going to Hollywood? Take my house' while he was in *Golden Boy* in New York. This is heavy civil rights time. A lot of guys we knew from CORE [Congress of Racial Equality] and from SNCC [Student Non-violent Coordinating Committee] would come to the house, stay over, go down into Watts, come back, so the house was busy. And because Marlon was such a good draw, we used to hold benefits. Marlon was in his house up on Mulholland Drive, but we would hold it in Sammy's house because Marlon's was not big enough."

Peggy Penn remembers that Brando "would interrupt my phone calls and say, 'This is Dr. Brando calling Mrs. Penn.' So I would get on and say, 'What's up? Is Fannie Lou Hamer[17] going to come?' And he'd say, 'Yes, she's going to come. I just wanted you to know.'"

Ten years later, Brando and Penn again worked together in a collaboration greatly anticipated in the film world. By then the actor had spectacularly revived his career with *The Godfather* and *Last Tango in Paris* (both 1972), and the director had come into his prime with *Bonnie and Clyde* (1967), *Alice's Restaurant* (1969), *Little Big Man* (1970), and *Night Moves* (1975).

The Missouri Breaks didn't start out as a rush job, but it became one. It was an original screenplay by novelist Thomas McGuane, who was commissioned by producer Elliott Kastner and bankrolled by tax shelter money at United Artists.[18] Kastner was a master of creative deal making, and the production services company[19] Devon/Persky-Bright was happy to help. *The*

Missouri Breaks would benefit from his skills as well as those of producer Robert M. Sherman. Sherman had just produced *Night Moves* (see chapter 19) and offered to get McGuane's script to Penn. Penn based his consent on the presence of two major stars, and Brando agreed pending Kastner landing Penn and Jack Nicholson. The only element that wasn't ready was the script.

"Everybody pretty much committed to this on a first draft," says associate producer Marion Rosenberg, "and it was always, 'Well, we'll fix it as we go along,' but it doesn't work that way." Elaborates Penn, "It was sent to each of us individually and we each said no. Then Elliott Kastner, the entrepreneur, went around and got two of us. He got Nicholson and said, 'If I can get Penn and Brando, will you do it?' and then he got me and Nicholson and went to Brando and said, 'If Penn and Nicholson do it, will you?' and Bang! Pretty soon we had a picture."[20]

But not, alas, a script. The first draft that got the ball rolling concerns a band of rustlers led by Tom Logan (Nicholson) in Missouri in the 1880s. A local rancher, Braxton, worried that his eight thousand head of cattle are at risk, hires a "regulator," Robert E. Lee Clayton (Brando),[21] who picks off Logan's crew one by one until he himself is gruesomely outsmarted by Logan. McGuane wrote Clayton as a religious zealot who deems his human prey to be "lost souls" whom he sends to "the paradise beyond the stars." In Brando's embodiment he became an eccentric Irishman who takes inventive glee in killing. Unfortunately for Braxton, Clayton cannot be stopped even when he oversteps his bounds.

"What grabbed everybody," says Sherman, "was the [penultimate] scene where Nicholson says to Brando, 'Do you know what woke you up? You just had your throat cut,'" a scene that would turn out to be nearly impossible to shoot.

Money helped. In addition to percentages if the film paid off, McGuane got $400,000, Brando got $1 million, Nicholson got $1.25 million, Penn got $600,000, and Kastner got $600,000.[22] Even at that price, says Sherman, "UA was anxious to do it. It was largely because they needed what was called in those days 'a locomotive.' Today it's called a 'tent pole.'" In other words, a blockbuster that would support the company and its subsequent releases.

With the package in place, people finally realized that the script had problems. As Penn admitted to Wayne Warga of the *Los Angeles Times*, "The film started shooting a trifle un-prepared" and "our schedule was one of the greatest fantasies of all time. It was made up in a board room some place."[23] Both charges were true. The script was incomplete because McGuane was in a London editing room trying to save his film of *92 in the Shade*. Writer and director had only a handful of discussions prior to principal photography, and the schedule was the result of panic when UA realized that, not only was there a locked-in Memorial Day release date, but the Directors Guild contract was about to expire, and the picture had to be in the can lest a DGA strike cause Penn to picket his own movie.

Such urgency left skid marks on McGuane's script which, despite its buzz, gave the two superstars only about four minutes of screen time together: a single three-page exchange two-thirds of the way through the picture, and the final brief encounter when Clayton awakens after Logan has slashed his throat.[24]

Panic set in. Eventually two more Brando-Nicholson confrontations were added by an uncredited Robert Towne (which irked the absent McGuane). The new material worked, but shaping it ate up shooting time. "That gave us an opportunity to improvise," Penn gallantly spun to the press, "and who could wish for two better ponies than Brando and Nicholson?"[25]

Brando's character presented the greatest challenge. It simply didn't exist. "We weren't sure who this man Clayton was," Penn told *Time Out*. "So we tried one way after another, and we thought to do it every way; that he's a chimera, something slippery and unknowable. Of course, Marlon leapt at it—it would have been dull just to play a hired killer. We wanted to invent, to take a relatively formulaic story and de-formularize it . . . much to the consternation of the studio. Jack never knew what was coming, but you can't throw him. He responds to what's there. For the same reason, Marlon was reluctant to learn lines. He didn't want the words to go stale."[26]

Perspective allows Penn to speculate, "Marlon had a kind of dyslexia which rendered full memorization at this time in his life as, I wouldn't say extremely difficult, but difficult. So he took a very logical, undignified course, which was to get the biggest obstacle out of the way—either a cue card, or have it on the shirt of somebody he was playing with. I never heard him enunciate it fully, but I did sit enough times with him in the trailer where we would read a scene while we were trying to sort out this character, and I would watch him struggle with cold reading. He knew the scene, he just didn't want to get the words in an exact order because, my guess is, that would diminish his spontaneity. People did resent it. On the other hand, it gave him the freedom to act in a way that not many people can do."

Brando created his own gravy. "The first three weeks were just Jack," Rosenberg recalls. "Just Jack's scenes up front. And it was very clear to everybody—the cast, the crew—that Jack was the star.[27] It was 'Jack this' and 'Jack that.' The minute that Marlon appeared, it was 'Jack who?' But Jack took it absolutely beautifully. He was so respectful of Marlon that you never heard a peep."

Nicholson, who marveled that "Marlon got it all with the deal of the cards,"[28] contrasted his approach to acting with that of his costar: "I think Marlon finds acting painful, and that has something to do with it. We do have a difference of opinion. He still doesn't think that much of acting, but I think a lot of it. But who knows? Marlon might mellow as he grows older and turn into a great elder statesman. Of course, it's unlikely."[29]

Tension increased when it appeared that Brando couldn't be wrapped in the twenty days for which he was contracted, and immense overtime fees loomed. "Everybody was terrified," Penn recalls. "'Twenty days? How're we gonna finish Brando?' We're near the end and I set up a scene day for night, and Brando said, 'Why are we doing this day for night?' I said, 'Because of you and your fuckin' contract.' He said, 'Go home, hey, everybody, go home.' And we came back the next night, and the next night."

On the final day, Kastner decided to pay a wrap visit, and Brando thought it would be fun to take him on. He feigned inability to read his cue cards no matter where a young production assistant held them. "Marlon started the take looking at the card," Penn smiles, "and then moved over here. So the kid had to run around. He got there and Marlon finished it, but Elliot said something to the kid—whatever was going on, I don't know—but finally, as I kept shooting the same sequence, Elliot took the cards. Now Marlon had him hooked! Elliot would get just into position, and Marlon would turn away: 'What do I say here?' And Elliot would just tear around. It was hilarious because he was the only one with pressure. He had to finish Brando or there was some kind of enormous penalty."

When the team's creative juices were flowing, nothing equaled Brando's inventiveness in the moment. "What you want to do is give him an environment where he can invent without being that grandiose about it," his director reveals, citing Brando's entrance in the film interrupting a wake where a ranch hand's body is laid out in an ice-filled coffin. "He came in with a toothache. I didn't know it was coming until he took a piece of ice from under the body" and pressed it against his jaw, creating a piece of business that brings the scene to life. So does an odd moment toward the end of the film when Brando feeds his horse and it starts to pee. "I'm not wildly taken with the idea of improvisation," said Penn, but "we realized he was about to get his throat cut and we hadn't seen him for five minutes in the movie, so Marlon got the [horse and mule he rode], some carrots and some food, and he said, 'I'll figure something out.' He started and we just kept the cameras going. We went all day, just rolling cameras. The horse urinated and he said, 'Ah, that's lovely, my darling.' He had this love affair with the horse and absolutely rejected the mule. He built an entire scenario himself inside that one scene."[30]

The enigma of Brando lies in his absolute pursuit of truth at whatever the cost. Marvels Penn, "To be as brave as he was in front of the camera—which was 'I don't care what shows, I'm gonna go for this'—was very courageous. I don't know of your experience, but if I put a camera up here, you'd put on a face. Everybody does. Everybody puts on 'I want to do the best I can.' Not Marlon. He'd be in the moment, and that's where he was. So it looked effortless, but the process to get there was by no means effortless. Every actor in the world should be so lucky as to have taken that journey and get there."

Finished just in time, *The Missouri Breaks* was accorded a nine-hundred-print release in May of 1976 into a market that had been unalterably changed the year before by the wide release and phenomenal success of *Jaws.* A thoughtful picture, it could not compete with the blockbuster mentality that had overtaken Hollywood. That, combined with the end of tax shelter financing, meant that film companies and theater chains were no longer content to build an audience—rather, they demanded all or nothing on opening weekend. By the May 1977 release of *Star Wars,* the "Decade under the Influence," as the 1970s have been called, was over.[31]

For Penn, this was a particularly harsh reality. The revolution he had ignited with *Bonnie and Clyde,* fueled with *Alice's Restaurant,* fanned with *Little Big Man,* and inflamed with *Night Moves* had left him in ashes. He wouldn't finish another film for five years.

14

Foggy Mountain Breakthrough

Bonnie and Clyde was no accident. It was the result of actor-producer Warren Beatty's single-minded plan to generate his own screen material and guide it through the Hollywood gauntlet, and director Arthur Penn's ability to apply the vision he'd been honing his entire career. Penn, Beatty, and their creative team were at the peak of their game. The only accident—and it's tempting to call it Fate—was that the picture succeeded entirely on its own merits, having been cast adrift by a studio that neither understood it nor recognized the emerging film generation that would rise to support it.

That last component is the most significant, for *Bonnie and Clyde* was arguably the first shot fired in the movie revolution that crowned the "New Hollywood." Even if, as Robin Wood insists, "there is nothing in *Bonnie and Clyde,* stylistically, technically, thematically, which was not already implicit in *The Left Handed Gun,*" the fact remains that American audiences were more attuned to Penn's syntax in 1967 than they had been ten years earlier. Indeed—again quoting Wood—"obviously, the intense identification audiences had with the characters is a major factor . . . in the film's box office success."[1] In other words, Penn and Beatty knew how to reach the changing audience, and the Hollywood system did not.

The audience shift had, in fact, begun in the mid-1950s when adolescent baby boomers emerged as a distinct consumer group. Kids suddenly had money and leisure time, and they spent both on comic books, records, candy, clothes, and, especially, movies. At the time, Hollywood made films primarily for general audiences. As the studio system began to wither in the 1960s, however, independent companies gained access to the marketplace with fare that grownups wouldn't be caught dead watching: biker films, monster movies, beach blanket romps, and pictures where kids were heroes and authority figures were buffoons. This increasingly reflected the unrest outside of movie theaters—quite literally outside of movie theaters, in the streets—as these same young audiences realized that their parents had been lying to them about Vietnam, civil rights, sex, drugs, and politics.

It was in movies that these chords of rebellion came together. Young people began seeking films that reflected their collective raised consciousness. They recognized film as a visual medium and didn't need to explain things neatly.[2] In short, they were primed. The tipping point was *Bonnie and Clyde*.

Countless scholars have traced *Bonnie and Clyde*'s genesis, but no timeline can reflect its creative zeitgeist.[3] Even Penn acknowledges that he "caught lightning in a bottle" with his most lauded work: "*Bonnie and Clyde* was one of those absolutely fortunate films where I made the movie I wanted to make, and it turned out to be a big hit."[4]

Looking back, it was Beatty who nailed it when he complimented—actually, conned—Jack L. Warner that *Bonnie and Clyde* was "a kind of an *homage* to your body of work, to all those gangster pictures that were so extraordinary." But it really wasn't; the old Warner Bros. gangster films were urban westerns where the bad guys were exciting but the good guys won. *The Public Enemy, Little Caesar, The Roaring Twenties*, and *Angels with Dirty Faces* were about Italians, Irish, Jews, and other ethnic types fighting for survival in a hostile urban culture. Bonnie Parker and Clyde Barrow, by contrast, were corn-fed products of that part of America that Warner and his brethren were both jealous of and excluded from. Robert Benton and David Newman, who wrote it, declared that they wanted their gangster film

Irving and Arthur (in front) when they lived together during Arthur's peripatetic youth, c. 1928.

Arthur, probably age eight, perhaps wondering with whom he is next going to live.

Arthur with his and Irving's manipulative mother, Sonia.

The teenage man-about-town, c. 1939. Arthur was introduced to culture by his brother, Irving, and Irving's first wife, Nonnie.

Private Arthur Penn when he wasn't billeted at Fred Coe's Town Theatre, c. 1943.

Defendants at the Nuremberg war crimes tribunal, c. 1945. Penn dropped in when Baldur von Schirach (last row, second from left) was on trial.

Penn traveled through Europe on this passport and the GI Bill, then returned to America to discover television.

"Arturo" and the people from his pensione in Perugia, including the four
sisters who ran it, c. 1951.

(Above) Shooting *The Left Handed Gun* (1957): producer Fred Coe (seated); Penn (in white); J. Peverell Marley (at camera); actors John Dierkes, Colin Keith-Johnson, and newcomer Paul Newman.

Billy the Kid, aka the Left-Handed Gun, in the famous tintype, which, when reversed decades later, made him the Right-Handed Gun.

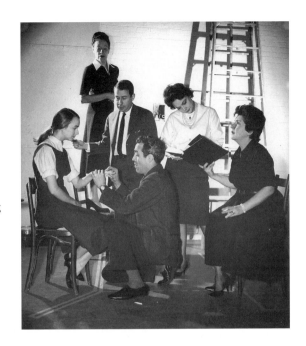

Rehearsing Lillian Hellman's volatile play *Toys in the Attic* (1960) with a volatile cast. Left to right: Rochelle Oliver, Penn, Jason Robards Jr. (kneeling), Irene Worth, Maureen Stapleton. Standing behind: Anne Revere. Penn banished Hellman from the theater when she made the cast nervous.

Playbill magazine, featuring a cover photo of Anne Bancroft for *The Miracle Worker* (1959).

Arthur and Peggy arrive in Brussels in March of 1963 to receive honors for *The Left Handed Gun,* a film ignored in America but embraced in Europe. (GJ "Le Soir" Bruxelles)

Arthur and Peggy Penn, c. 1965.

Peggy contemplates where to put things in their new apartment while Arthur contemplates the camera contemplating them.

Penn signaling "action." He became so involved during shooting that actors gauged their performances by watching him out of the corners of their eyes.

Arthur and Peggy in their dining room, c. 1968. The table is empty, but their plates are full. Note the Bentwood chairs that inspired the settings for *Nichols and May.*

At the time of this moody portrait, c. 1968, Penn had five hits running on Broadway and his choice of films. (Fred Schnell)

Arthur, Peggy, Molly, and Matthew gallivanting behind their home in Stockbridge, Massachusetts, c. 1969. Dede Allen edited *Alice's Restaurant* in the barn while Arthur was shooting it nearby.

Penn and Dustin Hoffman relax while making *Little Big Man* in 1969.

Penn at the height of his Hollywood power, c. 1970. The holes in his bush jacket are probably wounds from movie executives.

Bonnie Parker and Clyde Barrow. They were their own best publicists until Benton, Newman, Beatty, and Penn came along.

Arthur and Peggy dress in sync with the countercultural era his films helped to kindle.

Penn looking uncharacteristically dour for a man who had his choice of projects—for the stage, television, and movies—all at once.

Penn meets press while making his segment for *Visions of Eight* at the Munich Olympics.

Penn and playwright William Gibson, c. 1975. *Two for the Seesaw, The Miracle Worker, Golden Boy, Golda,* and *Monday After the Miracle* are legacies of their friendship.

Portrait of the artist as an elder statesman, c. 1995, but not quite emeritus.

Four Penns: Matthew, Peggy, Arthur, and Molly, c. 2008.

to have all the things you never saw in a gangster film. Consequently, *Bonnie and Clyde* became the first major studio release that gleefully flouted the prevailing Motion Picture Production Code's starchy admonitions against explicit violence, sex, and, especially, making crime attractive.

The real Bonnie Parker and Clyde Barrow may have thought they were rebels, but they were rebels without any knowable cause except their own pleasure, which came to a bloody end on May 23, 1934, when authorities pumped between 130 and 167 rounds into them (depending on who's doing the counting). She was twenty-three; he was twenty-five. It was Easter Sunday, which may account for the pair's resurrection as heroes.

In an era of gangsters, they were only hoodlums. Guys like Al Capone, Dean O'Banion, and Meyer Lansky ran syndicates and inspired fear. If anything, Bonnie and Clyde were freelancers like John Dillinger, who cultivated his Robin Hood image by stealing from banks, not people, and famously telling the press, "You'd do what I do if you had the guts." Judging by her self-glorifying poetry, Bonnie saw herself and Clyde in the Dillinger mold, much to Dillinger's alleged dismay. The reality was that the capricious young pair—when they met[5] in January of 1930 he was twenty-one and she was nineteen—were reviled by other criminals for their spree killing that brought the cops down on all of them.

It has been a disappointment to social scientists and romantics that Bonnie and Clyde were not psychos, children of abusive parents, existential killers, or political radicals. They were simply criminals who, in the 1930s, symbolized the feral survival instinct of a country that was betrayed by its leaders into the Great Depression. Likewise, in 1967, *Bonnie and Clyde* fueled a revolution among the children of that depression, who felt equally betrayed by a government that led them into war.

Penn turned down *Bonnie and Clyde* three times before saying yes. But it was also rejected, at various stages of its development, by George Stevens, William Wyler, Karel Reisz, John Schlesinger, Brian Hutton, Sydney Pollack, Jean-Luc Godard, and most notably, François Truffaut.

It was David Newman who encountered the material. "I was

a true crime buff and had picked up a copy of John Toland's *The Dillinger Days*,"[6] he told *Los Angeles Times* film reporter Patrick Goldstein. "It had footnotes about other outlaws of the time—and there were Bonnie and Clyde. In an appendix of the book, he'd published Bonnie's doggerel poem, 'The Ballad of Bonnie and Clyde.' Here was this uneducated white-trash West Dallas gangster who'd written this compelling poem. When I talked about it with Benton, who was from Waxahachie, Texas, he realized he had these memories, as a child, of kids getting dressed up as Bonnie and Clyde for Halloween. And we thought, This is the movie we want to write."[7]

Benton and Newman crafted a seventy-five-page treatment, including cuts and cameras angles, and got it to two would-be producers whom they knew socially, Elinor Wright Jones and her brother, Norton Wright. Jones and Wright were interested, and in the spring of 1964 asked their lawyer, Robert Montgomery, to approach Arthur Penn to direct. Penn, still licking his wounds from *The Train* and trying to get a production of William Faulkner's *The Wild Palms* off the ground while gearing up for *Mickey One,* paid scant attention. Benton and Newman next prevailed upon Helen Scott, who represented many French filmmakers, to get it to François Truffaut. Truffaut's knowledge of film was encyclopedic even if his grasp of English wasn't, and he demanded a translation before deciding whether to continue. In March of 1964 he came to America on other business and made time for a weeklong confab with Benton and Newman. The writers credit his input with giving the film its shape. He worked intimately on tone and structure, taking his acolytes to screenings and imbuing them with the sense that it's more important to be true to cinema than true to history.

When Truffaut finished mentoring Benton and Newman, he headed to Chicago, where Penn was filming *Mickey One,* which, on his recommendation, happened to star Alexandra Stewart and happened to costar Warren Beatty, who happened to be dating Truffaut's friend Leslie Caron, who happened to be married to Peter Hall, who happened to run England's National Theatre. Whether Beatty and Truffaut discussed *Bonnie and Clyde* at this opportunity is unclear. Meanwhile, in May of 1964, Jones and Wright bought an eighteen-month option on the treatment that allowed the writers to ditch *Esquire* long enough to take a research trip to West Texas. It was there, says Newman, that he and Benton heard the "Don't sell that cow" joke that Clyde's brother, Buck, tells endlessly throughout the film. On their return to New York, the writers spent their days with *Esquire* and their nights with *Bonnie and Clyde,* passing scenes back and forth until neither knew who had written what. The billing even switched on various script drafts; some were written by Newman and Benton, others by Benton and Newman.

For nearly a year the script languished on studio desks. Despite interest by David Picker at United Artists, his staid bosses, Arthur Krim and Robert Benjamin, balked at its sex and violence. Nevertheless, Picker remained interested until the budget rose beyond his $1.6 million limit.

After Beatty and Caron finished filming *Promise Her Anything* (1965) in England, he prevailed upon her to arrange a meeting with Truffaut in Paris so he could pitch himself as the lead in the director's pending *Fahrenheit 451*. Instead, Truffaut hooked Beatty on *Bonnie and Clyde*. Returning to America, Beatty phoned the writers and literally showed up on Benton's doorstep wanting to buy the script, only to learn that it was still under option to Jones and Wright. So he waited until the day the option lapsed (November 27, 1965) and phoned again. They sent him a copy. Recalled Benton, "He called that night and said, 'I'm on page 27. I want to do it.' And I said, 'Wait till page 47.' And he called back and said, 'I still want to do it.' Warren bought the script for $10,000."[8]

On page 47 was the ménage à trois.

Benton and Newman's spirits were considerably restored by Beatty's enthusiasm, and they suggested that Truffaut would make a fine director. Beatty wisely told them that they had written a French New Wave film and needed an American director. Then he began looking for financing. Reports vary on the sales technique used by the persuasive actor to wheedle the budget out of Warner Bros. According to reports from the studio's publicity

VP Richard Lederer, Beatty begged on his hands and knees to the company's CEO, Benny Kalmenson. Publicist Joe Hyams insisted it was Jack Warner before whom Beatty prostrated himself, and that the incident involved kissing J. L.'s footwear.[9]

"It never happened," Beatty insisted. "It was Walter MacEwan [Warner's production chief] who approved the movie. That stuff about me being on my hands and knees is all apocrypha. There's so much about this movie that people tend to hyperbolize." Then he added, tantalizingly, "The real stories, they're even better."[10]

"Trust me," Lederer maintained, "it's not something you could make up. I was there to see it."[11]

Whoever kissed whoever's whatever, Beatty got the go-ahead for $1,800,000. All he needed now was a director. Naturally, he wanted the one with whom he had disagreed the most, yet felt closest to: Penn. But Penn was tied up directing Lee Remmick, Robert Duvall, and Mitch Ryan in *Wait Until Dark* at the Ethel Barrymore Theatre at the beginning of 1966. For the third time, he turned down *Bonnie and Clyde*, and Beatty, who uses patience as a tool, went off to London to shoot *Kaleidoscope* (1966). There he met with Jean-Luc Godard as a possible director, toyed with casting Bob Dylan as Clyde Barrow, and decided against asking his sister, Shirley MacLaine, to play Bonnie once he resigned himself to playing Clyde. A succession of turndowns by other directors brought him back to America and the decision to pursue Penn.

In Penn's words, "I didn't stand a chance."

"Arthur was my first choice," said Beatty, "not only because I knew him but because I could get into an argument with him. So when he said he would make the movie, I said, 'I want to have one agreement: that if we make this movie we will have an argument every night. If we don't have anything to argue about, I want to find something to argue about, because there's always something that can be better or can be thought about more.'"[12]

Beatty was a man of his word. He and Penn had ongoing "discussions" from the October 11, 1966, start of principal photography to its January 6, 1967, wrap six days over schedule, and continuing through early May postproduction. Yet the resulting film is less the product of contrived conflict than the creative alchemy that comes from deeply committed filmmakers.

And few filmmakers are as committed as Warren Beatty. Although his protracted decision-making process gives the impression of indecision, what he is actually doing is waiting for the planets to accede to his terms. "He's a better actor than he is ever given credit for," Penn readily offers. "There's much more going on there. A lot of intelligence. He had a kind of a proprietorship where I think he felt that he had to set a good example. [On *Bonnie and Clyde*] he was not the actor personality of *Mickey One*. He was much more in charge."[13]

Penn admires Beatty's ability to play against his charisma. In the scene after robbing the grocery store at the beginning of the film, in which Bonnie is drawn to him sexually, he advises her, "I ain't much of a lover boy" and proceeds to feed her ambitions rather than her libido. At once he is distracting her, conning her, and trying to reassure himself, a remarkable acting trick. "I have to credit Warren with that," Penn admires. "He had a pitch in his mind on how to do it, and then he thought, 'Gee, it's a little too glib, I have to poison it,' and he bumps his head on the car window. That was really Warren."

What intrigued Penn was not the lines in the script but what went on between them. He saw the film as an essay on crime: not those of Bonnie and Clyde but the institutionalized larceny of banks that lent money to farmers in the 1920s and then foreclosed when economic conditions (caused by the banks' own profligacy) turned sour.[14] "I kept emphasizing that we have to set this against a socioeconomic time," he says. "You have to understand that the banks loaned us the money to get the farms, we couldn't pay it back, they took the farms, they got the money, so let's go get the money where it is. It was as simple as that."

Bonnie and Clyde were also lucky. The FBI wasn't granted interstate jurisdiction until 1934, and local police were likewise forbidden to cross state lines in pursuit of fleeing criminals. Moreover, the Barrow gang also made it a point to steal eight-cylinder getaway cars at a time when local constabularies drove less powerful six-cylinder vehicles.

The art direction of Dean Tavoularis was particularly important in establishing the era; Penn calls it "the best thing that happened to *Bonnie and Clyde*. Done in a minimalist style. I mean, the scene in which Bonnie and Clyde meet and rob their first store, it's three posters of Roosevelt, an old car, and a grocery store. And that was *it*."

Benton and Newman had labored so long and so hard on *Bonnie and Clyde* that it must have shocked them when Beatty asked Robert Towne—not them—to perform rewrites. "Benton and Newman, I think, were exhausted and had moved on," Penn opines. "Warren was tough on them for a long, long time. He had worn them down."

"His contribution to the picture is equally enormous," Benton allowed diplomatically about Towne years later. "I do think Bob is one of the two great screenwriters around today. I mean brilliant."[15] Towne is credited as "Special Consultant." Among his gifts are his ability to spot what's wrong with a script and then fix it within the style of the original material. In the case of *Bonnie and Clyde,* both Penn and Beatty knew that there were structural problems that Benton and Newman had not solved, but they weren't sure what they were. Towne did. And so did Peggy Penn. "The best idea that occurred in terms of the script came from Peggy," Penn says. "In that script the family reunion scene occurred earlier. Towne and I had been doing it on a corkboard with cards [on location in Texas], and we put it in this configuration, and we said, 'There's something wrong here.'

"I came back to New York with the script and Peggy and I read it. Because of the scene with Evans Evans and Gene Wilder where he says, 'I'm an undertaker,' and Bonnie says, 'Get them out of here,' and then runs into the cornfield followed by Clyde, Peggy said, 'She's got to see her family because the intimation of death has registered.' Where, before, it was a frivolous little scene, I realized that that was exactly right. When that came, it was Towne who was there. It's a small scene—only half a page—mostly nonverbal, with the mother saying, 'You live three miles from me, honey, and you won't live long.'"

The reunion scene stands out from the rest of the film in tone and mood. Penn and cinematographer Burnett Guffey gave it a veneer of misty nostalgia, and Penn's inclusion of a child rolling down a sand hill in morbid slow motion was, per Penn, "my adumbration for the ending."

Other than the Barrow gang, everybody in the scene was a nonprofessional actor. Of particular note is Mabel Cavitt, the woman who played Bonnie's mother. "That was not an actress," Penn smiles. "That was a woman who was watching us shoot, and Gene Lasko said, 'Look at that woman's face. It's Faye [Dunaway, who played Bonnie]!' It's true. She was a schoolteacher. I said, 'Would you try this?' A real Texas woman: 'Well—all right.' I said to myself, 'That coolness is not gonna hurt us one bit,' and I just laid back. Warren was great. He started to seduce her: 'I'm gonna take your little girl . . .'—it just flowed out of him. He was terrific."

The reunion scene cleared the way for Bonnie and Clyde to consummate their love so that, in terms of classic tragedy, once they achieve self-knowledge, they must die. "The scene in which he made love with her was a new scene," explained Towne, who wrote it, revealing how Penn works with writers as well as actors. "The scene in the hotel room in which she says, 'I thought we were going some place but this is just it,' was a new scene. I can't remember all of them. I was in a hotel room working on scenes every day, and I would be told, 'Try it this way.' My overall impression was feeling like a fool—it was one of my first jobs—because I was asked to rewrite scenes so many times, the original and my own too. I thought, 'Jeez, I must be terrible,' because Arthur Penn kept asking me to do it again and again. Then I realized Arthur was really using me the way a good director uses an actor: 'Try the scene this way. Try the scene that way.' It was very intelligent of him."[16]

The sex scene also called for a resolution of an issue that the filmmakers had to address. According to legend, Clyde Barrow was gay, Bonnie Parker was not, and C. W. Moss[17] serviced them both. The Benton-Newman script revealed this at page 47 (which became page 33 in the budgeting script), and to them it was an essential part of the story. Beatty originally deemed the idea "novel and unexpected," but, then, as Newman remembered,

"Our very first meeting with Warren, he came right out and said, 'I'm not playing a [homosexual].' He had plenty of aesthetic reasons, but he thought it would make him terribly unsympathetic to his audience."[18] Benton and Newman resisted changing it until Penn took Beatty's side. "I said, 'This is a film about bumpkins,'" Penn reports. "It was just too sophisticated. C. W. was a babe, a mascot; he was an innocent, and it's so much better the way we have it. Their source material was this one little lousy book written by an ex-FBI agent who had such contempt for these people. I said, 'No, it's a failed love story.'"

Concludes Benton, "Arthur said that we'd written a very heterosexual love story, and therefore one didn't go with the other. David and I thought that was very true. The other thing he said— and this is what made us change our minds—was that if you gave the audience any reason to believe that Clyde was homosexual, the moment the killing took place, they'd say, 'Oh, he's a fag,' and you would distance your audience from that character. There was just so much that the audience would abide; the audience would love those characters and accept the fact that they were killers—and that in itself was such an enormous thing for audiences to do—that when you lay on top of it this complex sexual relationship, it was too much."[19]

In the production script, the legendary ménage happens—or would have happened—twenty-four minutes and forty seconds into the film, right after Bonnie has coerced C. W. Moss (then called W. D.) into robbing the gas station where he works. In the missing scenes 23 and 24, the three pull up to Puetts Tourist Court, get out of the car, arm in arm and laughing, and enter the bungalow together. After four beats, W. D. comes out, "still dressed, but overwrought and disturbed, shaking his head back and forth . . . the sex proposition has just been put to him and he is reacting to it strongly negative." He steps to the side of the road and starts to hitch a ride, but when Bonnie and Clyde emerge from the motel and smile at him, he bows to their authority and joins them inside. The next morning all three are seen in bed together. After some silent interplay between Bonnie and Clyde, W. D. awakens and "suddenly he remembers what he did last night and his eyes open up as big as saucers and he leaps from the bed." The scene carries the stage direction that it should be comic and "indicate that for all three of them the experience of the previous night has been really far out and wild."[20]

As the film now exists, Bonnie and Clyde share a bed but C. W. is in a chair, where his presence presumably relieves Clyde of the burden of having had sex with Bonnie during the preceding night. In retrospect, Penn's decision was the wiser one. Additionally, by casting the cherubic Michael J. Pollard as C. W., Penn and Beatty were further stacking the cards against driving on a sexual two-way street.

The film was set up as a Tatira-Hiller Production, and the search for the rest of the principal cast began. Penn had seen Michael J. Pollard in Norman Jewison's *The Russians Are Coming, the Russians Are Coming* (1966), but Beatty was ahead of him, having appeared onstage with the gentle actor in William Inge's short-lived *A Loss of Roses* in 1959. He also brought Gene Hackman to Penn's attention, citing him as one of the few good experiences to come out of *Lilith* (1964). Penn quickly agreed, and Hackman became Buck Barrow, Clyde's brother. Gene Wilder, who made his screen debut as the mortician Eugene, was known to Penn from the Actors Studio. Playing Velma, Eugene's fiancée, Penn cast Evans Evans, an honorable choice given that Evans's husband, director John Frankenheimer, had replaced Penn on *The Train* three years earlier.

"Then came the period of 'Who's gonna be the woman?'" Penn says. "Warren had gone to quite a few well-known actresses, all of whom I objected to for a variety of reasons; either he had been linked to them romantically, like Natalie Wood, or he kept trying to get me to go with Jane Fonda. Finally we settled on Tuesday Weld.[21] Good choice. Gave her the script, went out to visit her after she read it. She said, 'I don't want to do this.' I said, 'Why?' 'I just don't want to do it.' She wasn't forthcoming. Years later I asked, 'Why did you turn this down?' and she said, 'Because . . . I was trying to make my marriage work.'"[22]

Enter Faye Dunaway, already tapped for stardom in *The Happening* and *Hurry Sundown* (both 1967). With Elia Kazan as mentor, the smoldering yet icily beautiful Dunaway had impressed Penn with her stage performance in Arthur Miller's *After the Fall* in 1964 and William Alfred's *Hogan's Goat* in 1965. Although neither of her films had yet been released, her experience making *Hurry Sundown* for abusive director Otto Preminger nearly put her off movies forever. Penn knew she had the chops and persuaded Beatty to give her the part. That did not, however, assure that the two leads would get along, and it would complicate matters down the road.

Gene Hackman would win plaudits for his role as Buck Barrow, Clyde's older brother. Hackman and Beatty had worked together previously in *Lilith*, the two men sharing a scene in which each was uneasy with the other. Their first scene together in *Bonnie and Clyde* retraced that landscape. Penn's direction shows how he was able to exploit the actors' moods for the benefit of the film. "I had that scene with Warren and Gene Hackman. Gene was uncomfortable, and he wanted me to say, 'Do something' and I sort of let it sit, thinking, 'Go ahead, be uncomfortable.' And then he goes, 'Woo! What are we gonna do? Have a good time!'" Hackman's most disturbing moment is his death scene. Buck has been shot in the head and pursued by police to a clearing where he dies in agony. "When he dies at the end of being shot," notes Penn, "he said, 'What do you want me to do here?' I said, 'Have you ever seen a bullfight?' He said, 'Yes, I have.' I said, 'You know, after the sword is in, what does the bull do?' Gene paused, then said, 'I got it.'

"You watch the life go out of a body instead of a movie 'die.'" Penn recounts. "It was just something I liked."

Estelle Parsons, who had studied law before a stint as TV's first political reporter (in 1952 on the *Today Show*), was known to Penn from the Actors Studio and the Berkshire Drama Festival. At first she was unnerved by Penn's process of putting up scenes and exploring them at the same time. "It's the actor's nightmare," she recalled, "getting up and doing it in your own words when you don't really know it so that things start coming out of you, and all of a sudden I thought, 'Yes, I am in the right place, I am in the right business.' When I see *Bonnie and Clyde*

I can't believe I was doing all that. Whatever was in me for that role, Arthur was able to bring it out."[23] Parsons would earn an Academy Award for her performance.

As befits a film about outlaws, the people who made *Bonnie and Clyde* also broke the law, chiefly Hollywood's creaky Production Code. Their crime, so to speak, was performed at gunpoint. The "face shot," as it came to be called, is one of the most significant moments in cinema. In the film, it's the instant at which the gang's (and the audience's) fun and games turn deadly serious. In terms of the motion picture medium, it is the first time that a studio-made film includes the gun, the shot, the victim, and the blood in the same frame. The script says coldly what happens when Bonnie and Clyde hop into C. W.'s getaway car and a bank teller jumps onto their running board: "Clyde fires through the window. The face of the man explodes in blood. Then he drops out of sight."

The studios were signatories to Hollywood's Production Code, which had, for over thirty years, hypocritically allowed violence but downplayed its results, particularly gunshots. "This really blew it out of the water," Penn says proudly, his eyes twinkling with the mischief of achievement. "The gunshot in the same frame was very conscious; I was going to do that. Because all you're doing is sanitizing if you have somebody shoot over here and you cut to somebody getting hit over here. That gap has changed everything."

It was assistant director Russ Saunders, a former stuntman, who agreed to play the teller when the original stuntman balked. The effect, especially upon audiences in 1967 (by way of comparison, *The Wild Bunch* was two years away), was as profound as it is upon Bonnie and Clyde themselves.

The violence in *Bonnie and Clyde,* plus its skill in making criminals attractive, sent shudders through the offices of the Motion Picture Association of America. The very next year, in a pragmatic move that has drawn fire ever since, the Production Code was practically eliminated.

And then there was the sex. The first scene in which Bonnie and Clyde share a bed and try to make love, the MPAA warned the filmmakers, should not look as if she is engaging in fella-tio. "She certainly was!" Penn laughs. "[Warner Bros. and the MPAA] were scared. There was no question about it. It frightened 'em badly."

Beatty, too, took note of the scene, but for opposite reasons. "They hadn't been able to consummate sexually by that point in the story," Penn says. "And when we got to that, Warren kept saying to me, 'C'mon, they *gotta* do it *once*.' Finally I agreed with Warren, saying that if they don't do it once, it isn't a love story, and you won't weep for them at the end."

As originally scripted, the ambush that ends the film was only indicated in still photographs, with the gunfire playing offscreen: "*At no point* [emphasis in script] in the gun-fight do we see Bonnie and Clyde in motion."[24] Penn thought the device wasn't cathartic enough, yet didn't know how to stage it in a manner meeting its dramatic needs. "That was what troubled me," he says. "First of all, it resembles the beginning of the movie (snap-shots), and that's a bad thing to do, to go back tonally to something very like the front. But also it just is not right. That's the end of a gangster story, but that's not the end of this film. A few days later I woke up and saw the ending. I saw the ending! I saw it just the way it is in the finished film. Warren said, 'What are you talking about?' I said, 'It's a kind of spastic ballet.' He said, 'I don't know what the fuck that means.' I said, 'Just trust me on this one. I know what I want.'"

Penn covered the scene with multiple cameras set to roll at varying speeds, but "they were ganged in one common point of view. I didn't want us to jump around. I just kept a consistent point of view and let [the actors] do all the movement. People have written about that and spoken about that. I didn't want to get wild; I just wanted to look at it. But it was intended to remove us from the vitriol of the direct shooting and to bounce us into another state of being."

The ambush was shot at Albertson Ranch in Triunfo, California, over three days beginning December 29, 1966 (the original wrap date of the film, incidentally), interrupted by New Year's. Beatty and Dunaway were wired with hundreds of squib with

cables strapped to their legs leading offscreen. A piece of pros-
thetic scalp was affixed to Beatty's head and would be yanked
off with invisible catgut in homage to the Zapruder film of the
JFK assassination. There was one little glitch, however. "The first
take, because we had to roll all these high-speed cameras, there
wasn't time to get up to speed and [use the clapsticks]," Penn
reports, "so I would [signal] Warren and he would squeeze the
pear and that was the signal for the special effects guys to start
firing, et cetera. Well, we spent the whole first morning rigging it.
And we get ready and it's tense, it's really tense around the set.
Finally we run the cameras and I go 'Pow' and Warren freezes.
He squeezes the pear but he stands there watching all this happening around him. Faye is dying the death of the damned and
everything is going on, and Warren hasn't moved. So that whole
morning was gone. It took all half-day to rig it. We got two takes
a day. You know, it's terrifying stuff because, finally, you've got
a bundle of wires coming out of your trouser leg of that kind of
thickness, and he's gonna roll, and so it's gotta be in back and
front and all over, and the wires kept off camera. The wires were
very close. Faye was tied to the emergency brake. But she was a
gamer on that. Warren had that moment. But it took us the best
part of three days to get that sequence."

"It was one of those insane moments where, as a director,
you're saying to yourself, 'I see it this way, I see it no other way,
so I'm not going to economize' and, meanwhile, you can see people whispering on the set, 'This guy is nuts. What the fuck is he
doing?'"[25]

Tension was at a peak. Although both parties were too professional to let it show, by this time there was palpable acrimony
between Beatty and Dunaway. Penn was concerned that this
might inhibit them as their characters look at each other for the
last time before the bullets fly. "They had to be mutually saying, 'Good-bye, I love you, and I don't know why this moment
is happening,' he explains. So he stood in their eyelines. "I was
the person that she looked at instead of Warren, and then, on
the reverse, I was in the car where Dunaway was when Warren
looked at her. By then the tension between them was a little bit

flammable, and I thought, 'These are just gonna be singles; let's get the best we can get out of it.' And that's why we did it." Seeing such tenderness before such carnage has affected audiences ever since.

When *Bonnie and Clyde* returned to the Warner Bros. studio in Burbank for process shots and looping, the sale to Seven Arts hadn't closed yet and Jack Warner was still the titular mogul. But he had no one left to order around. "They come to us and say, 'There's nobody in the lunchroom. Please come up to the President's lunch room.' [At lunch], Warren and Jack are funny, and Warren is saying, 'I hear you sold the studio, Jack. You know who you sold it to?' Jack says, 'Yeah, I know who I sold it to!' 'No, you don't know who's behind it. Look up on the water tower: those are my initials.' It was that kind of lunch. A lot of laughter.

"Jack has no function. At Warner Bros. the tradition had been that, on low budget pictures, they would give them a schedule and Jack would walk in and say, 'This wraps on Friday.' So we've shot all the rear projection. The only thing we have left to do are the stills that are under the titles. I said, 'We're not going to do that here with the crew'—we'd already set up a wrap party on the stage—'on Monday, Warren, Faye and I will go into a photographer's studio and we'll knock these out.' Jack came down and said, 'No, you wrap on Friday. This is Friday.' I said, 'Jack, it makes no sense.' He held fast. So we stayed there with a full crew and shot still photographs. It was truly the last hurrah." Title artist Wayne Fitzgerald used the period photos of Walker Evans as reference, and the sequence adds the sound effect of an old-fashioned box camera. "Suddenly it evoked the memory we all had from our childhoods of that clicking noise of the Kodak camera shutter," said Penn, "and it just made the titles come alive."[26]

Even a lame duck mogul can quack. Warner hated the sex, violence, and tone, and he didn't understand why anybody would like it. Furthermore, the film offended his patriotism. "They did all the gangster films where you could tell the good guys and the bad guys," editor Dede Allen analyzed several years after the film was released, citing how Warner was close to FBI director J. Edgar Hoover. "Jack Warner wanted to be a good boy very badly. He wanted to prove that he was the most American. And I think that *Bonnie and Clyde* struck him as slightly un-American."

The studio faced other problems, this time from producer Beatty. Faye Dunaway's contract called for her to have above-the-title billing with the actor Beatty. Producer Beatty, however, balked, even though he had initially wanted a female co-lead to take pressure off him. Consequently, he withheld his approval of the advertising and publicity materials, jeopardizing deadlines. His intransigence was such that Warner executives P. D. Knecht and Walter MacEwan debated taking the picture away from Beatty, and even brought Warner into the discussion. The matter was dropped when Beatty capitulated.

While the front office was settling its affairs, Penn and his editors were finding the film within the footage. When his previous editor, Aram Avakian, was unavailable, Penn met Dede Allen through director Elia Kazan, for whom she had just cut *America, America*. The Penn-Allen team continued through six pictures[27] and became a collaboration that even auteurist film critics would acknowledge, making Dede Allen one of the most recognizable and respected film editors in the world.

"Dede is a wonderful collaborator," Penn says. "She understands what an actor is doing, so my whole theory about rhythm is a theory that she shares. Dede also has characteristics that I don't have. She is daunting. She will stay even with something small until it works, until it's right. I will say, 'Okay, that's enough, let's leave it alone' and then I'll come back in the editing room the next day and it will be totally different and I'll say, 'When did you do that?' and she'll say, 'Oh, I stayed here all night last night working on it.' I'll say, 'Dede, you're crazy. You're crazy but you're wonderful.'"[28]

Their chemistry was not immediate. "It took us a while," says Allen, who calls herself a "gut" editor. "I'm basically as inarticulate as Arthur is articulate. He absolutely intimidated me. He'd use these big words and finally I couldn't take it any more. I looked at him one day and said, 'What does that word mean?' He caught on right away and he never did that again."

Allen declined to visit the set, telling Penn and Beatty, "I live in New York. This is where the film's going to come," a position that would later cause friction with the studio. By the time Penn wrapped and got back to Manhattan, Allen and her assistant, Jerry Greenberg, had a rough cut ready for him. "I was appalled, I was just appalled," the director still blanches. "I knew that Jerry Greenberg had been given the task of cutting the ending. He kept trying to make sense of it, he was trying to cut it literally. So, of course, it crashed in flames.[29] But then Dede—she's tremendous—at that point she says, 'Okay, now let's go to work. We know what to do.'"

While screening footage for Penn, Allen and her team discovered that the director had a "tell" that gave clues which takes to use. "We'd list all the dailies in the order of the scene on a yellow sheet of paper with enough space between so that I wouldn't have to take my eyes off the screen," she confides. "I used to tell my assistants that if Arthur does certain things like clenching his jaw in a certain way, to note what that line was on. I got to know his signals." It was the same directorial empathy that inspired Beatty, starting on *Mickey One,* to ask Penn to stand near the camera so he could use his silent reactions as a reference.

"*Bonnie and Clyde* had a pace and a tempo that could never go the opposite way," Allen summarizes. "It carried you along at such a pitch that you never were let down, even for a generation that's been raised in a different tempo. It was the most finely honed picture I ever worked on."

Two kinds of music enliven the film: the formal underscoring of Charles Strouse, whom Penn had known from *Golden Boy,* and the roots music of Lester Flatt and Earl Scruggs. Although it is Strouse's sparsely applied work that pays off the emotional scenes, most viewers cite Flatt and Scruggs's jaunty guitar/banjo duet, "Foggie Mountain Breakdown," as the film's iconic musical signature. Written by Scruggs and recorded in 1949 by the duo and their group, the Foggy Mountain Boys, its use in the freewheeling early scenes of *Bonnie and Clyde* beautifully captures the youthful hopefulness and the bucolic setting.

The film was set for an August 4, 1967, premiere at the

Montreal Film Festival, but its fate had already been decided by Warner Bros., which booked it for a U.S. bow on August 13. It was a Sunday, which was unusual and indicative of the studio's expectations of losing its $1,849,200 negative cost.[30] The film's triumphant Montreal reception, rather than inspiring confidence, only caused the embarrassed Warner executives to entrench.

"It started out and it was dead," Penn says. As if it wasn't damaging enough that the studio thought it was a loser, *New York Times* film critic Bosley Crowther used it as the center-piece of a series of articles against violence in American films. "When he saw [it] at the Montreal Film Festival, he is alleged to have said to somebody that he was going to blow that film out of the water," Penn said in a later interview. "Which he did, in his review. But it was the best advertising we could have had."[31]

"*This is during the Vietnam war!*" he adds, enraged by the memory. "What's the excess? Oh, in the *movies* you shouldn't; at *home* you can live with it! Out on the street you can live with it, but at home we don't talk about the war! It was a crazy series."

In reaction to Crowther's blast, Warner Bros. wanted to pull the film's New York booking and cut its losses. Instead, Beatty persuaded it to change the ad campaign to "They're young, they're in love, and they kill people."

And then the groundswell started, recalls Penn, "because this was during the change in the whole social setting of the country. The kids knew from each other—without the Internet—that there was this movie. And they began to line up. Then the exhibitors began to say, 'Hey, gimme back that movie that you guys took out of here after three days.' That's when it started to roll. Letters now in the 'Arts' section; you couldn't buy that publicity for anything. It just kept going, and by that point, it was running away from them."

Crowther wasn't alone in his pan; Joseph Morgenstern was equally negative in his *Newsweek* review. He had watched the film in Warner Bros.' Fifth Avenue screening room with Beatty sitting behind him. It didn't help him like the film. But after his review broke, Morgenstern's wife, actress Piper Laurie, did. She inveigled him to see the film again, only with her by his side and in a full house. "That afternoon audience needed no cues from critics," Morgenstern remembers. "The word had gotten around: this was something special. And they were just eating it up. It was a filmmaker's dream." Reflexively, the critic reached for a pencil and paper and started taking notes. "The audience was just in ecstasy," he continues. "I mean, this was a genuine popular phenomenon." The next week the following rereview ran in *Newsweek:* "Last week this magazine said that *Bonnie and Clyde,* a tale of two bank robbers in the 1930s, turns into 'a squalid shoot-'em-up for the moron trade' because it does not know what to make of its own violence. I am sorry to say I consider that review grossly unfair and regrettably inaccurate. I am sorrier to say I wrote it."[32]

"I made the transition with some public embarrassment," Morgenstern admits with hindsight. "I'm not pleased about all of that. I'm amused by it; it's certainly become a great curiosity and footnote to movie history."

Bosley Crowther did not do as well. His repeated attacks on *Bonnie and Clyde,* added to other instances of missing the changing cultural boat, led to his January 1, 1968, "retirement" from the *New York Times* after twenty-seven years. He was replaced by Renata Adler, who was roughly half his age.

The movie was nominated for ten Academy Awards and won two: Estelle Parsons for Best Performance by an Actress in a Supporting Role, and Best Cinematography, Burnett Guffey. In a particularly competitive year, Penn was nominated for the second time as Best Director but lost to Mike Nichols for *The Graduate,* and Benton and Newman's original story and screenplay lost to William Rose's traditional *Guess Who's Coming to Dinner.* The film itself was defeated for Best Picture by *In the Heat of the Night,* renewing the contention that the Oscar usually goes to films that confirm the Hollywood status quo rather than challenge it.

Nevertheless, *Bonnie and Clyde* is a demarcation in American cinema. It was an independent film that got made within the studio system only because the studio system was collapsing around it. It was the film that changed the way audiences saw heroes and villains in movies, and it was released at a time when the public was starting to revise its view of heroes and villains in real life as well.

As Clyde Barrow might say, "Ain't life grand."

15

Golden Boys

The collaboration between Arthur Penn and William Gibson is one of the most fruitful in American theater. While its public milestones are *Two for the Seesaw, The Miracle Worker, Golden Boy, Golda,* and *Monday After the Miracle,* the partnership also includes their families and fifty years of shared lives. Like all great friendships, theirs was tested in battle and survived, most significantly with the extraordinary rescue of the 1964 Broadway musical adaptation of *Golden Boy.*

Written in 1937, *Golden Boy* was more than the latest play in the socially relevant canon of Clifford Odets, scribe-in-residence of the left-leaning Group Theatre. It was created to rescue that organization from financial straits, which it did. An additional gift is that, some thirty years later, it also created a financial legacy for Odets's children, Walt and Nora.

In a plot that would later become the stuff of parody, but which was serious, even touching, at the time, *Golden Boy* follows the family turmoil, professional conflicts, and moral dilemma of Joe Bonaparte, a violin prodigy who can escape his lower-class life only by becoming a prizefighter. While the most obvious jeopardy in such a trade-off is to his musician's hands, the collision of art and violence, thuggery and family, and fate and free will provide innumerable textures.

Margaret Brenman Gibson—Odets's biographer as well as William Gibson's wife—notes that Odets wove his own strained relationship with his father, Louis, into the tensions between Joe

Bonaparte and his father, to whom he doesn't even give a first name. Fight promoter Tom Moody sees Joe as his ticket to success and sends his mistress, Lorna Moon, to woo the lad into staying in the ring. The drama comes to a head when Joe accidentally kills an opponent and ends when, brooding over his guilt, he commits suicide by running his car off the road, taking Lorna, the fallen woman, with him.

The idea of turning *Golden Boy* into a musical came from producer-manager-agent Hillard Elkins. Elkins, who had represented lyricist Lee Adams and composer Charles Strouse for the Broadway musical *Bye Bye Birdie,* caught a show-folk-only "midnight matinee" with Sammy Davis Jr. at the Prince of Wales Theatre in London in the early 1960s. Elkins says he had a "vision" during Davis's show in which Odets would update *Golden Boy* into the civil rights era, Adams and Strouse would write a "serious" score, Davis would headline, and Broadway would gobble it up. Sammy agreed, and Elkins began working with Odets, who was in declining health (he died on August 14, 1963) as well as declining ability.

Odets's update was rooted in 1930s sensibilities, something its young British director, Peter Coe (no relation to Fred), was incapable of noticing, and Odets, for obvious reasons, did not correct. The show was in trouble from the start.

"We were on the road with *Golden Boy* for twenty-two weeks, longer than most plays run on Broadway, because we were afraid to come in," wrote Sammy Davis Jr. in his autobiography. "We opened in Philadelphia and got rapped badly. We had four weeks there to fix the show before our next out-of-town tryout in Boston." The reviews for their Boston opening in the fall of 1964 were, in the producer's word, "blistering." Continued Davis, "Elliot Norton, their most astute critic, cut us to shreds. Hilly invited Norton to lunch and picked his brains."[1]

"We knew we had a problem on the road," Elkins agrees. "We knew we had a book that wasn't working. Our director went back to London while the show played, and I took the liberty of inviting Paddy Chayefsky to come up. Paddy saw the show and put his hand on my shoulder and said, 'Close it.' Then William

Gibson—whom I didn't know—came up to me and said, 'Would you like a first act?' I said, 'Yes, please.'"

Only later did Elkins learn that Gibson had been Odets's protégé and that he would do anything for the man and his memory. "People in the show were saying [Odets's] dialogue was 'dated,'" Gibson wrote in his preface to the published *Golden Boy*. "Simply untrue. It remained what it always was, the best dialogue ever written by an American; what they meant was that dialogue written for a white couple in 1937 was unbelievable in the mouths of a Negro youth and a white girl in 1964."[2]

Gibson delivered a rewritten first act and Elkins summoned Coe back from London for a reading. When he heard it, Coe responded, "Well, yeah, that's pretty good, but you could get any hack to stage that." Fumes Elkins, "Bill Gibson is six foot three, an Irishman, and his jaw is going like this. He's just done this for nothing, right? And I said, in this room full of people, 'I think you're absolutely right. I'm going to get another hack. *You're fired*.'" At that, Gibson turned to Elkins and said, "I'm going to ask Arthur if he's free."

Penn was. He and Aram Avakian were editing *Mickey One* in the barn on Penn's Stockbridge grounds. The director drove to Boston, watched the show in preview, cringed as expected, read Gibson's new first act, and agreed on the spot to take the helm. Together the two men began one of the most remarkable rescues in Broadway history.

In technical terms, they rewrote a new show "inside the old one." This meant that the cast would rehearse the new show during the day while performing the old one at night. They had no choice; the name of Sammy Davis Jr. had drawn such a massive advance sale that Elkins was obligated to bring the show to Broadway. The reality was, at this point, there was no show to bring in.

"While in Boston," says Elkins, "we were trying to decide something. In the original, Sam's character was a violinist. Then he became a surgeon. All unbelievable on any level, of course. I remember one meeting in Sammy's dressing room where he had just taken off his makeup and his shirt and trousers, and we were arguing about what he should be in the story. He said, looking in the mirror, 'Tell me, what's my problem?' Of course, it occurred to us to tell him that he was black and the girl was white; that was sort of a bigger problem than his being Italian, as the character was in the original play. Everybody got it, including Sam, as soon as he realized what he'd said. After the laughter subsided, we concentrated on the interracial relationship."

While Gibson went to work reshaping act 2, Penn put act 1 on its feet. The first thing he did was assemble the company and assure everyone that nobody would be fired. Two personnel changes did ensue, however. One was Louis Gossett Jr., who took over the role of Frank, Joe's brother, when the original actor asked to be released to take a movie. The other was choreographer Donald McKayle, whose concept of the boxing milieu irritated Penn from the moment the play began. "The first scene was a bunch of fighters in the gym, shadowboxing," says the director, "and, at the end of it, one of the fighters goes very gay and says, 'Oh, a mouse!' and runs away. Jesus!"

Rather than replace McKayle, however, Penn and Elkins asked Herb Ross to step in. Ross, who would later direct such films as *Funny Lady, The Turning Point,* and *The Goodbye Girl,* was beginning to distinguish himself in dance apart from his more famous wife, ballet dancer Nora Kaye. Ross was impressed by the theatrical sleight of hand that Gibson and Penn were attempting and committed himself wholeheartedly (for "a lot of money," Elkins adds). Ross and Penn restaged the opening, keeping it in the gym with the fighters working out but adding the rhythm of skipping ropes, punching bags, and shifting feet. "It was a gangbuster opening," Penn says. "It just rocked! They put percussion under it, and it drove the show. When we had that in, the show flew off the deck."

It went like that throughout the tryout period on the road. In Detroit, Penn had no choice but to hold the first act rehearsal in front of that night's paying audience. "We knew that it was not going to match the second act," says Penn, recalling that he and Gibson watched the patrons file out of the theater baffled at what they had just watched. "It was a mess. It was an utterly schizophrenic experience for the audience because there would be a heavy-duty scene and then *finale!* The second act was so lightweight. But they had seen Sammy."

The grueling process was worse on the star. "Sammy was very graceful," remembers Gibson, "but there was a strange event that happened. We were working Sammy like crazy and his voice was giving way. A singing star who can't sing was a terrible situation. And yet he would go away on a weekend and play a couple of dates in Vegas, things like that. He was incapable of resting. He would go up to Harlem with his wife, May Britt,³ who was the whitest woman I ever saw, and he would be booed by black comrades. And then he would get threats on the road for kissing a white girl in the show."

"Detroit was in the middle of race riots," Davis reported in his autobiography. "The onstage kiss between Paula Wayne and me outraged some people and Hilly got threats. 'We're gonna cut off that whore's tits. And the nigger's balls.' Paula had to be given a bodyguard. I already had one."⁴ "This was, by the way," notes Elkins, "the first time that a black man had kissed a white woman on Broadway. We had armed guards in the balcony. They shot our windows out at the Majestic Theatre."

A dozen years earlier, Penn had worked with Davis on the *Colgate Comedy Hour* when the then twenty-six year old was with the fabled Will Mastin Trio. Since that time the versatile performer had become an actor, a solo, and a Jew. The two men respected each other, and Davis was keeping to the unforgiving rehearsal/performance schedule. Until he just disappeared three days and three nights before opening on Broadway. "Sammy knew he was going to come back, but we didn't," says Gibson. "Then word came: Sammy was reappearing. He was gonna come at a certain time. I waited in the alley of the theater until the cab arrived, and I walked Sammy in because I thought he was walking into enemy territory. It turned out, as he said, 'If you're not gonna give me two days off or three days off, I'll take it, that's all.'"

Elkins tried tracking down the entertainer using his insider's connections, to no avail. Meanwhile, audiences expecting to see Davis queued for refunds upon learning that his understudy, Lamont Washington, would appear.

Nobody dared chastise Davis. Nobody, that is, except Margaret Gibson, who had, by virtue of her credentials, become the company's de facto shrink. "Margaret Gibson, who's a psychoanalyst, had gotten very close to him and felt that they were very tight," recalls Peggy Penn, who earned her own PhD in 2008. "But she wrote him a letter telling him, 'You are a Judas goat.' That's what she felt." "It was a ridiculous letter," Arthur Penn adds. "It did no good. I was pissed at her and I remained pissed at her for the rest of her life."

As director, Penn had to ride herd over the changes and the disoriented but grateful talents implementing them. Recalls Elkins, "If it was a general note that was not going to create a problem, he'd sit there with the cast and talk to all of them and say to Sam, 'In the third act, in that scene where you come in from the left, move to the right; you're blocking something.' If it was an inherently personal situation that involved the actor's relationship to the material, and discussing it in front of the company would not solve the problem, but would, perhaps, exacerbate it, he would put his hand around your shoulder and walk outside or downstage or upstage with the actor and give him the clue to uncovering that scene."

When *Golden Boy* opened at New York's Majestic Theatre on October 20, 1964, after twenty-five previews, it ran 568 performances on a $750,000 investment. It earned four 1965 Tony nominations: Best Musical, Best Actor in a Musical (Sammy Davis Jr.), Best Producer of a Musical (Hillard Elkins), and, ironically, Best Choreography (Donald McKayle). Although a hoped-for London production never came to fruition—Sammy desperately wanted to play the London Palladium—it was a personal triumph for Sammy and entered Broadway legend as a play that should have collapsed but was saved by the concerted efforts of all involved. And it achieved its other goal of throwing off royalties to the Odets children.

Five years later Gibson was again at work. He had been asked by Philip Langner[5] of the Theatre Guild to construct a play about Israeli prime minister Golda Meir. When quizzed, as he inevitably and tiresomely was, why a strapping Irish Catholic felt qualified to write about the diminutive Jewish dynamo, Gibson would repeat, "It was written by a Christian who carries in his consciousness two thousand years of history in which the crucified figure is that of the Jews."

Meir's and Israel's stories are inseparable. Born Golda Mabovich in Kiev in 1898, in 1906 she followed her father, Moshe, to Milwaukee, Wisconsin, where he had gone ahead of the family in 1903. After schooling in the United States she met and, in 1917, married Morris Myerson, a sign painter. In 1921 the couple emigrated to what was then Palestine. Returning to the States in 1934 without Morris but with their two children, she became involved with political groups pushing for the formation of a Jewish homeland and trying to get world powers, including the Roosevelt administration, to rescue international Jewry during the Holocaust, to no avail. Following the war and the May 12, 1948, birth of the state of Israel, she rose through a succession of posts—truncating her name from Myerson to Meir—until she was elected prime minister in 1969. She served until 1974 and died, at the age of eighty, in 1978. Morris had predeceased her in 1951. Gibson began writing his play in 1976.

Months of interviews with Meir's family, friends, admirers, and enemies (there were lots of each), plus several trips to Israel, left Gibson pretty much where he started—adrift—albeit with research. He knew from the start that the focus of *Golda* would be Mrs. Meir's leadership and triumph in the 1967 Six Days' War between Israel and Egypt, Jordan, and Syria. But when he started to write, he realized that his challenge was not content but form. "I made a fatal error in the beginning by thinking, 'This is a big, historical theme and we should have a big production with visuals and movies in the background, and all that,'" he admits, "and I wrote this into the play."

After Gibson read his work to Golda (he never called her anything else), she told him, "The only thing you have to take out is Remiz." Gibson had discovered that David Remiz, an Israeli labor leader, was Mrs. Meir's lover.[6] "I figured it out," the playwright insists. "Nobody had told me. I told her I figured it out from who was where, when, and how she solved a problem by going back to the kibbutz and then going back to Jerusalem, and leaving Jerusalem and working for the party, and that meant a breach with her husband, and that was the end of the marriage. I started to explain this to her, and she said, 'I didn't ask you how you found out; you just have to take it out.' I said, 'Why?' She said, 'I don't want my grandchildren to know.'

"What I wanted to get at was what goes on in these people who run governments? I said to Golda, 'What does it feel like when you tell soldiers to go into such a raid?' She said, 'It's the worst thing I've ever had to do, but I always ask the generals, "How many fatalities, how many soldiers might we lose on this?" because I always try to get an estimate. But then I figure, if I can't do it, get out, and get somebody who can.' In *Golda*, the moment is captured dramatically as Golda says, "In heaven I'll—maybe—forgive them for killing our boys. One thing I'll never forgive is making us kill theirs."

What was not captured in the play—because Gibson didn't know about it until later—was Dimona. Dimona, in the Negev Desert, is the place where everybody in the world except Israel says Israel developed its nuclear weapons.

Gibson asked Penn to bring this kinetic, multimedia vision to life. Santo Loquasto designed a complex set that incorporated rear projection, light cues, images, and sounds, and then took it on the tryout road. "And God thought it was terrible," Gibson jokes, "because He burned the set down in Boston." The electronic and mechanical set caught fire at the Wilbur Theatre, and the show was moved across Tremont Street to the Shubert Theatre, where it played on a bare stage while the set was rebuilt in New York. It was then that producer Philip Langner drew Penn's attention to his observation that the audience paid more attention to the play when they weren't distracted by the pyrotechnics. No one listened—or noticed—and *Golda* opened at New York's Morosco Theatre on November 2, 1977. It was there that Golda herself attended a performance and, in Gibson's words, "was horrified," not only with the produced play but with the performance of its star, Anne Bancroft.

"Annie had gone over there and spent a couple of weeks

with my wife traveling around with Golda before the show was done," Gibson reports. "The idea was that Annie would soak up some of Golda's stuff and be able to use it. Annie and Golda fell in love with each other; these politicians love actors, and vice versa, I suppose. But when she came to see the show, I went backstage, and there were Annie and Golda in Annie's dressing room, nobody else around, and they were sitting in silence. The only dialogue I remember between them was that Annie was taking off her nose and Golda said something to the effect of, 'I wish I could.'

"Then there was a meeting the next day in Golda's hotel room where she said, basically, 'If I had seemed to the public the way you [Annie] do, I never could have been elected prime minister.' What Golda objected to was what she felt was a caricature performance by Annie. What I objected to was that the whole production had no reality to me." The grumbling took its toll on Bancroft, who started missing performances. Rather than accommodate her, Langner closed the whole production after ninety-three performances.[7]

"I hated the whole experience," Penn fumes. "I was dealing with ignorance. What we should have done was close it before it was born. Bill Gibson had given Golda Meir the right of censorship, and she, on seeing it, very deftly removed all the drama, saying, 'Israelis don't behave like that.'"

It might be unfair to call *Monday After the Miracle* a sequel, but William Gibson knew that *The Miracle Worker* was only the first half of the extraordinary story of Anne Sullivan. His problem was that, for a generation, everybody had been referring to his 1959 drama as "the play about Helen Keller." *Monday* picks up ten years after the action in *The Miracle Worker*. Helen is in her twenties and is studying for a degree at Radcliffe while Anne, now thirty-seven, is still her teacher. Tension grows between them, however, when twenty-five-year-old John Albert Macy applies for the job of editing Helen's autobiography, and an unusual love triangle develops—one involving not sex but devotion. Anne wants John, but first demands that he win

Helen's approval. Helen feels threatened by her teacher's romance because she fears that if it flourishes, she will be sent back to her parents' home in Tuscumbia. The solution is not a resolution; the three wind up living together as man, wife, and burden. Anne wants a child by John, but John finds himself drawn to Helen. In the end, there is no room for John in Annie-Helen world, and he leaves (interestingly, his second wife was a deaf-mute).

The piece is fraught with challenges. Unlike *The Miracle Worker,* there was no emotional catharsis that brought audiences to tears. Instead, Helen has become a young woman very much aware of her growing stature in the public eye, and Annie has become increasingly resentful that the student, not the teacher, is being venerated.

The project began after business manager Raymond Katz had packaged a television remake of *The Miracle Worker* starring Patty Duke in the Anne Bancroft role and Melissa Gilbert in Duke's breakthrough role. After an abortive production at the Actors Studio with Ellen Burstyn and John Heard, Katz, Penn, and Gibson recast it with Jane Alexander and Karen Allen. They workshopped it at Spoleto in Charleston, South Carolina, and again at the Kennedy Center, and then came into New York. Poor reviews followed by soft ticket sales led Katz to close the show. Penn was not happy. "Ray Katz never produced a play in his life," says the director. "He was a business manager. We opened in New York and got a bad review from Frank Rich, which we really didn't deserve, I promise you, and Ray said, 'We're not gonna lose any money on this, I'll close the thing.' It was like that—" he snaps his fingers "—and it broke our hearts."

"My experience in life is that no dream turns out to be what it seems to promise," Gibson says. "*Monday After the Miracle* is an exemplification of that, I suppose. It was the last time Arthur and I worked together." That was 1982.

Margaret Brenman Gibson died on May 10, 2004. The cancer took her slowly, and Bill nursed her through the ordeal in the sunroom of their Stockbridge cottage as Peggy, Arthur, and a stream of her psychoanalytic colleagues paid visits. As for the grief, he says, "You get on top of it. I've been writing, in this recent period, about Margaret's death. I'm writing and crying my eyes out all at the same time. But if I write about it, then I'm in charge of it, and if I don't write about it and I'm just subject to the passions and the emotions, then they are in charge of me. That's a big difference, and as much as one can be in control of one's life, art, for the artist, is what makes him be in control. Dylan Thomas said something like, 'I was found when I was lost and I was lost when I was found.' I think the reason Dylan Thomas drank himself to death is that he had lost his genius, he had lost his muse. That muse keeps you above the disasters which otherwise would sink you. So, yes, writing about it certainly helps."

The partnership with Arthur Penn—as neighbors, as friends, and as part of show business lore—ended on November 25, 2008, when Gibson died.

"I never felt that I was very remote from anything Arthur felt or said," Gibson had held. "He and I were close and we knew we were close, and that was how we worked together in the theater. He'd say, 'You know that moment when Jerry says—' and I'd say, 'Yeah, but—' and we'd have these unfinished sentences, but the thoughts would be completely communicated. I never worked with a director like that otherwise. It was always a pleasure to me when Arthur and I worked together. Arthur has been half of my professional life!"

16

Curtains

With one Broadway hit after another in the 1960s, Arthur Penn was at the top of every producer's list. "I was offered everything," he reports. "I can't say it quite *that* broadly, but there were a *lot* of plays." He was also available as a doctor. "I had certain friends and I could get called up if they had a show out of town, or they had a show in trouble: 'Would you come up and talk to us?' I did that for quite a while without remuneration because I was in the theater community. I also had enough money at that point, what with five hits and *The Chase*."

Over the years there were hits, misses, and false starts. After *Two for the Seesaw* in 1957, he became intrigued with doing a musical about New York mayor Fiorello LaGuardia and offered his research to producers Harold Prince and Robert Griffith. When they expressed interest, he proposed that Arnold Schulman write the book. Unfortunately, Schulman got carried away and began writing lyrics too, not knowing that Prince and Griffith had already engaged Sheldon Harnick and Jerry Bock (*Fiddler on the Roof*). Penn and Schulman withdrew, but *Fiorello!* ran two years and won 1960 Tonys for Best Musical, Best Director (Abbott), Best Actor (Tom Bosley), and the Pulitzer Prize for Drama. "It was a big hit," Penn smiles, "and I still have a little percentage of it."

Of those plays that he did direct, some were hits and some were not, but, like surgeons, Broadway tends to quietly bury its mistakes. *In the Counting House* lasted two previews and four performances at the Biltmore Theatre after trying out in Boston, where it received an impatient, if supportive, send-off to New York. The story of a middle-aged businessman of principles who forsakes them one by one as love and pragmatism intrude, it starred Howard DaSilva, Sydney Chaplin, Kay Medford, and Nancy R. Pollock. Playwright Leslie Weiner worked with Penn to build sturdier connective tissue for what was never more than a series of vivid individual scenes, and the results opened at the Biltmore on December 13, 1962, before they could gel.

Different obstacles awaited *Lorenzo,* Jack Richardson's ambitious 1963 drama set in Renaissance Italy. Starring Alfred Drake, Fritz Weaver, David Opatoshu, Herb Edelman, and Camila Ashland, it followed the adventures of a troupe of actors caught in a regional war. When two of them are killed, the others decide that the show must go on, even though war, specific or generic, makes no sense. "That was a good production, but it was during a newspaper strike," the director laments, "so we came and we went." *Lorenzo,* at the Plymouth Theatre, like *In the Counting House,* also shuttered after four performances.

Then came a hit that audiences are still screaming about. "You wait for that click, or as in the case of *Wait Until Dark,* you just want to play in the theater, you want to play with it! I knew that I wanted to get to a point where the audience came out of their seats and screamed. And there it was!"

Although he also wrote other plays, Frederick Major Paull Knott (1916–2002) is best remembered for two joyously manipulative thrillers: *Dial "M" for Murder* (1952) and *Wait Until Dark* (1965). With *Wait Until Dark,* he again hit the mark. His play tells of three miscreants who taunt a blind woman because they think she knows the whereabouts of a doll containing heroin that her husband has unknowingly smuggled into the country and hidden somewhere in their apartment. A classic one-set play told in nearly continuous time, it gleefully etches a rising line of unbearable tension with characters who go after one another as well as their intended victim. In other words, the writer and the director play the audience like a harp.

"Freddy Knott was a very pristine, small Englishman but he

wrote these two wild plays," Penn describes. After he got the script, he "took it to Fred Coe, and financing was a snap. The script was just too actor-friendly to not want to do it."

Lee Remick (who was nominated for a Tony) starred with Mitch Ryan. But the standout was Robert Duvall as Harry Roat Jr., the creepy chameleon who takes perverse delight in taunting his sightless prey. "That was when Duvall was new to us," enthuses Penn, who had used him in a small role in *The Chase*. "The word around New York was about this guy coming on and, boy, when we went into rehearsal and he started doing stuff! I remember, one rehearsal, Mitch Ryan just stopped in the middle of a line and said to him, 'You are a fucking genius!' He just couldn't believe what Bobby was doing."

The climax of the play has Remick alone in her blacked-out Greenwich Village apartment thinking that the evil Roat has been killed. What she doesn't know—but the audience does—is that the door to her refrigerator has been opened, allowing just enough light to spill into the living room and make her visible. At precisely the right moment, Roat springs out of the darkness, attacking Remick and, more commercially, sending everyone in the audience ten feet into the air. The real challenge in saying "Boo!" to eight hundred people, says Penn, was not just a matter of scaring them, but of mollifying the fire marshal.

"It was a question of getting a good set, which George Jenkins did, building it so that the refrigerator light would be what it was, and we took it out of town. There was a little bit of honing, but nothing of any consequence, and we get to that point where Duvall comes blowing back onto the stage and they yelled and screamed! But the only trouble was, in Boston we couldn't get the theater dark; they turned out all the lights except the exit lights, which, by law, they had to keep on.

"So we get to New York and we start working on who we know, and we got the exit lights turned off. But we had to pay a fireman to be in the house with his hand on the switch at every performance because, when it went dark, it *really* went dark.

"You forget, when you're in the theater, how much ambient light there is. We went flat-out black. The audience wasn't even conscious of it, but they knew they were in the black and *bang!* On came the refrigerator light. When the light goes on, the audience realizes that she has been duped, as they have been, and then out of the shadows lunges Bobby, and you would literally see them jump out of their chairs."

Wait Until Dark enjoyed a remarkable run, overstaying the availabilities of three successive theaters between February 2 and December 31, 1966, until it accrued 374 performances. When it was sold to Warner Bros. that year, Audrey Hepburn was cast in the Lee Remick role and asked Penn to direct her. He had to decline because he was busy doing another picture for the same studio and couldn't work it into his schedule. The film, of course, was *Bonnie and Clyde.*

"But I'll tell you what I'll do," Penn told studio manager Walter MacEwan. "I'll write up a series of cautionary notes about *Wait Until Dark* based on our experience on the road before New York." He handed his notes to MacEwan, who said, "You don't expect to be paid for this, do you?" "Of course not," said Penn, insulted, reminding MacEwan that they were both making Warner Bros. pictures and that he was a team player. Penn now smiles, "He just thought that was bizarre." The resulting film of Knott's play was directed by Terence Young.

During one of his later sojourns from film—between *Dead of Winter* and *Penn & Teller Get Killed*—Penn was given a play, *Hunting Cockroaches,* by Janusz Glowacki. It was a comedy about a Polish couple, played by Dianne Wiest and Ron Silver, who battled bugs along with an overload of their own memories and nightmares in an infested Manhattan apartment. "They're caught between their cultures," Penn told *CineAction!* magazine, "a nostalgia for the culture they left behind, but not a nostalgia for the horrors of that culture."[1] Glowacki wrung dry humor and symbolism from his work, translated by Jadwiga Kosicka.

"Janusz Glowacki was a well-known Polish playwright and writer who had had a very tricky escape from Poland before the big [1980] strike," Penn reports. "He had been invited to England and then the curtain fell. His wife and daughter were in Poland; he was in England, but she worked for the *New York*

Times and they got them here. Janusz barely speaks English, but he wrote a play about two immigrants living in a cold-water brick building on the Lower East Side."

The play received enthusiastic notices when it premiered March 3, 1987, at the Manhattan Theatre Club. "We had just one bed—that was the set—and a bathtub," says Penn. "But the actors had a passageway built under the stage where they could come up through the bed, in the bed, through the mattress. These were the nightmares out of the past, and KGB guys came through. It was that kind of theater. There was wonderful comedy in it. Plus horror."

The director's ambitions matched the playwright's, and he tried to get the producer to bring it to Broadway, which, he felt, was losing its ability to present serious themes. The move was thwarted, not by finances but by a fellow filmmaker: Woody Allen needed Wiest for retakes on his film *September* (1987) and she was obligated to withdraw from *Hunting Cockroaches*. Undiscouraged, Penn staged a revival with Swoozie Kurtz and Malcolm McDowell at Los Angeles's Mark Taper Forum later that year where it won *Drama-Logue* awards for outstanding play and Kurtz's performance.

And then there was *One of the Guys*, produced by Joseph Papp at the Public Theatre. "Oh, Christ!" Penn groans. "One of the worst experiences I've ever had." It was written by Marilyn Suzanne Miller, who had a solid background in TV sitcoms and the heyday of *Saturday Night Live*. She and Penn never hit it off. *One of the Guys* opened January 30, 1990, and closed after twenty-four painful performances. Miller's official biography does not cite the Penn production; she credits only Sydney Pollack with directing a workshop version with Bill Murray at Papp's New York Shakespeare Festival in an unspecified year.

Penn returned to Broadway in 2002 to direct *Fortune's Fool*, Mike Poulton's adaptation of Ivan Sergeyevich Turgenev's 1848 play whose Russian title is more appropriate: *The Parasite*.[2] An early work by the eventual author of the novel *Fathers and Sons*, it offers a pointed take on class differences and the foibles of nobility. First presented at the Rich Forum at the Stamford Center for the Arts, *Fortune's Fool* is a deft drama of manners that become coarse when an impoverished aristocrat is disgraced, then enraged, by a jealous antagonist. It is a play of incident built in moments, not outbursts.

Fortune's Fool took shape in England when Alan Bates got a production together at the Chichester Festival in 1996. He drew praise, but the production didn't, so, after he made a success Off-Broadway in 2001 in Christopher Hampton's translation of Yasmina Reza's *The Unexpected Man,* he persuaded producer Julian Schlossberg to mount *Fortune's Fool* on Broadway. Schlossberg had been trying to entice Penn for years with projects, and he was surprised when Penn accepted with the caveat "If you're crazy enough to do it, I'll do it too." Once Penn agreed, the director began working with adapter Mike Poulton to shorten and shape the work.

"I'm sort of jealous of this play," Bates told the *New York Times* just before its April 2, 2002, opening. "It was written 150 years ago and nobody's seen it. And I sort of want to keep it to myself until we're absolutely ready."[3] As the show was coming together in New York, the sixty-seven-year-old Bates's health became a factor. An insulin-dependent diabetic who would die of pancreatic cancer a year and a half later,[4] he was becoming weaker, yet insisted on forging ahead. He was locked in as the faded aristocrat, Kuzovkin, and Frank Langella was first choice for his lubricious bête noire, Tropatchov. Smiles Penn, "I was on the phone calling Frank Langella and saying, 'Come on, Frank, this is a wonderful role for you,' and he would call me back the next day and say, 'I *must* do that part! I *must* do it!' and I'd say, 'Yes, you must.' [Pause] 'Lemme think it over . . . ' Alan also wanted his son, Ben Bates, to be in it." Bates *fils* would play the fiancé, Pavel.

Schlossberg, whom Penn invited to rehearsals, became enamored with the director's ability to "make the actors comfortable, let them really get to know their intention, and actually throw away the script. He's not big on the script at the beginning. He wants them to understand who they are and what they are. Later, the words will eventually mean something, but not initially. The intention is what matters."

Schlossberg cites Bates's drunk scene as an example of the process at work. In the London production, Bates played drunk. For the American production, Penn held the actor back. "Immediately," Schlossberg reports, "Alan wanted to do what actors can do well: get drunk. Arthur said, 'No, no, not now. Don't do that now.' And that went on for a while. Finally, after about two and a half weeks, because Alan was really chomping at the bit to do it, Arthur said, 'Go ahead and do it. You can now play drunk.' But he didn't *have* to then. He had become drunk with *power.* He was still inebriated, but he wasn't going to do what he had done in the English production."

Penn was aware that Turgenev, though of noble birth, resented the way serfs were treated in czarist Russia, and in *Fortune's Fool* the playwright used them to upstage their masters by their presence alone. A scene in which Bates's character is supposed to be humiliated but, instead, defuses the barbs is illustrative. "It was like a string quartet," the director marvels. "It played on the stage with that kind of deftness between Frank Langella and Alan Bates. It was supposed to be a scene where they made a mockery of Alan Bates. They made it, and then it happened again. When it came to the second time, I said to Alan, 'Let's shift the dynamic here, so slightly.' He was supposed to get up and make a long speech about his family and his ancestors. And they were making a mockery of it—teasing him and so forth. The slight tipsiness allowed him to turn the story into something amusing, throwing the attention upon him and taking away from them the ability to tease him.

"One day, while we were rehearsing, he dropped a napkin and, as Alan, started to reach for it. I said 'No!' I just screamed from the back of the theater and he looked at me and *he got it!* He *understood!* The holy grail was being able to get that napkin, and he was doing it for, like, three minutes." Confirms Peggy Penn, "it was incredible. He was the best actor I think I ever saw." Arthur continues, "It was not like Broadway. It was beyond, it was class, it presumed a level of sensibility in the audience that you wouldn't expect from a play. The pity was that he was running out of gas."

Bates's diabetes had become so advanced, and the effort of performing so taxing, that the actor had to give himself insulin injections offstage in order to keep going. *Fortune's Fool* was to be the last time Alan Bates was on a stage.

Before the play had gone into rehearsal, Penn told the *Hartford Courant*, "What I think we've been missing in the theatre for quite a number of years are plays of a certain substance and an intellectual complexity and beauty."[5] The Broadway that, between 1957 and 1960, gave Penn five hits at once has, in the decades since, profoundly changed. From the $80,000 it took to mount a straight play like *Two for the Seesaw* on Broadway in 1957, it rose to between five and ten times that fifty years later. "The fabulous invalid" may be thriving physically, but its mind is on the ropes.

Julian Schlossberg, who produced *Fortune's Fool,* sadly concurs. "The reasons I did it were threefold," he says. "Arthur, because if there ever was a person who could do this property, it would be he; secondly, Alan, of course; but the real reason was that I fell in love with what I used to love: it was a play that I would have seen when I was a kid, and I hadn't seen those kind of plays on Broadway in years."

17

Hippie Sunset

History may not exactly be bunk, as Henry Ford famously proclaimed,[1] but it is generally written, as Alex Haley noted, by the winners. Motion pictures have an unusual ability to contort history because they exist in time-present even when they are set in the past. The screen looks real, even when it lies, and filmmakers exploit this phenomenon by the cinematic equivalent of having their cake and eating it too.

Alice's Restaurant (1969) is an extrapolation of an actual incident that occurred in 1965 when then eighteen-year-old Arlo Guthrie and his friend Richard Robbins helped Alice and Ray Brock clean out the garbage from the deconsecrated church where they lived in Great Barrington, Massachusetts. It was Thanksgiving, and when Guthrie and Robbins saw that the town dump was closed for the holiday, they chucked the trash on a roadside in adjacent Stockbridge where somebody else had already done the same, figuring, "one big pile is better than two little piles, and rather than bring that one up, we decided to throw ours down."[2] They then returned to the Brocks' church for "a Thanksgiving dinner that couldn't be beat"[3] and went to sleep, only to get a call from Stockbridge police officer William Obanhein that an envelope bearing Guthrie's name had been found amid the refuse, making him a suspect. When Guthrie and Robbins went to remove the garbage, they were arrested. In the end, they paid a $50 fine and hauled off the junk anyway, and that was supposed to be that. But it wasn't. Because a short while later, when Guthrie took his preinduction draft physical, he was deemed unfit for military service—which in that era meant being sent to Vietnam—because of his prior conviction for (blush) littering. The sheer ludicrousness of it inspired Guthrie to adapt a song he was writing about a restaurant that Alice had opened in Great Barrington into "Alice's Restaurant Massacree," an eighteen-minute narrative ballad he debuted at the August 1967 Newport Folk Festival. At that time, Arlo was known only as "Woody's kid," Woody being Woody Guthrie, the politically conscious troubadour of the Depression and Dust Bowl. Over the course of the weekend, Arlo performed his song three times to increasingly large and appreciative crowds, closing the festival with a group sing-along that included every folkie from Judy Collins to Joan Baez.

"The next day I started getting the phone calls from all the record companies and the execs and stuff," Guthrie recalled, "and we recorded "Alice's Restaurant" in a studio in New York City with a live audience. One take. Spent $6,400 to make that record. It became fairly popular."[4]

Ranging from a gentle satire of small-town America to powerful criticism of a national policy that held a littering conviction to be worse than bombing civilians in an immoral war, "Alice's Restaurant" established Guthrie as both an entertainer and a partisan who voiced the soul of his hippie generation just as his father had spoken for the disenfranchised thirty years earlier.

The "Alice" of restaurant fame is Alice Brock, who met her husband, Ray, an architect and builder, when they worked at the Stockbridge School. In 1964 the Brocks took over the Trinity Church on Van Deusenville Road in Great Barrington and made it their home. Alice's actual restaurant—one of several that she ran over the years, all of them successful—was at 40 Main Street in nearby Stockbridge and truly is, as the song says, "around the back, 'bout a half a mile from the railroad track."[5] She and Ray divorced a year later.[6] The restaurant is now called Theresa's Stockbridge Cafe.

When he listened to the album in his Stockbridge home, Penn, who was already familiar with the local story, became aware that he was witnessing the end of an era before the era itself was over. Excitedly, he called Hillard Elkins, with whom he had just worked on *Golden Boy,* and played it for him, enthusing to the energetic producer, "I'm going to make this movie."

"And I said," recalls Elkins, continuing the story, 'You're right; that'll make a great picture.' He said, 'Would you produce it?' I said, 'Arthur, I'd love to produce it; I think it's terrific. I think the talent's great. I think your involvement's great. The only problem, as your friend, is that I've never produced a film. I've produced a lot of stage shows.' And Arthur gave me perhaps the best advice I've ever gotten in my career: he said, 'Same shit.'"

Penn tells the story a little differently: "I made the mistake of mentioning that I was gonna do a film of *Alice's Restaurant.* Hilly Elkins heard me say that, and he acquired the rights to it—not fully, but partially, in some way, from Arlo's manager—so I *had* to involve him." But then Penn adds with a grin, "He was a good producer. We made out very well on *Alice's.* Both of us."

Elkins and Penn immediately approached Warner Bros., for which Penn had just directed *Bonnie and Clyde,* and whose record division owned the Guthrie album. Astonishingly, the studio—then headed by brothers Eliot and Kenneth Hyman—passed on making the movie.

"That's when I called David Picker at United Artists," reports Penn, still fuming from his studio's ingratitude, "and said, 'David, guess what. Warner's passed.' And David said, 'Go ahead, make it.' Just like that."

Penn immediately moved forward on two fronts. First he asked Off-Broadway playwright Venable Herndon[7] to cowrite the script (the only time he has ever taken writing credit), explaining, "I needed somebody who was able to go out and stick with these kids while I had the job of trying to assemble this town." The latter would prove to be only a momentary obstacle: "They knew the song, and they were okay with the song, but they didn't understand that we were gonna drop a million bucks. When they *did* understand that, they came around."[8]

Expanding an 18-minute song into an 111-minute film was

not a simple matter, as Herndon and Penn quickly discovered. At first they considered making it a kind of *Rashomon* in which conflicting points of view would drive the story forward. The problem was that, since Guthrie and Robbins had pleaded guilty, there was no real dispute over what had happened. Instead, the film front-loads the story so that the events of the album don't start until about an hour in, just before the Thanksgiving feast. The rest is constructed from moments in Guthrie's past, symbols of the times he lived in, and thin air.

It's important to remember that, when *Alice's Restaurant* was shot in 1968, it wasn't nostalgia; the events it portrays were barely three years old. Yet the world that had seemed so optimistic in 1965 had, by then, turned dark. It was the year that Martin Luther King Jr. and Robert Kennedy were assassinated; that Chicago police beat demonstrators at the Democratic National Convention; that North Vietnam launched the Tet Offensive; that American troops committed atrocities at My Lai; and that the Kerner Commission reported that America was becoming two societies, one black and one white. Suddenly a snapshot about hippies seemed naive.

Penn felt otherwise. "This was that period in America when the conservative Right was rattling its chains," he explains. "They had succeeded in assassinating the cream of the Left, and interestingly enough, the Left, as a political movement, didn't respond. Young people *individually* responded in *individual* statements about society—from burning draft cards to changing their dress to changing the music—but it was more or less individual until it became contagious. Then it was the youth movement. I had a lot of admiration for that generation and was grateful for what they did. That became *Alice's Restaurant*."[9]

Penn had matured in an era when politics were much clearer: "Labor was good, capital was bad. No one ever fancied that labor could turn out to be exploitive, exclusionary, racist." He was raised on the activist songs of Arlo's father and observed, "Where Woody sought to militate, Arlo attacked through ridicule."

The film bent events to fit its enlarged purpose, letting Penn assert, "I felt no great obligation to accuracy. Arlo would say, 'That's not the way it happened' and it was, indeed, not the way it happened. I had to heighten everything. Looking for evidence at the dump, I had helicopters and many more police. I wanted to kick it up to a wonderful fable of a fabulous time that, it was clear at that point, was going away." And Arlo's verdict? "His verdict," says Penn, "was the same all the way through, which was, 'Hey, it's your film, it's not mine. I made the record. I'll do what you want.'"

"You gotta realize that this is older people's versions of what we were doing," Guthrie later countered. "There's my story that has to do with garbage and draft and stuff, and everything else is other people's versions of what we were doing and how we were living and stuff, and so this is their take on what hippies did."[10]

The age difference is one of the film's strengths, posits editor Dede Allen. "It was a bunch of people in their forties making a picture about a bunch of people in their early twenties," she notes, "and I think that one of the reasons the film worked on the level it did was that it wasn't made by the young people about themselves, it was made by more parental figures."[11]

The movie Ray is, of course, not Ray, but actor James Broderick. Alice is actress Pat Quinn. Even though Penn found the real Ray and Alice to be "very nice, tender, laid-back folks," he needed professionals to meet the complexities of film acting. Almost everyone else, however, was either a neophyte or a nonactor. Especially Arlo. Says Penn, "Arlo, right from the beginning, said, 'You tell me what to do 'cause I don't know what to do.' And I really had to show him every moment. Others in the group, to a lesser or greater degree, were in the same state as Arlo. They were the kids who hung out there. Many of them were beautiful young girls, but they were stoned out of their heads during production."

Producer Hillard Elkins shares Penn's diagnosis, citing that the cast was housed in Stockbridge during the shoot. "I don't recall which motel the cast was staying at," he says, "but if you got within a quarter of a mile of it, you got high."

Directing people who didn't have technique sent Penn back

to his early days. His solution: "Show 'em. Show 'em to do this; do this. But it was fun; I enjoyed it. I got to know Arlo better, and we got to be good friends."

Says Guthrie, "The thing that was funny about Arthur Penn was that he was one of the first people that actually believed that the song about Alice's restaurant was not fiction. Like I say, he lived in the town of Stockbridge where it actually happened and he said, 'You know, these hippies are not making this up. These are real people.' I don't think he understood everything that the culture had to offer, you know. I don't think that the people who were in charge of the production had a sense of what was happening with who we were and what was happening at the time. It was a different world. But I thought it was a valiant attempt to make a movie about it, anyhow. He was nice to work with. He was really wonderful."[12]

And then there was Officer Obie. William J. Obanhein, in his early forties when the events took place, was police chief of the City of Stockbridge. It was he who, per Arlo, compiled the "twenty-seven 8 × 10 color glossy pictures with circles and arrows and a paragraph on the back of each one" with which he damn well intended to get a littering conviction against miscreants Guthrie and Robbins. He was thwarted in court when the judge assigned to the case was replaced by Judge James Hannon (playing himself), who was blind and therefore unable to inspect the evidence.

Obie was, from most accounts, respected and beloved. He had modeled for Stockbridge resident Norman Rockwell (he was the cop sitting beside a runaway boy at a soda fountain in a famous illustration) and agreed to play himself in the film, saying, "If anyone is gonna make a fool out of me, it might as well be me." "He was a good guy," Penn smiles. "He was a sweet guy. He liked these kids. He had a terrible life." In 1985 he was forced into retirement after an altercation with another policeman. He died in 1994.

Arlo is a part of this world and yet not, just as his voice-over narration places him outside the story as well as within it. Though devoted to Alice and Ray, he leaves town to perform in coffeehouses, to visit Woody again (in a scene in which Pete Seeger joins Arlo in a memorable duet), and to sort out his options in a life that may, at any moment, ship him to a rice paddy in Southeast Asia.

"What's involved is a clash of value systems," Penn says. "What we have, in a way, is an almost too-good story. Imagine if you are a part of a certain generation which says, 'I am repudiating the values of the older generation, that immobility that I feel in my parents.' And imagine having this characterized by a man (Woody Guthrie) who's experiencing increasing paralysis as a dramatic event which ends, finally, in death. It's almost too perfect, too well chosen. Point two, it's a hereditary disease and it's possibly going to affect Arlo or his kid brother.[13] Three, that your father was the voice of the Old Left. It begins to resonate like a well-toned bell because it begins to tell all kinds of stories in all directions."[14]

And yet the clash of value systems isn't only between the old and the new. It can be seen as fractures that will split and ultimately destroy the New Left itself within twenty years:

> After singing for his supper at a coffeehouse, Arlo asks for a cheeseburger. So not all hippies were vegetarians.
>
> Arlo turns down sex with an underage groupie out of moral compassion, but rejects sex with the woman who owns a coffeehouse in an act of blatant ageism.
>
> Everyone smokes tobacco more than they do pot.
>
> Women are defined in pre–women's movement roles, mostly as appendages to the men, except for Alice who, by the end, begins to question Ray's domination.
>
> Gas-guzzling cars and a consumer culture abound.
>
> Dropping out, not social engagement, is seen as the way to peace.
>
> Men can be randy, but women are expected to be monogamous.

It would be cynical to say that the sixties contained the seeds of its own destruction, but *Alice's Restaurant* makes it clear that any movement that gloats in its own self-righteousness is doomed. Two incidents in the film trigger this. The first is the suicide of one of the young people, and the second is Ray's drunken proclamation that, despite all they've been through, he wants to sell everything, including Alice's Restaurant, and buy a farm. He does this on the day that he and Alice are set to renew their wedding vows. The dream dies when the dreamers change.

In his preface to the published script, cowriter Herndon writes about Brook Farm in West Roxbury, Massachusetts, where people actually planned the same kind of commune that arose spontaneously in Stockbridge. In the end, both imploded when the spiritual fuel was depleted.

"They're destined not to endure," Penn agrees, "because what happens—what I was meaning to be doing here—is saying you fall in love with this environment, and then Life begins to erode the love, either directly with you, or with the death of somebody like Shelly in the film. There were some people at Black Mountain College who just couldn't handle the freedom and cracked up and had to leave. I knew that was coming with the church that Ray and Alice bought, and I thought, 'I've got to have a visual image.' And that's the last image."

The last image in the film has been cited repeatedly as one of the most unsettling in modern cinema: a long, slow dolly away from the church, past sparse trees, yet zooming in on the door so that, as the distance increases, the framing remains the same. The effect is to make the viewer feel at once free and yet trapped. In the doorway stands Alice, abandoned, wearing a wedding gown for a ceremony that will never take place, her marriage effectively in limbo, thinking, "It's over." She should be angry. Instead, she is almost in shock. "The final image of Alice is imprinted on Arlo's life story," Penn says. "It is meant to suggest that he will wear it for the rest of his life. It's also imprinted on the viewer."

The shot is iconic. The camera pulls away from Alice while she stays the same size in the frame, with the trees and world pressing in upon her. "It is a moving static image," Penn describes, "so it's interacting with Arlo, but also, that moment was, I thought, a defining moment in her life, his life, and Ray's life. The film was over, but it was still in motion, and that was the crucial ingredient: to get motion into it while you had stasis. It's really a kind of a Proustian moment, a moment that will stay with you forever although it can't endure. It's over, but you won't forget it. And that woman is the woman in the bridal gown, and from this she's got to move on. I was really imbuing this with a certain sadness about Black Mountain."

It took three days to get the shot right. "I knew that I was gonna dolly back and zoom in and stay neutral. We cut tree trunks and worked it out mathematically where we would slide them into the camera path, because they couldn't be in the dolly track until we got almost to them, and they had to be eased in just at that moment."

If *Alice's Restaurant* today seems more of a lament than a memorial, it certainly isn't an apology. "I'm not saying these guys were right," Penn maintains, "but the other guys weren't right either. And they weren't wrong."

Adds Guthrie, "The sixties wasn't just a fun time of getting stoned and wearing jeans and stuff. It was a serious time when people went out of their way to really change the course of history. And they succeeded, 'cause we're still here."[15]

18

Little Big Mensch

Despite being able to film *Alice* in their backyard, the Penns were not rolling in money. UA deemed the project too American to expect wide foreign success (they were wrong), so they held Penn and Elkins to a budget that wouldn't make anybody rich unless it scored at the box office (which it did), but the returns wouldn't start until the picture was released on August 20, 1969. As it worked out, that was ten days before Woodstock, which earned Arlo Guthrie superstar attention. Meanwhile, although the Penns owned outright their Manhattan and Stockbridge homes and had been able to set aside college money for Molly and Matthew, they could not call themselves well to do. The huge profits from *Bonnie and Clyde* had not begun to trickle down, and times were tough. So perhaps it was foolhardy to forge ahead on a film that the director had been nurturing for six years and that, even if it were green-lighted, would not make him rich. Still, he loved the project, and it was finally starting to come together. It was *Little Big Man,* and its pro–Native American message was also a long time coming.

"Slowly certain films began to show an ever-so-slight bias in the direction of the Indians—*Soldier Blue* (1970), for one," Penn told interviewer Tony Crawley. There was also a newly minted star to play *Little Big Man*'s Jack Crabb: Dustin Hoffman, whose *The Graduate* (1967) had made him bankable. Plus Penn was coming off *Bonnie and Clyde.*[1]

As the advertising campaign would claim, "Jack Crabb was

either the most neglected hero in history or a liar of insane proportion." Once again history was in the eye of the beholding camera, and this time the person telling it was a 121-year-old "Indian fighter" who claims to be "the sole white survivor of the Battle of the Little Big Horn."

Little Big Man is a revisionist western framed by the flashback device of an anthropologist's interview with a wizened Crabb in an old-age home. During a twenty-year span in the mid-1880s, the old man claims to have been an Indian warrior, a preacher's ward, a swindler, a mule skinner, a gunfighter, a drunkard, a hermit, an Indian scout, and a polygamist. It paints General George Armstrong Custer as a psychotic racist who gleefully implements the American government's policy of Indian genocide as his stepping-stone to the presidency. Although the film's overall tone is cynical and slyly comedic, its credibility was bolstered by being released at a time when the American government had engaged in so many betrayals, from civil rights to Vietnam (Watergate was two years away), that audiences accepted that the Republic had been founded on chicanery.

"The question is," Penn told Michael Lindsay, "whether or not the audience will be able to sort out fact from lie. That's the technique of the film, which is to say, How much of this is fable and how much of this is real? In the final analysis, none of it matters because what we're saying is another version of history than the white version, which is equally fable. In that sense, we're not trying to set the record straight."[2]

Based on Thomas Berger's 1964 novel, *Little Big Man* begins in 1847 and follows young Jack Crabb as he goes between white and Indian worlds, ending up at Custer's Last Stand as a white man seeking revenge on behalf of the Indians (who call themselves "the Human Beings"). As picaresque as the later *Forrest Gump* (1994), only more biting and astute, *Little Big Man* is a gallant lie wrapped around a shameful truth. "It's prejudiced in the sense that I thought there was a good deal of history that ought to be told the other way with at least as much passion as 'the whites are the good guys and the redskins are hostile savages' as we've been told over the years," Penn said, explaining his passion for the project. "I sort of loaded it in the other direction, but I like to hope that I at least informed the audience that I was loading it. I don't mean to have this be representative of what I think of as being historically accurate."[3]

On the other hand, he continues, "It shows the lifestyle of the Indians a little more accurately and certainly in greater detail than it's been shown before in a commercial film, and certainly better than we do the white world. We do the white world in a slightly more caricatured way throughout. [But] we are stacking the cards. He, himself, as a character, tells you that he's stacking the cards right from the very beginning of the picture by the blatant lie that he's the only white survivor and he's 121 years old and lived through all these occasions because he manages to be in all the places in the west where things were happening."[4]

Custer's attack on the Sioux and Cheyenne at Little Big Horn on June 25, 1876, was a reckless military decision that backfired when he was slaughtered with his men. "Apparently," reports Penn, "it was the first time that the Indians ever did mount so complicated a military campaign and were able to stick to it."[5] Repeated encounters with Custer had taught the Indians a thing or two about the white man's battle strategy. Ordinarily used to fighting as individuals, the six thousand braves who amassed at Little Big Horn under Chief Crazy Horse worked as a coordinated force.

The Custer legend dies hard, but the truth is that he epitomized the country's racist, expansionist ethic, which history has gradually emerged to verify. Public (white) reaction to the "Custer Massacre" gave Presidents Grant and Hayes a mandate to pursue a program of annihilation against the tribes they held responsible.

The campaign to produce the film began in the mid-1960s when Penn was trying to write about the Holocaust, then realized that a film about white America's campaign against the Indians addressed many of the same themes. He and playwright Jack Richardson[6] began working on an original script about how the white man brought disease to the Indians. Then, says Penn, "When I read a review of Thomas Berger's *Little Big Man* in the

New York Times, I knew that was the book I would base the film on. I mentioned it to Jill Jakes [his assistant] and she said, 'Tom Berger? I'll call him.'"

After some shopping, Penn found newly formed Cinema Center Films to back the project, and he pressed forward, assuring Gordon Stulberg, who was running the company, "This is going to be my response to concentration camps—to genocide. And he kept saying, 'But it's got to be funny.' I said, 'It *will* be funny. And it also will carry that tone.' He was utterly confused by the conversation. I thought he was gonna scotch the deal, but he said, 'Okay. But make sure it's funny.'"

One reason the project was so hard to set up was its subject. "Budgeting departments at the studios didn't like the fact that it was sympathetic to the Indians," Penn charges, "so they would budget the film out of sight and then, naturally, the studio would decline to make it. That prevailed right up through the very end. The last budget we got from the studio was twelve million dollars. We delivered the picture for nine. It was a prejudice that was very hard to overcome. The Hollywood community is a working community, really pretty conservative. They had their ways of doing things, they had their logic about history, and their natural conclusions were that the Indians were the bad guys."[7]

From the very beginning, Penn and Calder Willingham planned Crabb's voice-overs as a commentary that added texture and counterpart to the visuals. It was decided early on that when Jack was among the whites, Dustin Hoffman would affect a western drawl, but when he was with the Human Beings, he would speak neutral English. In addition, the Human Beings talk in what Penn calls "a truncated language; for instance, they don't say *killed* in this picture, they say *rubbed out,* and we chose kind of modern, slangy expressions to make that the Indian vocabulary. It's clear and less expressionful: 'Your presence gives me pain between my ears' or the exchange 'You're blind, Grandfather?'—'Oh, no, I still see, but the light no longer reaches my heart.' Gorgeous, gorgeous writing. That's all Calder."

Another, more significant, change from the novel is that Jack is less passive. A la *Candide,* he was content, in Berger's more leisurely narrative, to observe events and tell the reader what he thought. Film demands a more active character, and so the screen Jack was made to embrace the Indian cause, angrily asking Old Lodge Skins, after yet another cavalry attack, "Do you hate them? Do you hate the white man now?" until he confronts Custer, at the brink of Little Big Horn, daring him, "General, you go down there. There are thousands of Indians down there, and when they get done with you there won't be nothin' left but a greasy spot. This ain't the Washita River, general. And them ain't helpless women and children waitin' for you. They're Cheyenne brave, and Sioux. You go down there if you got the nerve."[8]

Berger's novel contained so many characters that it was necessary to eliminate or combine many of them. The role played by Faye Dunaway is an example of the latter, as well as a lesson in the politics of filmmaking and the insight of a gifted actress. Recalls Penn: "Faye stopped me in the street one day and said, 'I want to be in your picture.' I said, 'You can't; I don't have a part.' She said, 'I want to be in the picture!' I said, 'Faye, come on, you're a big star now.' 'I wanna be in the picture!' So I came back up here and met with Calder and [producer] Stuart [Millar], and Calder's eyes lit up and he said, 'I have something way better!'" Willingham merged the character of Mrs. Pendrake, a minister's oversexed wife who adopts Jack early in the film, with Lulu Kane, a prostitute who has a fling with Wild Bill Hickok. The trick impressed Penn and created a part worthy of the star.

The picture was shot in 1970 on an unusually large number of sites throughout Nevada, Montana (on Crow and Cheyenne land), California, and Alberta, Canada. The battle sequences were staged along the Little Big Horn River in Montana where the actual event had taken place. The battle employed between five hundred and six hundred Crow and other Indians and several hundred cavalry over a period of eight days, plus additional days for close-ups and inserts.

There were, regrettably, production casualties. Trip wires were used to make horses take falls, endangering the animals and enraging the ASPCA. There were human injuries, too; although the prop departments provided Indians with rubber-tipped arrows, sighs Penn, "the young Crow braves would get so jazzed up that they'd take the tips off the arrows. And that's what happened: in one instance an arrow hit a stuntman in the tear duct and he lost that eye. We had to go around and be very careful, take after take after take, that they wouldn't touch those tips. There's a scene around Little Big Horn where these Indian riders come over the hill. We sent out word that I wanted 300, expecting to get 150, which is the ratio. But I said, 'You gotta ride bareback.' So the 150 show up and said, 'Yeah, of course we can ride bareback.' And of course they couldn't, and they came tumbling over the rise falling off their horses, the horses tumbling down. It was a charade."

As one of Hollywood's few pro-Indian films, *Little Big Man* attracted cooperation from the Indian community. In return, Penn ordered the caterer to bring extra food to supplement the inferior supplies issued in government the welfare packages they received. "That was the food they took home to their families," Penn says sadly.

Dede Allen was cutting the footage on location as it came in and remembered that "it put a gigantic strain on my relationship with Arthur," particularly when it moved into postproduction in Penn's despised Los Angeles. Cinema Center Films was having financial woes ("going down the tubes" is how some described it); the company had sunk a lot of money in the picture and demanded that it be ready for the lucrative Christmas playing season. But the audio mix was proving more complex than Penn had imagined, and his favorite mixer, Dick Vorisek, was three thousand miles away, based in New York. "I don't know that the result was what either of us had wanted," says Allen.[9]

Surmounting the pressures, *Little Big Man* emerges as an eclectic film reflecting Penn's sensibilities. Penn uses silence as powerfully as he does sound, and the sparse use of roots music, rather than a traditional orchestral score, adds another layer of consciousness.

Connecting these disparate elements is, of course, Dustin Hoffman, who imposes both a tone and a point of view on the proceedings. A vital part of his character was the makeup that aged him not only from the actor's then 33 years to 121, but also "youthened" him to approximately 25, the age at which Hoffman took over from young Alan Howard (with Hoffman's voice dubbed in). To accomplish the latter they used adhesive lifts to tighten Hoffman's skin. It's the old-age makeup, however, that garnered attention and applause, and it was both invented and crafted by Dick Smith. "That was beyond what Hollywood was capable of doing," praises Penn, who worked with Smith at NBC. "He changed the world of makeup." "A makeup artist can tell the actor how to get the best effects from the physical makeup," Smith explains, averring, "The only good makeup is the makeup that you don't see as makeup."

Because he was in charge of all the film's makeup, Smith was present on the set throughout the shoot. He witnessed the camaraderie between Hoffman and Chief Dan George, which, he says, was something the two men worked on together. "In the very beginning of the film," Smith says, "Chief Dan was an unknown quantity, so to speak. So they do some scenes and nothing very exciting is happening, and Arthur did not give any instruction or any directorial help to Chief Dan until a couple of days later when something happens and there's an intimate scene, and it just works. It came alive. Dustin is all excited; it happened between Dustin and Chief Dan, and it was one of the really bright things in the film, was Chief Dan in that relationship." "Dick didn't know that I was doing that intentionally," Penn offers. "I wanted Dustin and the chief to bond and for the chief to get used to speaking with his 'son,' Dustin."

What happened to Jack Crabb after Little Big Horn? In 1998 Thomas Berger published *The Return of Little Big Man,* which picked up the tale thirty-five years later. Still fueled with hot air, Crabb tells another interviewer how he knew Wyatt Earp, Doc Holliday, and Annie Oakley; toured with Buffalo Bill and the Wild West Show, becoming Cody's assistant; witnessed the murder of Sitting Bull by government agents; spied on the gunfight at the O.K. Corral; and met Libbie Custer, the general's widow, who lived to age ninety-two fighting to preserve the lie of her late husband's heroism.

However Berger may have fabricated Crabb's future, Penn had to face reality when pondering his own. Film companies were trying to assess the change in audience tastes and scrambling to find their corporate and commercial footings since having become conglomerated. At the same time, studio management was adrift over what to fund, and suddenly Penn, despite his track record, was without work. He took a teaching post at Yale and tried to get a film together about the 1971 Attica prison riots in which New York governor Nelson Rockefeller called in SWAT teams to quell unrest. For much the same budget reasoning/racism that stalled *Little Big Man, Attica* didn't work out. "It was just too expensive," Penn reported at the time. "They say it's mostly about black prisoners and 'black films' have never made back eight or ten or twelve million dollars. And the last time I checked, this one was going to cost thirteen million. So it's kinda political, the way pressure is exerted in an industry like film, via economics, which is the fundamental ingredient of it."[10]

Then an offer came in from producer David L. Wolper to be among a handful of directors to make short films about the upcoming Munich Olympics. For Penn, who had just made two features back-to-back in which Truth was a matter of conjecture, the Wolper invitation meant that he would make his first documentary, a genre that extols facts. As it turned out, the facts in *Visions of Eight* would be more shocking and dramatic than any fiction script he would ever encounter.

19

A State of Great Disorder

"No civilization in history ever survived by turning over its reins to the young," insisted writer-director John Milius, one of the young filmmakers to whom Hollywood turned over its reins in the 1970s. Milius was in the forefront of the "film generation" that resuscitated—though some say homogenized—American cinema in the decade after the final collapse of the studio system.

Like every other institution that eventually kowtowed to the youth juggernaut, Hollywood became a land of rebellion, optimism, experiment, and naked fear. Foreign films were arriving and bringing with them a broader worldview to those whose eyes were open. An art house circuit sprung up in major cities giving venue to specialized films that were a thoughtful alternative to the spread of mall multiplexes. Midnight shows, repertory, and revival theaters celebrated the remembrance of pictures past, though not always respectfully or quietly. Filmmaking equipment was getting cheaper; videotape was leaving the TV stations and hitting the streets; and colleges began offering courses in screen studies. Audiences from fans to aesthetes chose sides when the *New Yorker*'s populist critic Pauline Kael took on the *Village Voice*'s auteurist critic Andrew Sarris. The only thing everybody agreed upon was that cinema was *the* art form of the twentieth century.

Everybody seemed to know it except Hollywood. Despite the guerilla success of 1969's *Easy Rider,* which showed that a raw, low-budget film could score as long as it told the truth, the studio ostrich still had its head in the celluloid sand. The triple punch of *Bonnie and Clyde, Alice's Restaurant,* and *Little Big Man* conferred oracle status on Arthur Penn, and after *Little Big Man,* he should have been able to get any funding he wanted. Yet his *Attica* project was deemed too risky for its cost, and he took himself out of consideration for *The Autobiography of Malcolm X* and *The Confessions of Nat Turner* because he didn't feel qualified to direct the black experience. At a time when it seemed like everyone had a camera, Penn hadn't been behind one in a year.

David L. Wolper didn't care about cameras. He didn't need them; he spliced together pieces of other people's movies. First with the compilation documentary *The Race for Space* (1959) and then with *Hollywood: The Golden Years* and the *Biography* series (both 1961), he did what no independent documentary producer had ever done: he cracked the television networks with independent productions. He also bent the rules of nonfiction filmmaking with the philosophy "Documentaries are not reality, they are the creative interpretation of reality."

In 1970 Wolper, who had expanded into fiction films, was shooting *Willie Wonka and the Chocolate Factory* in Bavaria when he was invited to make the official documentary of the Twentieth Olympiad, to be held in Munich in 1972, the first time the Games were to take place in Germany since Hitler hosted them in 1936. Mindful that by the time his film hit the screens, live television coverage would have sapped his audience, he decided to take a bold approach. He commissioned ten international filmmakers to see the event through their eyes and planned to assemble the resulting short subjects into a single anthology feature. "This film wouldn't be reportage," Wolper declared. "Instead, it would capture the feeling of the Olympics. I wanted to make poetry rather than prose."[1]

The film, which Wolper intended to call *Visions of Ten,* was accorded a $1.5 million budget. Each auteurist poet would focus on one aspect of the Games: England's John Schlesinger the marathon; Japan's Kon Ichikawa the hundred-yard dash; Sweden's Mai Zetterling the weightlifters; Germany's Michael Pfleghar the women; Czechoslovakia's Milos Forman the decathlon; France's

Claude Lelouch the losers; Senegal's Ousmane Sembene Senegal's basketball team; the USSR's Juri Ozerov the moments before the race; Italy's Franco Zefferelli the Torch; and Arthur Penn boxer Bobby Lee Hunter.

Almost immediately, a petulant Zefferelli cancelled in solidarity with the African nations' withdrawal over the Olympic Committee's insistence on the presence of racist Rhodesia. Later, Ousmane Sembene left the project for unspecified reasons and never finished his piece. "Which," concludes Wolper, "is how it finally came to be called *Visions of Eight*."

Penn's segment was to be on Bobby Lee Hunter, a young black boxer who had qualified for the Games despite being jailed as a convicted felon. "There was so much 'We want to win' going on that I think they played fast and loose," Penn says of the U.S. Olympic Committee. "He was destined to win his weight division in the world; he was the best fighter. I thought, if I'm gonna do a fighter, it's not the fight that interests me, particularly under Olympic rules. What interested me was how he got here. The idea was that we would do the whole backstory, and then come to the Olympics and have one punch and end it. The other side of the story was a more romantic one, which is that he would win at the Olympics and then get pardoned. I was dubious about that, and I certainly didn't want to hang the movie on it. But he never made it through the eliminations. He lost before he got into the Olympics."

Committed to the project but now scrambling for a new subject, Penn—arriving in Munich with his family three days before the Games began—decided on a large theme told in small details. "I thought that some part of the film should be devoted to man's struggle against gravity, whether it's just the plain high jump or the pole vault. That's when I decided that the only thing I could do that was interesting—because mostly it's just a guy running down the runway holding a pole—was when he was in the air."

His solution was to shoot the event in excruciatingly slow motion with a Swiss laboratory camera.[2] Said Penn, "When you photograph the pole vault in ordinary speed, ordinary time, 24 frames per second, you discover that you see practically nothing.

Even watching it with the naked eye, it's very difficult to see. The indication, then, is to go to slow motion. Another thing I noticed in the tests was that there was some terrific kind of excitement when we couldn't discern the complete figure, couldn't read it. I thought to take it out of any accurate representation and just simply put it at the level of sheer and simple motion."[3]

The pole vault event lasted seven hours and yielded sixty-five thousand feet of film from six angles at varying speeds. It had to be edited down to ten minutes. Penn's piece—shot by Walter Lassally, edited by Dede Allen, and scored by Henry Mancini—was called *The Highest*. It met Wolper's demand for poetry and, once again, used the syntax of cinema to call attention to reality at the same time it exploded it.

Then came September 5, 1972. Most of the directors had already wrapped production on their segments and had headed to their various home countries, although Schlesinger, Sembene, and Penn were still rolling film. Matthew and Molly Penn were packed to go home, and Peggy was preparing to enjoy a little private time with Arthur as soon as he finished. Then everything changed. "Peggy and I took Molly and Matt to the airport to fly home with our nanny," Penn recalls. "We stayed hours and we stayed and we stayed and the flight didn't go. We knew nothing about what was happening in town. Finally, without telling us anything, the flight took off. They'd obviously been searching it. We headed back to town. It was like a sea change. Before then, they'd all been in the Munich costumes. Now they were in uniforms and command cars and halftracks and the place was an armed camp. When we got back to the hotel, our freedom was seriously curtailed. We couldn't get to the windows to see into the Olympic Village. We could hear the helicopters coming in, and rumors would say, 'That's Moshe Dayan' and this guy and that guy. Apparently it was Israeli generals who were coming to take over the operation from Germans, who were not experienced, as they later so well proved."

Eight Palestinian terrorists had broken into the Olympic Village, killed two members of the Israeli team, and had taken nine more hostage. The world waited while Black September—the group that had staged the attack—appeared in masks on the balcony of the Olympic Village. In a failed rescue attempt on September 6, all nine remaining Israeli hostages were killed along with one policeman and five of the terrorists. "Peggy and I got so sick at heart—there was no resolution at that point—and I said, 'Let's get the hell out of here.' We got a car and drove to Italy and we were watching television in Italy and we saw the end of the whole thing down there. It was terrible."

There would be subsequent criticism of whether the German police were capable of—or even interested in—saving the Israelis. When *Visions of Eight* was released on August 10, 1973, it was dedicated "to the Eleven Slain Israeli Athletes, Tragic Victims of the Violence of Our Times."

Violence was not exclusive to Munich. The early 1970s seethed with upheavals across every threshold of world society. Dictators and chaos in the Middle East, Salvador, Haiti, Uganda, South Africa, and Northern Ireland were matched in duplicity by the Nixon administration's continuing Vietnam atrocities, domestic spying, and Watergate. A then independent press showed a stunned America that its own elected government was not to be trusted.

America was adrift in a "Me Decade" that also saw the rise of the women's movement, gay liberation, and assorted religions, both fundamentalist and new age. And, of course, there were drugs. "We all went into a kind of induced stupor," Penn told writer Tag Gallagher. "I really think we're bankrupt, and that the Watergate experience was just the *coup de grace*. We've been drifting into this state for the last twenty years."[4] The 1968 assassinations of Martin Luther King Jr. and Robert Kennedy were still weighing on Penn. He fell into "a deep pessimism after *Little Big Man*. I couldn't find the right film, the string I wanted to be attached to."[5]

Producer Robert Sherman shared those feelings. Sherman had been working with Scots novelist Alan Sharp, whose muscular scripts for *The Hired Hand* (1971) and *Ulzana's Raid* (1972) had become two distinctive westerns. Sharp was writing a detective story called *An End of Wishing* and was, like its main character, torn between breaking the rules and following them.

"He needed some living money," Sherman says, "and I arranged to cover his rent. He said, 'Should I make this a typical detective story about a guy trying to solve a crime or should I make this what I really would like it to be, which is about a guy trying to solve himself?' I thought that was a more interesting way to go about it, and that was my answer to his question." Sherman acquired the script and sent it to John Calley, head of Warner Bros., who agreed to make it for $4 million. Calley wisely gave it to Penn.

"I had a particular passion for *Night Moves*," Penn says. "I was very depressed by the assassinations and felt that we needed to give voice to our grief. It was a beat-up culture."

Sharp soon changed the name of his script to *The Dark Tower*, and then, during production, Penn hit upon *Night Moves*.[6] The story: Harry Moseby (Gene Hackman) is a low-end private detective who is so emotionally disconnected from life that he realizes his marriage is in trouble only when he sees his wife (Susan Clark) with another man (Harris Yulin). He takes on a routine job of returning a runaway nymphet, Delly (Melanie Griffith), to her mother. Harry brings Delly home but she is later killed, and Harry feels compelled to pursue the case, which leads him to a movie stuntman (Edward Binns), Delly's garrulous stepfather (John Crawford), and a wise and sexy Paula (Jennifer Warren) who is nobody's fool. The mystery—but not the explanation of it—ends in the waters off the Florida Keys. The last moments find Harry alone in a damaged motorboat circling in the open sea.

As symbols go, the image of a powerless man adrift after solving a crime without understanding it was seductive to critics and audiences alike when *Night Moves* was released on June 11, 1975. The film's tagline, "Maybe he would find the girl . . . Maybe he would find himself," added fuel to Penn and Sharp's existential fire. The title is a pun that suggests the story's noir trappings but is, even more obscurely, a reference to a classic chess match in which a player lost because he missed a crucial clue. Sharp addressed this when he novelized his script and wrote of Moseby, "He lay watching, helpless, as indeed he had been from the start, moving through his life by the rules that allowed him to pretend he was in control, disguising himself from his essential plight."[7]

"It was a standard pastiche detective thing," Sharp says modestly. "I didn't think the script was remotely up to being submitted to Arthur Penn and felt very uncertain about it because it hadn't resolved itself. But they sent it off, and I went to see Arthur and was astonished, a bit surprised, that he was interested in going ahead with it. When Arthur came on board I thought, 'Well, I can kind of have a whack at this threnody for loss of American innocence, which the Kennedy thing represented for me. And, of course, Watergate was going on while they were shooting it because I can remember sitting and watching television of the committee."[8]

The Kennedy thread was important not only for comparing Moseby's loss of innocence to America's but in establishing rapport between the sassy Paula and the brooding Moseby, who share a kind of emptiness. Harry covers his with distance, Paula with impudence. On one level, Paula is the requisite icy blonde who draws the private eye into the proverbial web of intrigue. But she is also the only person in the story who doesn't lie to him. She just never quite tells him the whole truth.

"Paula was a great character, a wonderful character," judges Penn, "and she remained intact. But it was tough to cast her. Jennifer Warren was a New York actress, not greatly known. I auditioned a lot of women, and they would have one aspect but not the other. She, finally, was just perfect: smart, sexy, not self-caring. She *got* it! Paula was really a soul mate, and I was sorry to see her die in the story. But she had no loyalties to anybody."

Melanie Griffith, fourteen, made her acting debut as the absconded teenager Delly. Gene Lasko discovered her and brought her to Penn's attention. As a minor, she came with a tutor. She also came with a boyfriend: Don Johnson. "Somehow I guess they found ways to get [the tutor] to go off shopping and she and Don would get together," Penn smiles. "She was really raw. She had some scenes with Gene Hackman. We had to nurse her through. Gene Lasko worked with her, and then I'd get her on the set with him. We started out sort of artificially, outside, and then it began to come in. And then when Gene Hackman comes in—when you get somebody else like that who's apparently believing you—it all follows. That's what good actors do for each other."

"I thought it was a modeling job," Griffith recalls of her audition. "I said, 'I don't want to be an actress. My mom's an actress [Tippi Hedren] and I don't like the whole thing.' They said, 'Well, just meet with Arthur.' At the same time, Don [Johnson], who I was with at the time, had said to me, 'Go out and get a job and do something to help support our life.' That's why I was modeling. So when Arthur gave me [script pages] to take home, I said to Don, 'I have to go back tomorrow and read for this; will you help me?' He helped me, and we worked on it, and I went back and read for Arthur. And I went back again the next day. I think I went back four or five times. I remember he made me pound on the chair to get really mad—I didn't know how to do anything then—I just pretended I was that person, and all of a sudden I got the job. It was like, 'Wow, I'm costarring in a movie with Gene Hackman!' And then, all of a sudden, something happened, and it was sort of magical, and it was just easy. Gene made it very easy for me, and fun, and I loved it. It changed immediately."

Penn and Sharp worked on the script cordially enough, but Penn's method of exploring, rather than declaring, put a burr under the moody writer's saddle. "Even though I'd done a few movies and worked with a few directors," he says, "I assumed that directors were auteurs and that you brought them the material and they shaped it into their vision. It didn't occur to me in the screenwriting process that Arthur didn't really know any more about it than I did. In a way, he was just trying to figure where the story went; he didn't have a vision to put on top of it, particularly. Then, when I was on the set watching him shooting, I realized that that wasn't his thinking."

Sharp took exception to Penn's process of shooting a lot of angles so he could find the rhythm during editing. "I got the impression that he basically acquired a lot of excellent footage and then retired to the safety of the editing room with Dede Allen and made his decisions there. I thought he would be more on the set doing it. But it was a more than affable and amiable working relationship. He's an admirable person and smart as a whip. And Gene Lasko was a pretty significant figure. He had quite a lot of input on the script in a good way."

"Interestingly enough," says Dede Allen, "Arthur never gave me the script of *Night Moves* to read before he filmed it. The only time he ever did that. I never thought of it until later. I'm now assuming that means he wasn't satisfied with it, because it's very unlike him not to give me a script. And that's one of the things I felt was frustrating. I didn't feel free, I didn't feel as candid about that picture. I was troubled by a lot of things that I kept thinking would turn out all right and that Arthur would somehow solve. And that troubled everybody, including Arthur. There were marvelous things about that character that didn't quite work."[9]

"I don't understand why Dede would say that," Penn responds. "We collaborated totally on all six films together and this does not sound like anything I can recall. In fact, nobody was paying attention to editors; I drew the press's attention to Dede Allen and started them writing about her and her large contributions. She's a very complex lady."

In many ways, the history of *Night Moves* echoed its plot, and both would serve as metaphor for the country that inspired them. Along with *The Long Goodbye* (1973) and *Chinatown* (1974), *Night Moves* in 1975 forms the iconic detective film trio of the 1970s. Each features a central character (Philip Marlowe, Jake Gittes, and Harry Moseby, respectively) whose morality is higher not only than those of the people in his life but of society in general. In *The Long Goodbye*, Marlowe does a friend a favor and winds up becoming implicated in a murder, the Mob, and a suicide. In *Chinatown*, Gittes is blindsided and, while exonerating himself, stumbles upon a scheme to swindle an entire community out of its water. *Night Moves* drinks from both streams: hired to retrieve a runaway, Moseby uncovers a smuggling ring that is looting an ancient culture. Thus the crime is both specific and metaphoric, and Moseby is stymied by his own impotence. To a country buffeted by Watergate, Vietnam, and a decade of assassinations, it is, in Penn's words, "a description of a country gone boundless." *Night Moves* turns the genre upon itself just as Harry Moseby is forced to look within rather than without.

"We didn't pay that much attention to plot," Penn admitted at the time of the film's release. "We thought that plot was not going to be achievable, that you were never going to be able to delineate a mystery properly. There was never going to be a way of saying 'Ah-ha!' in the last reel when you find out that so-and-so did so-and-so. And my only excuse or explanation for that is that we're part of a generation which knows there are no solutions."[10]

Penn, Sharp, and Sherman all say they were attracted to the project by the "Baltimore bench" scene in which Moseby describes how he used his detective skills to locate his estranged father, but didn't have the nerve to follow through and make contact.[11] Though it may suggest resonances to Penn's relationship with his own emotionally distant father, it came more directly from a quest by Sharp, who was adopted, to locate his natural parents. "My father was dead so I didn't have to find him," he says, "but I found my mother. You take something that's in your own life like that—finding your parents—which is a big event."

Most importantly, Penn wanted to *show* the solution to the mystery, not *tell* it. "The task I set myself was to have a detective story where we could resolve it more or less without spoken language," he says. "That's what that last sequence is with the plane, the hitting of the tank. Alan and I worked on it for a long time, and then we had the idea for the ending not being spoken in any form, which meant we had to work backward to build the plot. I think that film plotting has changed so you don't need those 'and then this happened's and 'and then that happened's.'"

This narrative parsimony gives the film an unusual and sometimes frustrating edge. Relationships seldom begin, they simply exist; Harry arrives after things happen and has to catch up; it's as if the viewer is dropped into the middle of a mystery and has to find the beginning and the end at the same time. This is the result of losing scenes that were removed for pace and the filmmaker's confidence that audiences could connect their own dots.

Shooting took place in the latter half of 1973 at Sanibel and Captiva Islands in Florida and in Los Angeles. It was not a happy experience. Hackman, always sullen when working, was reportedly under personal stress, and Sharp was facing challenges in his marriage as well as a growing frustration with the way his script was being realized. "I suppose I was disappointed that the collaborative process hadn't worked better for the piece," he says. "Arthur was, for all his precision of mind, quite vague. I came to realize that the things you need from a director are that he's got to tell you what he wants, and then he's got to recognize it when you bring it back, or not. I'm not one of these writers who has a chip about his words. I'm quite happy to go again. And Arthur had a few conversations with me about his own indecisiveness."

"It was all quite amiable at the beginning," Penn says. "It was going along rather swimmingly. Most of the changes didn't sit well with Alan although, at the time, he was enthusiastic. It was only after the picture was finished that he called me in New York and said, 'Can I come over and see you?' I said, 'Sure.' He came by and said something to the effect of 'Well, you got what you deserved,' meaning, '. . . having fucked up my script and imposing this other version.' I guess he was talking mostly critically and financially. I didn't have the sense that Alan had this hostility until after the film."

It was a challenging time for the director. "I sometimes got into such dark moods after a film like *Bonnie and Clyde* that I thought, 'I don't want to go back into that dark area for a while,' because it's painful," he says. "You're in it for a long, long time. It's a year, a year and a half of immersing yourself in the misery of a film like *Night Moves*. I miss my family more. I really do. I feel very lonely during those films. I get so inside that I'm sure I'm a lousy father and husband at that point, because you end up touching personal, painful material."

Nine days after *Night Moves* opened came a cultural event that would change motion pictures: *Jaws* was released, amassing more money in less time than any film in history. No one knew it then, but contemplative films were doomed, and the era of the manufactured blockbuster had begun. Whereas *Night Moves* could be expected to play off gradually across the country, *Jaws* splashed on hundreds of theater screens on the same day. Studio sales departments took keen notice and, because of rising marketing costs, pushed their production slates toward *Jaws*-like movies to the increasing exclusion of personal films such as *Night Moves*. By the time *Star Wars* was released in 1977, the die was cast.

As for *Night Moves*, Penn succeeded in his challenge, which was "to not have a plot-heavy story. To try to go through a certain minimum action but to have the personality revealed. And that's what it is, really, from Hackman's early fight with his wife up through the developing story with Eddie Binns, and then the story of his father told, now, in a reconciliation with his wife. That was essentially the extent of the plot. The other part of the plot is, 'We go out here, we get these things, and we lift them up and steal them' with stunt pilots as the elements. But it was always the personal story that grabbed me."

Does Harry Moseby die in the circling boat? According to Sharp, in earlier drafts of the script, he lost his leg. Penn offers a more philosophical answer: "I don't think he physically died. I think something in him died. It was a lovely, lucky final image."

The aimlessness of Moseby's boat became a metaphor for Penn's career as well as the collective culture. Media consolidation, right-wing coercion, shortened attention spans, and growing anti-intellectualism were making the country less introspective.

As he usually did when the movies got to him, Arthur Penn turned to the theater. In this case, he also went back to Italy, circa 1606.

20

Sly Foxes

When *Sly Fox* opened on Broadway on December 14, 1976, its director was 54, its author was 48, and the play was 370. Based on Ben Jonson's 1606 Elizabethan drama *Volpone*, with influence from a 1924 German adaptation by Stefan Zweig, *Sly Fox* is a comedy about fraud, greed, death, and deceit between friends. Jonson composed his version, it is said, in five weeks. Playwright Larry Gelbart and director Arthur Penn took considerably longer, but they emerged with an adventure as well as a hit.

Set in Venice, Italy, Jonson's original work presents Volpone, the fox, an elderly miser, whose clever servant, Mosca, the fly, is his accomplice in a scheme to cheat three of his friends out of their fortunes. Mosca sends word throughout the city that Volpone is dying and has vowed to leave his entire estate to whichever of his friends proves the most loyal and generous to him in his waning days.

It would be an understatement to say that *Volpone* offered its premiere audiences a lesson in venality. Although it proved to be the ill-tempered Jonson's most popular play, it paled in comparison with the more accessible folio of his contemporary William Shakespeare.

Sly Fox came about as a way to squeeze television for money—not to benefit a scoundrel pretending to be dying but to help the Actors Studio, which actually was.

"Some of the best things in life sometimes come at us from straight out of the blue," muses Larry Gelbart, whom Penn called in 1972 with the idea of setting *Volpone* in California's post–gold rush era.[1] "Though we'd been close friends for years, Arthur and I had never done any professional work together. All too often, doing the latter turns out to be a surefire recipe for ending even the closest of friendships, but working together on *Sly Fox* made the bond between us—and our families—stronger than ever."[2]

Penn's grand plan was to make *Sly Fox* as a network TV special for the benefit of the Actors Studio, feeling he could entice such Studio luminaries as Al Pacino to star in it, and use newly portable video technology to shoot it on location. But first he needed a script, so Penn asked Gelbart—whose stellar credits include *Caesar's Hour, A Funny Thing Happened on the Way to the Forum, Tootsie, City of Angels,* and most of TV's *M*A*S*H*—if he had ever read *Volpone.* "Quick as a flash," Gelbart says, "because we had been so close for so many years, I immediately lied and said that, of course, I had."

Penn's agent, Sam Cohn, assisted by asking international showman Lew Grade for development money. Grade said yes.[3] When California-based Gelbart turned in his first draft in March of 1976, Penn held a reading in New York. As Gelbart's miscreant, Foxwell J. Sly, Penn enlisted Art Carney, who had appeared for him in *Charley's Aunt* on television and had just won the Academy Award for *Harry & Tonto.* Lee and Anna Strasberg were also in the reading, which was performed before an invited audience at the Actors Studio. The next day Penn phoned Gelbart in California to report that it was "indecently funny." Energized, he took it to the networks, figuring that the combination of Gelbart, him, and the Studio would make a sale a no-brainer. And that's what happened: the TV people had no brains.

"It was okay for PBS to do it," Penn reports sarcastically, "but the major networks wouldn't. I was trying to impress on them that we could get these people and go out and just do it and end up with a television show as a benefit for the Actors Studio. The guy at CBS said, 'What have you done since *The Miracle Worker?*' This is after *Bonnie and Clyde!* He wouldn't hear of it. Neither would NBC. Then Peggy—after we had the reading at the Studio and it was so damn funny—said, 'You're crazy not to do this on Broadway.' So I offered it to the Studio [to produce on Broadway]." Unaccountably, they passed on their own fund-raiser.

"There was a business man who was dubious about this, and jealous," Penn says, "and, although the Studio—either then or later—backed *The Best Little Whorehouse in Texas,* he wouldn't back this. We didn't need his money, we just needed the auspices of the Studio; we'd have gotten the money privately. So Lew Grade came in with Marty Starger as his American representative. Then the Shubert Organization came in, and that was pretty much the financing of it."

While the money was being raised, Gelbart went back to the typewriter to restructure a six-act TV play into a two-act stage play. Penn sent Gelbart's rewrite to both George C. Scott and Walter Matthau. Matthau immediately said no because he didn't want to brave New York City's winters. As for Scott, his wife, Trish Van Devere, read it first, saw a part for herself, and recommended it to her husband, who said yes for both of them. "So we were in business," Gelbart beams, "with one of the best actors of our time."

Then reality set in. In New York to finally hear his play read out loud on the first day of rehearsal at the Minskoff Studios on Broadway, Gelbart deemed his comedy "indecently awful. Sketchy, stilted, desperately unfunny."

"Go to your room," ordered Penn.

"Not as punishment," Gelbart adds quickly. "He didn't mean 'Write this play five hundred times on the blackboard' (although I think, except for the blackboard, that's what I eventually wound up doing). He meant 'Make this play as good as you think it ought to be.'"

Why didn't it work this time? Says Penn, "It wasn't Art Carney, and they weren't performing for an audience. The night we heard the reading at the Studio there were perhaps a couple hundred people, and we were sitting there and there were a lot of laughs." At the Minskoff it was just family.

Gelbart's take on Jonson was in keeping with the spirit of *Volpone* (which he insists he still hasn't read) only funnier, while remaining not only in character but in style. Now set in San Francisco in 1849, the year after a glistening discovery at Sutter's Mill triggered the gold rush, *Sly Fox* isn't merely an essay on greed and duplicity; it's a well-constructed sequence of set pieces with strong characters and a payoff that flows from the motivations of its unindicted co-conspirators.

The Gelbart-Penn concoction has Foxwell J. Sly (George C. Scott) dispatching his assistant, Able (Hector Elizondo), to spread word that the master is dying and will leave his entire estate to whoever shows him the greatest tribute in his waning days. Lawyer Craven (John Heffernan) offers a gold goblet, Jethro Crouch (Jack Gilford) contributes a jeweled ring, and accountant Abner Truckle (Bob Dishy) brings gold. But what Sly really wants is Truckle's wife (Trish Van Devere), the mere suggestion of which drives the jealous Truckle apoplectic. Complications have Able suggesting that lawyer Crouch marry the fallen Miss Fancy (Gretchen Wyler), that Truckle volunteer his voluptuous wife to minister to Sly, and that Crouch disinherit his son, the captain, who eventually brings the law down upon everyone. Appearing before Judge Bastardson, the troupe is shocked when Sly is wheeled into court alive and Captain Crouch is convicted for being self-righteous. After the trial, Able tries to outfox Sly, but Sly trumps him by saying, "There's only one way to take it with you, my boy; send it on ahead." Curtain.

"Jonson was all about punishing the title character," says Gelbart. "It was Arthur who had the wonderful idea of changing the ending of the play. Arthur's take was: 'We're living in post-Nixon times. Crime *can* pay.' That's why, in our incarnation, Sly's final exit is one of triumph rather than one of shame. Volpone is made to pay for his transgressions; we let Sly keep all of his ill-gotten gains."

Referencing Zweig's version, Gelbart deleted several subordinate characters and added the role of Miss Fancy, a prostitute, whose presence allowed risqué humor. He also heeded the lessons that he and Burt Shevelove discovered when they wrote *A Funny Thing Happened on the Way to the Forum*, which was to write in a contemporary style while avoiding anachronisms "at all costs." The rest—as at least seventeen drafts between October 26 and November 24, 1976, attest—was rewriting.

"You stand there in the back of the theater, with your chin on the rail looking like Kilroy," Gelbart describes. "I was lucky enough to be standing next to someone who picked up on all of the play's possibilities—and all of the wrong notes I had orchestrated—not so much in text but in tension and nuance. Arthur has a built-in radar. I came to trust his instincts and welcome his suggestions." Penn directed Gelbart to "play the situation" and make scenes "serious for all, then break them down." Above all, he urged, make lines "better, or cut." Says Gelbart, "What I started to feel, thanks to Arthur, was a greater confidence in my ability to write the play and to inject as much humor into it as I possibly could. Arthur freed me to be able to do that."

It was George C. Scott who helped them solve a problem that was both structural and commercial: after Fox dies, the star of the play disappears for half an hour until after the trial. Scott's solution was that he play both Fox and the judge. The reveal is one of the comedy's high spots, but forever afterward it has caused Gelbart to be plagued with inquiries about whether the judge is another of Fox's schemes. Like Annie Sullivan's brogue, the doubling of Sly and the judge has become tradition, even though it was a device. That it became so powerful describes the enigma of George C. Scott, an actor who was at once brilliant at his craft and disdainful of it. Observes Gelbart, "George would often glare at the audience during his curtain call with a look that always seemed to say, 'How *dare* you watch me act? How *dare* you see me do what I do?' He was a closet aristocrat, George was. I'm convinced he would much rather have made his mark as a writer and not as an actor."

Part of the complication was that Scott was an alcoholic. "He'd sip Smirnoff vodka with Budweiser chasers all day long," Gelbart recalls, "but I'll be damned if I ever saw him unable to perform. I don't doubt that he might have caused Arthur some trouble." "He showed the behavior cycle of a guy who was a drunk," Penn confirms. "He came back from a bender, everything was great. And then little things would start to accumulate that nobody knew about, and *boom!* Ten days later the lid would blow off and George wouldn't show up for a couple of days."

One such blowup happened during a rehearsal. It had to do with a chest that Penn placed at the foot of Fox's bed that held the riches he had bilked. "George hated that chest," says Gelbart. "He hated having to maneuver around it during a performance; he was always asking Arthur to put it somewhere else. The first time I ever saw him tell the world just how much he hated it was also the first time I ever heard the word *cocksucking* used as an adjective. Both firsts occurred when, during a rehearsal, George told Arthur to 'Get rid of this cocksucking chest!' And then kicking the offending prop for all his big toe was worth."[4]

The playwright dodged Scott's invective until a party after the tryout opening at Baltimore's Mechanic Theatre. "Waiting for what would be our first reviews," he says, "I asked George if he was worried. 'Me?' he said. 'I'm fine! I'm not the son of a bitch that's rewriting Ben Jonson. *You're* the one they're gonna go after.'" But "they" didn't, except with praise, and *Sly Fox* moved on to Boston's Wilbur Theatre, then to New York's Broadhurst Theatre, where it ran 495 performances.

Sly Fox was the first full-out comedy that Penn had directed since *Nichols and May,* and he'd lost none of his touch. "My theory—which I use in the theater and everywhere—is 'Comedy comes last,'" Penn explains. "Everything has to be credible, the circumstances have to be sound and stand up on their own, and now you start doing the comedy."

Bob Dishy, who played the jealous Truckle, remembers Penn discussing the "dark underbelly" of the play. "That's what the initial emphasis was on," Dishy says, "the serious nature of the play. To explore that bottomless pit of jealousy, envy, greed, duplicity, lust, et cetera, embedded in the characters. That's what I understood Arthur to mean by the 'dark underbelly.' There was no talk of comedy. That came later. I think this approach built a solid foundation that was a major factor toward the play's success. Later we added the whipped cream." For all Penn's seriousness about comedy, says Dishy, "Arthur doesn't have the answers. That's what's so great. It's not as if he's starting out with all the answers. He's leading you with him and the other actors to try to find out, and what he's after is something that's new, something unexpected."

With people like Dishy and Jack Gilford, though, it's hard to stray from the comic prize. Penn cites Miss Fancy's visit to Craven when she starts seducing him, "and he falls asleep. When it was done, the audience was in on it every step of the way, and there were screams of laughter with every drop of his eyelids."

If Gilford could reduce an audience to puddles by closing one eyelid, Dishy added moments of manic madness that displayed his character's inner torment. "Dishy is one of the funniest people in the world," Penn praises. "He gets there by intensifying the circumstance beyond credibility. He turned himself into an absolute paranoid nut about how people were looking at his wife. It grew and grew and grew and was very funny, and it pissed George off because Dishy was getting laughs at Trish's expense."

"As a director, Arthur can be very provocative," Dishy says. "He can be very tenacious in goading you on in a way that can be irritating. Ultimately you find he's doing it to help you, to free you to make a discovery. A surprise! He's not imposing a result. He's searching with you. I can't quite put in words what Arthur does, but he creates an atmosphere (if you go with it) to allow actors to function at the top of their game."

After the Broadway run ended, the national company of *Sly Fox* boasted Jackie Gleason as Sly, Cleavon Little as Able, and a level of tension created by the egocentric, self-crowned "Great One." Penn pauses before commenting. "Jackie was a pig. We had Cleavon Little (an African American actor) playing Able. And Gleason would say, 'Hey, boy, come here, I want to talk to you' to Cleavon Little. After a day or so, Larry and I both intervened and said, 'Jackie, you can't do that! This is a well-known actor, he's a dignified human being, don't do that any more.' He said, 'What'd I do? Call him boy? He's younger than I am!'" Penn throws up his hands at Gleason's inability to grasp his offence. "He was not to be understood."

After several frustrating attempts to make *Sly Fox* into a motion picture (most of them involving fears that the youth market would not embrace a film with stars over forty), a revival of the play was planned as early as 1993 when Penn and producer Nelle Nugent tried to enlist Tom Hanks to bring his prodigious talents to the complex role. Nothing came of it. In 2004, Penn remounted *Sly Fox* with the backing of Julian Schlossberg (*Fortune's Fool*), who headed a financing consortium but did it as a labor of love. With Scott dead by then, they needed a box office name—film box office, that is, because that's what Broadway had become—and Oscar-winner Richard Dreyfuss was available, supported by Eric Stoltz as Able, René Auberjonois as Crouch, Bronson Pinchot as Craven, Rachel York as Miss Fancy, and "Professor" Irwin Corey as the appropriately addled court clerk. Bob Dishy was inveigled to return because, as Penn says, "We just could never think of anybody who was as funny." But something had changed in the three decades between productions: Jonson's nasty satire of greed and duplicity às embellished by Gelbart and Penn seemed redundant in George W. Bush's America. Initially, Schlossberg thought this would make the revival more commercial; "Greed had become more pervasive," he reasoned. Instead, the years had seen an erosion in the public's taste in humor. People now preferred crassness over wit and one-liners over character comedy. They also didn't cotton to being lectured on the evils of venality when venality had arguably become the law of the land.

And there was another problem. "Just simply," Penn says, "Richard, for some reason, could not learn his lines. Could not. Gave us rationalization after rationalization: 'I'm working on a TV show'; 'I'm doing this'; 'As soon as I get done with those I'll get to the lines.' I said, 'Richard, we're two weeks into rehearsal, you know?' I don't know what the hell was going on. But what happened as a result of that, it's like the military: if you don't maintain a tight, tight ship, it becomes an epidemic, it spreads to everybody. Everybody gets slack, everybody gets to improvising their own jokes. And that's what happened with this company. I never got them under my control. Never. And it was not a good show. We just had no precision, no clarity. Richard would have a very funny line and would just invert a word, and it would lose its effect."

"There was definitely no dark underbelly in the second production," agrees Dishy. "I'm sure it was very painful for Arthur and Larry. It seemed to be going well in rehearsals. Out of town it just didn't seem to work as well. In the end, the play worked, for want of a better word, as a crowd-pleaser."

Explains Gelbart, "Julian Schlossberg loved this play. He was a close friend of George and Trish's those many years ago when we first did the show, and I guess one of his ambitions was to be involved in doing it again. And so, God, ever the stand-up comic, punished him and let him do it. You need a name on Broadway, and Richard Dreyfuss, having appeared in, I think, five of the top-ten all-time movie money grossers—things like *Jaws* and *Close Encounters of the Third Kind*—fit the bill, and was the star we got." He declines further comment.

The revival ran 173 performances, from April 1 to August 29, 2004, at the Ethel Barrymore Theatre.

The odyssey of *Sly Fox* intensified the friendship between Peggy and Arthur Penn and Pat and Larry Gelbart, who had originally met at a restaurant called the Lodge in Stowe, Vermont, in the late 1950s and thereafter became sort-of neighbors across the New York–Massachusetts border. "They are," declares Gelbart, "just the most admirable people we've ever known. But then I'm a pushover for excellence."

21

The Studio

The building was not much to look at, but, like what was taught to those who studied there, the important thing was what went on inside. The address 432 West Forty-fourth Street in the Hell's Kitchen area of New York City had been the Old Labor Stage until 1947, when Elia Kazan, Cheryl Crawford, and Robert "Bobby" Lewis opened the Actors Studio. It was built in 1850 as a chapel, which is fitting, given the religious fervor with which the faithful studied the craft of acting. The religion became known as the Method, although, when it was proposed by Konstantin Stanislavski in his teachings, he called it the System. It might also be called the Process, because those who follow it engage in a lifelong exploration of self, craft, and a level of realism that didn't exist on the stage before Stanislavski codified its creation.

Konstantin Stanislavski was born Konstantin Sergeyevich Alekseyev in Moscow in 1863. He adopted the stage name Stanislavski in his early twenties, partly as a show of youthful independence but also to avoid the scandal he felt would befall his well-to-do merchant family were he to retain theirs. For while Russians loved culture, including the theater, actually getting up on a stage was too common for someone of Alekseyev's privileged station. The young man flirted with formal acting but felt increasingly burdened by adherence to its presentational style, a convention in which one actor waited for another to finish before speaking, and then addressed the audience instead of his fellow performer. Actual emotion was indicated rather than expressed, and certainly never felt.

It was while watching a performance of *Othello* in the 1890s that Stanislavski began to believe that the artifices of acting that had so burdened him in earlier studies could be stripped away so that only true emotions remained. In 1918 he established a school to teach his technique to young actors and began writing a series of papers that would become his seminal text, *An Actor Prepares.*

Stanislavski's troupe toured America only once—in 1922–1923—performing in Russian, but the superiority of the acting impressed New York–based actors Stella Adler and Lee Strasberg so much that when two members of the Moscow Art Theatre began teaching at the American Laboratory Theatre, they sought to study under them. Those actors were Richard Boleslavsky and Maria Ouspenskaya, both of whom had profound and continuing influence on the development of the American derivation that came to be called the Method.

Summarizing the Method can be both risky and incomplete, for it is a consuming regimen that requires both personal and professional devotion. In the broadest sense, it is a technique by which a performer calls upon personal experience, which can be painful, in order to create what is necessary for a performance. It is through training that the actor learns not only how to summon these feelings when they are needed but also to present them meaningfully to the audience.[1]

The Studio had its roots in the Group Theatre, which was formed in 1931 by Harold Clurman, Cheryl Crawford, and Lee Strasberg. It lasted ten years before falling victim both to World War II funding shortfalls and the poaching of its talent by Hollywood. After the war Kazan, Lewis, and Clurman re-Grouped, so to speak, added Anna Sokolow, and opened the Studio. Entry entailed an audition before a group of peers followed by an evaluation by the board. Even today, only a handful of people are accepted each year, but membership and access are for life, a reassuring guidepost in such a chancy profession as acting.

The Actors Studio changed American acting. At a time when

America itself was beginning to confront the responsibilities that came with its postwar position as a world power, the actors, directors, and writers who passed through the Studio likewise developed an attitude toward reality. Detractors, however, criticized them for their obvious stylistic differences with the past, notably their subtlety and introspection.

"There was a period that the torn undershirt and Brando's mumbling became sort of fair game for making fun of the Studio," Penn conceded.[2] What the actors were actually doing, of course, was exploring a verisimilitude hitherto unknown on the stage and screen. The trick was not only creating it but at the same time making sure that it worked—a thorny balance of id and ego that some observers mistook for navel-gazing.

Penn joined the Studio in 1953. He had been using the Studio as a casting resource for the live television dramas he was directing. "I couldn't get there very often because their sessions were Tuesday and Friday and I'd be in rehearsal most of the time," he says, "but I'd get there every once in a while and would see this wonderful work.

"It was Strasberg's contention that through affective memory—memory of your own emotional experience that was, in some way, closely related to the event of the play that you were engaging with—lay genuine art. Stella didn't agree. Harold [Clurman] was sort of on the fence about it because Lee was the director of the group. Harold was the intellectual, the dramaturge, but didn't really venture to direct early on, and Cheryl Crawford was the business. As Stella grew in stature and reputation, she also grew in displeasure with Lee and with what he was insisting upon. With Harold, she went to Paris and met the older Stanislavski, who was either vacationing or seeing doctors. They found some time with him—I think out on a park bench—where they discussed this."

The conversation remains controversial. "Either Stanislavski had been misinterpreted to a degree about affective memory," Penn notes, "or he had changed from the inner self-scrutiny to what later was called, in the *New England Journal*, 'active analysis.' But whatever had transpired—probably the latter, because he was quite elderly when Stella saw him in Paris—Stella came back and said, 'Lee, you're wrong! You're wrong! I spoke to Stanislavski.'[3] Lee said, in effect, 'Bullshit! I'm teaching it!' Stella gave it her contempt.

"Now Harold, who was really the major intellectual, is between the two of them, but has also started directing himself, and has developed a closer relationship with [Clifford] Odets than the one that Lee had. So you see all the splittings-off and breaking apart, and, through all of this, Kazan is emerging with all this flashy theatrical skill that supersedes Lee and even Harold. They were doing a kind of Talmudic scholarship of this while Kazan was doing the work: 'This is how you do it!' And that is, I think, how the Method became the American system."

By the 1950s, Studio acolytes were making their way to Hollywood. Some were even coming back to teach and continue their studies. Marlon Brando, Montgomery Clift, Paul Newman,[4] James Dean, Shelley Winters, Kim Hunter, Eli Wallach, Geraldine Page, Steve McQueen, and Anne Jackson were only a few marquee names who returned to nurture those they left behind. With Kazan and Lewis busy directing, Strasberg inherited their courses. Brilliant, perceptive, charismatic, relentless, controlling, and often cruel, he put students through the wringer. But they loved him.

"It was, for my taste, excessively reverential toward Lee," Penn says. "He and I always had an issue. I'd say, 'God damn it, get out of their way. Let the actors go.' I didn't have the courage to say that out loud when I was doing just television, but once *Seesaw* opened and I brought Annie [Bancroft] into the studio, I had a living example of learning how to act by doing physical things like that entrance I described.[5] Lee used to say, 'It's gotta come from the inside. I expect it to take two or three years.' We don't *have* two or three years; we have to be able to put on plays in three or four *weeks!* Lee never confronted that, so he could have this austere, hermetic position, because he wasn't doing plays. Kazan and I were doing plays. Lee couldn't carry that theory into a rehearsal."

Another difference was the kind of talent that was seeking

community at the Studio. Change was in the air. "This is my contention," Penn opines. "The period after the war was a very rich period because there had been at least half a generation that had been away from conventional life expectations and in harm's way. I found that to be true in live television: most of the directors were veterans. Almost all of us. [Sidney] Lumet. George Roy Hill was a fighter pilot, [Frank] Schaffner was in it, I was in it. There was a certain kind of—I don't know what—I would characterize it as 'It doesn't scare me.' Here we were in a new medium, inventing it every day. As a new piece of technology came in, we would then utilize it. And that was true, as well, in the ineffable aspect of actors' talent. This group came out of there—some of them very talented—and went right into the biz, from Paul Newman and Jimmy Dean to Steve McQueen and Marlon Brando."

By this time, Penn had developed his own directing vocabulary, and it wasn't Strasberg's or Stanislavski's. "I couldn't use Strasbergian talk because it was not functional," he maintains. "It didn't get the work done. The better way is to leave the actor to find it. I don't believe in all that active introspection. I direct differently."

By the mid-1990s, the Studio was in financial peril. "For a certain long period, Paul Newman supported the Studio," Penn recalls. "In the early days, if Kazan had a film and wanted to have a premiere, they'd have a benefit for the Studio in New York and make a lot of money. By the time my pictures started coming out, film studios weren't doing that any more because it cost them a lot of money. By then we were scratching for money. And then we got to a point where Paul said, 'That's it, I can't do it anymore, I have a much better place where I want to put my money.' So they came to me and said, 'We want you to be president.' I said, 'I can't see being president of an essentially bankrupt organization.'"

Two events occurred between 1994 and 1995 to reverse the slide. One was the affiliation of the Actors Studio with New York's progressive New School for Social Research (now the New School), whose president was Jonathan F. Fanton. "We got along famously; we had a couple of big meetings with Ellen

Burstyn, Lee Grant, Norman Mailer, et cetera, deciding to do this, and agreed that the faculty would be entirely from the Studio and under the auspices of the Studio," Penn chronicles. "For a year we worked out a contract that threw off a considerable amount of money to the Studio." In June 1994, Penn accepted the posts of president and artistic director of the Studio.

"We're returning to the Stanislavski method of acting as a unified system," he explained when plans were announced. "We're taking the tangential elements of the Stella Adler approach, the Lee Strasberg approach, and the Sandy Meisner approach, and putting them back together into a comprehensive Stanislavskian method." Penn and James Lipton worked together on the syllabus, which included an idea for seminars with notable Studio graduates.

The second idea quickly overshadowed the first. It happened on June 12, 1994, on the Bravo cable network and was called *Inside the Actors Studio*. "We naively started *Inside the Actors Studio* with the anticipation that it would be very serious," Penn laments. "But what happened was that it caught on so quickly that press agents called us to take their clients who had never set foot in the Studio. Well, we didn't resist it. We took it, Bravo took the show, money came flying in, and the president asked me to be a member of the board of trustees. So I was president of the Studio and on the board of trustees of the New School."

Although *Inside the Actors Studio* started off with a bang by calling on such notable graduates as Alec Baldwin, Paul Newman, Sally Field, and Shelley Winters, the real star that emerged from the intimate chat sessions was its host, James Lipton.[6] At about the same time, Lipton became program chair and dean of a three-year master of fine arts degree program in Theatre Arts at the New School—a program created by Penn. "The president of the New School wanted to revive the tradition of a dramatic school at the New School that was the stepchild of the theater school that Irwin Piscator had started there prewar. That's where Lee Strasberg trained, and Stella Adler. Marlon was there, and so was a very funny actor who became a big star, Walter Matthau."

The master's program was to begin with forty people in the

first class and eventually expand to three hundred people, one hundred in each year. *Inside the Actors Studio* was to serve as its "craft seminar." At that point, the president of the university essentially came to me and said, 'We're gonna take this program and make it a school of the university.'" Shows were staged at the Actors Studio Free Theatre at Raw Space in 1999.

"After a while, after we had quite a bit of money in the bank," Penn says, "I thought we should be able to put on plays, since it was not enough for the Studio to keep doing just this TV exercise. So I started a little free theater using Studio money. But the Studio objected that I was spending their money. I was saying, 'Look, if the Actors Studio is going to survive, it has to be productive and be something to the community that is not as abstract as "We're developing some twenty actors who are gonna dazzle you."' I told them, 'We're at a real fork in the road. I don't want to just keep getting money for the Actors Studio to train sixty actors of now-dubious talent unless we are a production unit.' They said, 'We'll never do production because Lee Strasberg said we must never do production.' Well, that's bullshit."

One of the features of the Studio was the Playwrights Unit, which was begun by Clifford Odets and Molly Kazan in New York in 1952, with a Studio West counterpart headed by William Inge. It lasted only a short while but was revived in the mid-1980s when Norman Mailer and Penn formed a haven for novelists who had a secret desire to write for the theater. Penn asked Kazan to alternate with him. "As somebody there said," Penn quotes, "'This is the place to be on Monday afternoon,' because the *writing* was not all that good, but the *criticism* was *superb.*" Kazan and Penn ran it in tandem until other commitments pulled them away, so they asked Joseph L. Mankiewicz—who was going through a spell of writer's block—to be a third leader.[7]

Novelist and essayist Jerome Charyn was also invited by Mailer to join the group, which convened at the Studio. "It met once a week on an afternoon," he says. "They had a little theater on the top floor with benches and a tiny stage. Kazan was there and he was a very, very big force; Norman Mailer himself; Harold

Brodkey; Rom [Romulus] Linney the playwright, and Eve Ensler the playwright. There were other people, but I remember them the most. What I also remembered is that Arthur was a great teacher. There's just something about the way he moves and the way he spoke. He was both reassuring and strong without ever being sarcastic."

"It was a terrific place," Penn remembers happily. "All the good writers were there plus a lot of novelists and journalists, and they would read their pieces or have actors from the Studio read it. It would be benign and okay. And then the criticism would start! It was our job, after all, with this sort of literary criticism, to provide a kind of dramatic overview, so that's what we each did in our own way. We would say, 'Well, this is a novelist's form, but if you were to do so-and-so, at least there would be dramatic mechanics which would thrust it forward in a way that you go laterally, because you're a prose writer, et cetera.' Inevitably, because they were hard-edged novelists, it would start out talking about drama and then go into *writing*. There were long knives out, but it was long knives of a group that had mutual respect. They were all big PEN writers, and boy, that place would rock."

"For a few years it was *the* most important sort of place in my own life," Charyn recalls. "I always saw [Arthur] as a kind of magical rabbi who really didn't have any ego investment in this. He didn't have any hidden agenda. He was just trying to make it better."

Penn resigned as president of the Studio on May 1, 2000, because, he says, of the Studio's refusal to back his free theater. He became executive producer and show runner on the television series *Law & Order*, accepting the Studio title president emeritus. Ellen Burstyn, Harvey Keitel, and Al Pacino were announced as co-presidents, replacing him.

Not long after, there were reports of internecine tensions that were beginning to take on all the passions of a religious schism. Trouble over academic accreditation and control had been brewing between the Actors Studio and the New School ever since former U.S. senator Bob Kerrey had become the

New School's president in 2001. Kerrey began a program of streamlining and reorganization, drawing equal parts praise and criticism, generally along political lines in the traditionally progressive institution. On May 26, 2005, Kerrey decided not to renew the Studio's contract with the New School and, three months later, named Robert LuPone to take over the master's program. Since 2006, the master's program has been affiliated with Pace University.

But there's more to the story than is indicated by the press release. Some say it began with the heart attack death of Lee Strasberg on February 18, 1982. In 1969 Strasberg, while serving as artistic director of the Studio, had set up the competing Lee Strasberg Theatre and Film Institute in New York and California.[8] He continued teaching while making occasional film appearances, notably *The Godfather Part II* (1974) and *Going in Style* (1979). The institute was taken over by his widow, Anna Strasberg, and their son, John. According to Penn, when Strasberg died, there was immediate jockeying for his mantle.

"Ellen Burstyn, who was a latecomer to studying with Strasberg, out of her peculiar spiritual orientation, has elevated him to a guru position and herself to his acolyte where she almost speaks for him," Penn says. "For example, right after he died, there was a big show business memorial at the Shubert Theatre. Lee's wife, Anna, was there onstage, and Ellen is there onstage. Before Anna gets a chance to speak a word, Ellen said, 'Dear Anna, Lee came to me last night in a dream and said, "Take care of Anna."' Peggy turned to me and said, 'She just cut her legs off.'"

Penn summarizes the rest: "Here's this program at the New School, going for ten years, beautifully. They're making money, the Studio is making money, the Studio for the first time in its life, at that point, had 4 million bucks in the bank as a result of the New School having *Inside the Actors Studio*. Bob Kerrey comes in as president, at which point Burstyn then comes to them and says, 'As head of the studio'—which she is—'I have to be in charge of the curriculum.' Kerrey said, 'Well, I'll certainly solicit your advice, but you don't mean you'll be in charge of the curriculum; that's an academic function.' 'No, I mean I'll be in charge.' This went on. Unable to agree on control, the Studio and the New School separated.

"I think the Studio was wrong," Penn declares. "I sided with the New School and they [the Studio] asked me to resign from the board of directors. I said, 'With pleasure.' I was now free to voice my opinion about the arch and oily performance of James Lipton as the public face of the Actors Studio on the television show."

It was the middle of 2000 and Penn was heading back to television. As he would soon learn, television had changed.

22

A Sea of Mud

The story has been told so often that it has entered the Hollywood apocrypha: a Seasoned Director pitches his project to a powerful but very young studio executive. Depending on the telling, the Old Master is variously Fred Zinnemann, John Huston, George Stevens, Frank Capra, or William Wyler. "What other things have you done?" the zygote asks blithely. The Seasoned Director then leans across the desk and says to the executive, in italics, "*You first.*"

By late 1978 Arthur Penn was practicing his italics. The film revolution that he ignited with *Bonnie and Clyde* had installed a generation of filmmakers who'd leapfrogged over him without looking back, never mind genuflecting. Their tastes had been shaped by movies, TV, and comic books—not by life—and they had precious little interest in what they called "character-driven" stories.

Penn wasn't alone. Paddy Chayefsky—who foretold the dismal future of the mass media in *Network* (1976)—held to traditional values while warily eyeing the future. He conceived a novel about a scientist who uses a sensory deprivation tank to regress to humankind's primitive past, then adapted it into a screenplay that offered plenty of potential for special effects. It was not only a science fiction love story (the scientist is rescued from his genetic netherworld by the love of a Good Woman), it was a paean to the folly of using technology to define humanity. *Altered States* became a best seller. The movie became a nightmare.

Chayefsky asked Penn to direct it. For the cast, Penn hired a newcomer from the Juilliard Drama School by the name of William Hurt, then added Blair Brown as his wife and Bob Balaban as his laboratory antagonist. The innovative makeup effects would be created by Dick Smith and would turn Hurt's character into a Cro-Magnon man (actually dancer Miguel Godreau) as well as what can only be described as a large pink embryonic blob. Chayefsky told interviewer John Brady that he came up with the idea—a shameless twist on *Dr. Jekyll and Mr. Hyde*—during a bull session with writer Herb Gardner and director-choreographer Bob Fosse at the Russian Tea Room.[1] Penn and Chayefsky hadn't worked together since *First Person* in 1953, and they looked forward to the reunion.

"And then I found out that he was the producer," says Penn. "He came in one day and said, 'I've seen the first set and it's no good, it's wrong.' I said, 'What are you talking about?' He said, 'I saw this big set, and it's wrong. I think of this as a small scene.' I said, 'Yeah: we're in the middle with all this equipment and we're gonna shoot in various areas of the set, Paddy.' It was a test of me and him, and we had known each other all this time from the Soldiers' Shows in Paris. Finally I said, 'Paddy, it's not gonna work.'"

There were also script problems that had surfaced during the six-month preproduction period, something Chayefsky readily admitted. "When I sat down to do the screenplay, all the holes came out. You can get away with a lot in prose that you can't get away with at all in drama. I tried to follow the book, and it didn't work."[2]

By this time the film's advocate at Columbia, Daniel Melnick, had bolted, leaving the agreeable Frank Price in charge. It was then that both Penn and Price discovered that Melnick had given final cut to Chayefsky and his producing partner, Howard Gottfried, not to Penn or even the studio. The director realized it was madness to continue. He was paid out, and Ken Russell took over. Not long afterward, Columbia dropped the project and Warner Bros. picked it up, by which time the budget had bloated to 15 million 1978 dollars. Chayefsky didn't like the Ken

Russell experience, either. "They were sending him dailies," Penn says, "and he'd taken his name off by this point."[3] The two men bumped into each other on Manhattan's West Side. "He'd say, 'Arthur, Arthur, you don't know what they're doin' to our piktcha.' He disavowed Ken Russell's stuff totally."

Altered States was released in 1980 with an ear-shattering gimmick called "Mega Sound" that goosed subwoofer levels to the point of physically shaking the theater audience. Even that didn't move anybody. "This," pronounces Penn, "was the height of Hollywood at its most dysfunctional: you throw money at things."

It wasn't money but passion that led Penn to *Four Friends* in 1981, a partly autobiographical original screenplay by Steve Tesich, who had won an Oscar with his blue-collar *Breaking Away* two years earlier. The story of a girl and the three men in her life who persist in their youthful romantic dreams despite the encroachment of age and reality, it was the film's secondary themes that attracted Penn. "It was a film about displaced adolescence and a kid who was an immigrant to the United States," he says, "and his ability to function with his father. In that sense, there are a lot of personal details that correlate with my own life. More than that, I think—well, I don't know what I think. I was going to say, 'I think that one of the things about the film is that there is, inherent in it, a certain forgiveness.' And I guess that's my subterranean connection to it. Some way we finally forgive each other and find a way to move on."[4]

For this reason, *Four Friends* is an example of the screenwriting adage that the *plot* may be what *happens* in a film, but that the *subplot* is what the film is really *about*. *Four Friends* covers some twenty years of American social and political upheaval, during which the youth of America became estranged from, and then reconciled with, the generation that sired them. It is a quietly ambitious epic that has so much plot to cover that it sometimes loses focus, yet Penn remains close to it.

The film follows young Danilo Prozor, who arrives in East Chicago from Yugoslavia in the mid-1950s with his mother to meet his emotionally remote father, who has ventured ahead to establish a life for them. By high school, Danilo has formed close friendships with David, Tom, and the free spirit Georgia, who appeals to them all not as a tease but as a life force. The story takes all of them through the next two turbulent decades of political, social, and moral change, and ends with Danilo and his father reconciling, not because the parent has changed but because the son has.

The emotional glue that holds the three male friends together is Georgia, played by Jodi Thelen (the original title, and the one used internationally, is the more accurate *Georgia's Friends*). She is not unlike Jeanne Moreau's character, Catherine, in François Truffaut's *Jules et Jim* (1961). By contrast, the men evince the kind of emotional and sexual reserve that constricted their whole generation until it was liberated in the 1967 Summer of Love. Much in the film is unsettling and disorienting, and that was intentional. "It was an era in which it was very difficult to have a conventional hero, or to have somebody who could genuinely enlist your sympathy," Penn observed.[5]

However much *Four Friends* was Steve Tesich's autobiography, certain elements also resonated with Penn, including both his political and filial anguish. "Parts of Danilo's life were related to personal experiences of mine, and I felt a lot of sympathy for that poor soul," he said. "Also I felt a lot of sympathy for the immigrant personality, from which I'm only one generation removed. It's a peculiarly odd role to have immigrant parents; the growing up in a culture to which they are not directly related. They'd be appalled to hear me say that because they were both very intelligent, forward-looking people of their own time, politically and intellectually active. But, somehow, to a child born in this country, and probably even to a child who came over at the age that Danilo did, his parents would seem quite hopelessly out of style. And that might account for the hungry social leap that Danilo attempts in the film—not the most attractive social move, certainly, but one I suppose that crossed the minds of an awful lot of first-generation immigrant children in America."[6]

Amplified Tesich, "Only Arthur knows for sure, but his life, although factually different, emotionally was very similar to mine—his own parents being immigrants, his own mother being the source of a kind of inspiration, his father being a rather hard man. So the two of us saw eye to eye and that was an attraction to him for the script. Although the film is parallel to my own life and my relationship with my parents, it could have been written about Penn's own life."[7]

Four Friends allowed the director to express these feelings of alienation from both family and society, yet he emerged from it to make what could be his least sentimental film despite the fact that it is also about reconciliation between a father and son: *Target* (1985). It's a snazzy thriller about an average family (Gene Hackman, Gayle Hunnicutt, and Matt Dillon) whose lives explode when the mother is unaccountably kidnapped by foreign agents and the father has to free her. It turns out that the father used to kill people for the CIA and his past has returned to haunt him while his son, who accompanies him on the rescue, is torn between astonishment that his milquetoast father was a spy and betrayal at having been lied to his whole life.

Penn reveled in the melodrama. "It's almost a television depiction of an average American family," he enthused. "Then the situation becomes progressively more absurd: the mother wired to explosive devices in a hangar is like the heroine being tied to the railroad tracks. The confusion of identity that the boy goes through is, by definition, a rather absurd thing to happen to you."[8]

The father-son tension was paralleled offscreen when Gene Hackman blew up at the then twenty-year-old Matt Dillon, who had made a name for himself playing alienated teenagers. "Matt had a scene," Penn reports, "and he showed up and said blithely, 'I just thought, you know, we'd try to do . . . ' and Gene said, 'That's not what you do' and gave him about five minutes of what it's like to be a serious actor and artist. You know, he was this cute kid and he was also of that generation where nothing is serious. Well, Gene said, 'It's serious, what we do.' Matt says, to this day, that it changed his life. What Gene was saying was, 'Have respect for the art.'"

Hackman's devotion was doubly ironic, given that he didn't

want to do the film in the first place. But his marriage was falling apart and there was talk of business reversals, so he presumably needed the money.[9]

At least there were the European locations. Although the Penns had traveled extensively throughout Europe, this would be the first time since being thrown off *The Train* twenty-one years earlier that he would be making a picture there. Powerhouse producers Richard Zanuck and David Brown (*Jaws, The Sting, The Verdict*) promised additional adventures. "Zanuck is obviously a sort of representation of his father," considers Penn, "decisive, that way. Brown is a total gentleman, elegant living, so while we were in Paris, if we had an early lunch or were on a weekend, we would lunch with Abe Ribicoff or this one and that one. David was married to Helen [Gurley], who was quite a figure in the magazine world. We had a very elegant time in Paris, and we zipped along.

"When the film had all that Paris stuff in it, I said, 'I've got the crew.' David said, 'You *know* these people?' I said, 'They're friends.' And it was true. The cameraman [Jean Tournier], production manager Bernard Farrel, the set designers, and most of the grips were people I knew from *The Train*. So we had a very nice time in that respect, and we worked the French hours, twelve to seven. I'd been back to France numerous times and had kept in close touch with the people. Peggy was friends with Jean Tournier's wife. We all saw each other—they would come here, we would see each other. Years later, Willy Holt, the designer, had a show at MOMA, and I was there with him."

The Penns took up residence on the Left Bank, and the Browns staked out the Right Bank. "He simply adored Paris," Brown recalls. "He reveled in it; it was though he was born to make a film in Europe." Penn brought his exuberance to the set, says the producer, who describes the director as standing beside the camera, "totally obsessed, and his face reflected the take. You would see him smile. Every time an actor hit something or nailed a scene, Arthur would light up like a Roman candle."

Penn enjoyed making his first genre piece. "It's not an elegant and thought-through film," he offers. "It was designed for quite other purposes on my part. I don't know whether it was a life crisis of my own, where I wanted to say that I was still alive and functioning. Maybe I thought I'd like to show that I can do this kind of high-kinetic, action movie: 'Damn it, I can do those, I can do them better than those damn whippersnappers.' But I just wish that I could have put a disclaimer on that saying, 'Don't take this seriously; it's just a movie.'"[10]

By his own admission, Penn's creative juices were now flowing again. But his bank account wasn't. Nevertheless, Penn chose his next project—rather, it chose him—not for money but as a favor, and proved yet again that no good deed goes unpunished.

Dead of Winter began as a script by Marc Shmuger and Mark Malone, two classmates of the Penns' son, Matthew, at Wesleyan University. Not credited as a source is Anthony Gilbert's[11] novel *The Woman in Red,* which was also the source for Joseph Lewis's 1945 film *My Name is Julia Ross.* A classically constructed gothic story (woman alone, boyfriend elsewhere, isolated house, phones cut, blizzard, creepy doctor, crazy servant, easily fooled local cops, blackmail, money, murder, and so on), *Dead of Winter* starts out simply enough. Recounts Penn, "It's about a woman who gets a job to replace an actress in a film, and is slowly made over to look like the actress. But then she discovers that this is not exactly the case.

"I thought the script was not a bad sort of thriller, but I was never familiar with the Joseph Lewis film that it steals from. I got Alan Ladd Jr. [at MGM] to agree, but he said, 'You have to godfather.' I said, 'Look, these guys are bright, out of Wesleyan, they know what they're doing.' And indeed they didn't; Shmuger spoke the most erudite film game you ever heard . . ."[12]

Unfortunately, production in Canada almost immediately slowed to a crawl when the novice filmmakers tried to, in Penn's words, turn *Dead of Winter* into *Citizen Kane.* Facing disaster, Ladd called in his marker and made Penn take over. "When I got to Toronto it was chaos," Penn sighs. "Producer Johnny Bloomgarden was shooting some film on his own; they had enlisted an editor [Rick Shaine] who was doing what the main film was trying to do with Shmuger. It was chaos. The crew and the cast were badly demoralized. So I pushed. But it was never a source of contentment."

The resulting picture, however chaotic in creation, is pure popcorn. "I think you're taking it all so seriously," Roddy McDowall chided at the time.[13] "You're seeing it as laborious. All it is, is, ultimately, a damn good piece of entertainment. I suspect, if it wasn't Arthur, who has this magnificent reputation—everybody goes to see Arthur Penn with the preconceived notion that this film has to be heavy—people would just sit back and enjoy it. If a newcomer made *Dead of Winter* you'd say, 'That's a talented piece of work.' One of the great things about working with him is that he is a masterful filmmaker and a formidable actor's director. He's terrific, and he has the soul of Peter Pan."

For young movie audiences of 1987, who were flocking to see *Dirty Dancing, Lethal Weapon, Three Men and a Baby, Fatal Attraction, Beverly Hills Cop II,* and *Good Morning, Vietnam,* however, *Dead of Winter* seemed out of step and quickly disappeared.

Penn was not deterred. Soon he was back at work on another movie, this time one that would again challenge the very nature of the motion picture medium. It started taking shape in 1987 in the subversive minds of Penn Fraser Jillette and Raymond Joseph Teller, the team professionally known as "Penn & Teller: the bad boys of magic." The duo had just come off a twenty-two-month run of their Off-Broadway illusion show and decided that they would try writing a film. They started meeting with prospective directors and quickly found that they were talking another language.

"The studio kept bringing to us all these whiz-kid directors who had seen us on *Letterman* and *Saturday Night Live*," recalls Teller, who speaks everywhere but in the act. "And they would just be parroting what the studio said about What The Film Should Be." When none of them "got" Penn & Teller's take, their agent suggested they talk to another of his clients, Arthur Penn. (This could get confusing so, from now on, "Penn" will continue to mean Arthur Penn and "Jillette" will mean Penn Jillette).

"They'd been interviewing directors," Penn says. "The three

of us met and started talking, and I realized that they were serious guys, but that the people they had been talking to had been treating them like comedians. So I said, 'Tell me the story,' and it was the story of Penn and Teller getting killed. I said, 'It's operatic.' And Teller said, 'My God, that's it!' That was the beginning."

Unlike those young executives before whom esteemed filmmakers had to recite their résumés, Penn, Jillette, and Teller recognized the absurdity of the situation. "*We had to audition Arthur Penn!*" says Jillette, with no small amount of irony. So they did: "He came in and said, 'I really want to do your movie.' And we said, 'Are you Arthur Penn?' He said, 'Yes.' We said, 'Done.'"

What Teller and both Penns designed was nothing less than a feature-length magic trick that uses the medium of film against itself. Appearing on a TV talk show, Jillette unwisely muses how exciting it would be if somebody were actually trying to kill him. The challenge triggers a series of practical jokes, Grand Guignol illusions, and fake threats, all of which are an effort on the part of Teller and the boys' manager, Carlotta (Caitlin Clarke), to teach Jillette the folly of his arrogance. Their lessons fall by the wayside, however, when a real-life murderous stalker (David Patrick Kelly) emerges, believing that he can rid himself of his obsession with Penn & Teller only if he kills them with a deadly twist on one of their own tricks.

And he does. And they die. End of movie.

It was Penn who suggested how to focus the script to better realize its theme. "He had us add a scene earlier in the picture that said Penn & Teller were compulsive practical jokers," Teller says, "It's something called 'exposition.'" "See," adds Jillette, "we figured everybody already knew about us, but Arthur said that we should add the scene at the airport that shows we play practical jokes." (It turned out to be a classic of timing, execution, and editing.) "Arthur said to us early on that he thinks the film is the first comedy for the assassination generation," says Teller, who wasn't entirely joking. "But he did realize that what we wanted was not what we had on the page when we started."

Filming began on April 19, 1988, in Atlantic City, including the casino and theater of Trump Plaza, and at assorted other locations there and in neighboring Ocean City. Interior sets were built in an abandoned New Jersey meatpacking plant. After eight weeks, the company pulled two days of shooting in New York at JFK Airport and a Forty-second Street studio.

Penn & Teller Get Killed dives into uncharted waters as their succession of practical jokes becomes increasingly dark and their comedy skates on the edge of disaster. When Jillette is actually wounded by a sniper, the tone changes, and the viewer is drawn into a universe where the medium is no longer the message, but the lie.

"I had a concept for it which was to do an absolutely pop movie," Penn said. "You know, Godard's idea of 'film is the truth twenty-four times a second.' And I thought that it's also a lie twenty-four times a second."[14] And that's the point: *Penn & Teller Get Killed* becomes one of the very few American movies to examine whether film is a reliable medium, even of telling its own truth. Even the magic is fake. Not special-effect fake, but fake-fake.

"We didn't do any magic in the movie for that reason," Jillette says. "You can't compete with the real magic that's going on, like being able to change from one scene to another. We were trying to avoid it altogether, but Arthur [said] he wanted people to see what we did for a living. So we created a bit that is, indeed, impossible: the drill table [in which Teller is impaled]. To take the curse off it, we said we would never knowingly expose a trick, and then we did, but, of course, the trick we expose could never work, though it looks like it kinda would work. But look at the movie and go out and try to build it."

Adds Teller, "Arthur says that making a movie is making a deal with the devil: when you get something, you always have to pay for it."

For a director who started his career telling the great comics how to relax and be funny on TV and then directed Mike Nichols and Elaine May and then *Sly Fox*, it is noteworthy that *Penn & Teller Get Killed* is Arthur Penn's only screen comedy. Even then, it is funny only in counterpoint to its seriousness.

Proving (or perhaps because of) the studio's lack of faith in it, the film was given only limited release in late 1989, and despite enjoying a cadre of fervent fans, it remains that kind of anomaly that Hollywood just can't abide: an exception that challenges the rules and therefore must be crushed.

It is also Arthur Penn's last theatrical film. It's almost as though, by exposing what the medium had become, the man who tried to keep it on a certain moral and intellectual plane would no longer be allowed to make films. But then television called, and he was ready to go home again.

23

Back to Basics

Like the proverbial bad penny, television reenters Arthur Penn's life at the strangest times. In July 1967, with his salary from *Bonnie and Clyde* spent and the film facing a profitless studio write-off, he was so strapped for cash that he took on a project that reminded him how far the once-mighty medium had fallen.

NBC paid playwright William Hanley $112,500 for *Flesh and Blood* and determined that it would be one of the first TV movies to be shot on video. The story of a troubled family living in an abandoned apartment building, it starred Edmond O'Brien, Kim Stanley, Suzanne Pleshette, E. G. Marshall, Kim Darby, and Robert Duvall. Penn agreed to direct it and asked for Stanley, not knowing that the actress was in crisis.[1] Both she and O'Brien were drinkers, and at one point during rehearsals Stanley went off on a binge that threatened the whole production. Colleen Dewhurst was hired as a standby.

Recalls Penn, "There was sober and drunk, and with drunk came a paranoia, the feeling between Eddie and Kim of terror, of people coming to get them, of the FBI. It was just ghastly. Whether they infected each other with the paranoia, I don't know. Certainly Kim was worse than Eddie at that point. It was about as agonizing as anything I've ever done in my life."

Penn coaxed a performance out of the actress, the show was taped, and it aired unhappily on January 26, 1968. By that time, *Bonnie and Clyde* had taken off, and Penn didn't have to look back. Not for another twenty-five years would he seriously entertain another TV offer, and when he did, it turned out to be another shotgun marriage.

The Portrait, adapted by Lynn Roth from Tina Howe's 1982 play *Painting Churches,* dramatizes how Margaret "Mags" Church reconciles with her aging parents, the headstrong Fanny and Gardner Church (Lauren Bacall and Gregory Peck), as they begrudgingly sit for her to finish a long-neglected painting of the two of them. At the same time, they are downsizing their home in advance of Gardner's retirement from academia (he is a poet); Mags has broken up with yet another beau; her parents insist on denigrating her choices while pretending to encourage her; and Gardner may be in the first stages of dementia.

The film held importance to Peck, who arguably committed to the project to benefit his then thirty-four-year-old daughter, Cecilia, whom he cast as Mags.[2] He also served as executive producer. "He wanted her to be an actress," Penn observes. "She didn't really want to be, I think. I stayed as superficial as I could and just tried to give her physical liberty and get her to be physically different from Greg's age group. He didn't fight me on that, but he would be sitting there in the scene with her, registering his disapproval, which, of course, she was enormously sensitive to."

Over the course of rewrites and preproduction in 1991 and early 1992, Penn and Peck adjusted the script. Peck, in particular, made handwritten notations of line readings not only to his own dialogue but to Cecilia's. After a week's rehearsal in New York in spring 1992, the four-week shoot commenced in North Carolina with Duke University serving as Harvard, Lake Crabtree as the Charles River, and the lush Durham area doubling for Cambridge, Massachusetts' historic Brattle Street. Production went smoothly, although it was obvious that there were personal agendas. Playing Peck's wife, Lauren Bacall ("Betty" to her friends) kept her distance, and the director noticed. "I knew Betty for a long time around New York," Penn says. "She was very close with Greg Peck. They were very dear. But she's a realist, and she could see what I could do with that daughter and what I couldn't do. Every once in a while she'd give me one of those [*he rolls his eyes*]."

The Portrait addresses matters seldom explored in public, namely, that parents are not perfect, plus the fact that two people in their seventies have a sex life.

Once again Penn was excluded from the editing process by the network, TNT, although he was sent various cuts to screen on tape. He commented, sometimes sharply, via fax to Peck, whom he asked to use his prestige to intercede. "They will damage the film," the director wrote in a memo, "and I don't want to be a part of that. Please use all your skills. You are the most persuasive person I have met in a long time and I am delight [*sic*] you are 'taking' this meeting."[3]

The notes were eerily reminiscent of those Penn had received from Warner Bros. for *The Left Handed Gun:* more close-ups. "Close-ups *per se* are meaningless unless they punctuate a moment of drama," Penn held. "Otherwise they cause undue emphasis on wrong matters." He then added, passionately, "Here I want to interject an opinion that I believe we need to bear in mind. I don't accept the contention about close-ups. The fortunes of TNT were made by the acquisition of motion picture libraries, a medium where the art and skill of filming and editing were raised to a very high level. No constant use of CU's there. My God, in 1953 in live TV we were already desperately trying to get away from 'talking heads.'"[4]

In Los Angeles during editing, Peck supervised the ADR (looping) sessions, adjusting Cecilia's performance. Not until the final sound mix was Penn called in, and when he saw how badly the climax had been edited, he took charge. The ending hangs on whether Gardner and Fanny will attend Mags's gallery opening. The scene is the emotional payoff of the film, but it had been assembled in Penn's absence in a way that was merely functional instead of dramatic. "I knew Greg was anxious about it," Penn says, "but he didn't articulate it. I remember looking around the room, wondering, 'Is *this* what you all wanted?' Greg was sitting next to me going, 'What?' I said, 'That's not the scene.' He said, 'What do you mean?' I tried to explain it and I couldn't, so I said, 'Give me a cutting room.' I don't think he'd ever seen a director get in there and change the meaning of the scene," Penn says of Peck. "Which I did. But I knew the scene and the editor clearly didn't."

The filmmaker brought it to life by the use of subjective sound to turn the Churches' arrival into a mystical event: room tone drops out, conversation fades, and Mags becomes aware of their presence by feeling, not by sight. The film ends in a group hug, and the credits roll.

Years later Penn closes the book on *The Portrait* by deeming the experience "the absolute personification of Hollywood: powerful and dumb. It's like I never made that picture."

Inside (1996) was quite a different experience and remains so for all who were lucky enough to be involved. How ironic that it should have been a pleasure to make, given the tragic seriousness of its subjects: apartheid, murder, informing, and revenge. The project reunited Penn with producer Hillard Elkins and actor Louis Gossett Jr., whose career had advanced from *Golden Boy* to *Roots* (1977), for which he won the Emmy, and *An Officer and a Gentleman* (1982), which brought him the Oscar. Partnered with Elkins, Gossett developed a script by Bima Stagg about a white South African journalist (Eric Stoltz) who dies under torture in a South African prison in 1988. After the repeal of apartheid in 1993, the colonel (Nigel Hawthorne) who was in charge of the interrogation is himself investigated by a black questioner (Gossett), and the tables are turned. Rather than become a formulaic story about racial revenge, however, the piece shifts back and forth in time, cleverly feeding the viewers bits of information and keeping them not only wondering whether the questioner will nail the colonel, but also whether the journalist was, in fact, guilty of the radical activity for which he was jailed. The contrast in empowerment between Gossett and Hawthorne in the present, and Hawthorne and Stoltz in the past, adds resonance, particularly when it emerges that Hawthorne arrogantly feels he will never have to face the consequences of his deeds.

Elkins set up *Inside* at Showtime, which had just initiated a series of $2 million films designed to increase its prestige. With Gossett's concurrence, he asked Penn to helm it. Together they brought Stoltz and Hawthorne aboard. Showtime's then production chief, Jerry Offsay, beams at having been able to get Penn. "I had the luxury of being the person who could hire people who weren't the flavor of the month," the likable Offsay says, "and I had that charmed and privileged job where I got to work with people whose work I had seen twenty, thirty, forty years before and admired, and I didn't think they had gotten stupider over those twenty, thirty, or forty years. Getting Arthur to do a movie was a big deal. In those days everybody was nervous about working with us. We didn't have that much money, and I made no secret about the fact, so it was worth almost anything to get in the Arthur Penn business; that was a stamp of approval that maybe [Showtime] wasn't just schlock purveyors."

"It was a good script," Penn says, then corrects himself: "I mean, it was a good *idea*. Bima was of the Left movement but was not really a dramatist. He could write a lot, but he couldn't write quintessentially. I was pressing on that script right up to the day we started shooting. The night before, he gave me what he thought of as the last draft. I remember sitting with Nigel, Eric, and Lou Gossett, and we just took out dialogue, knowing that these people were so eloquent as actors that they could fill that moment."

The network still worried whether a seventy-three-year-old director could hold to a four-week schedule. "It was a funny experience," chuckles Penn. "They were concerned about whether I could still shoot a film. We got to South Africa and we got the cast together, got all the prep work done, and there was [a woman from Showtime] on the set—sharp, pretty, but tough, obviously. I had rehearsed with Eric and Nigel, and I had a wonderful cameraman, my great friend from Denmark, Jan Weincke, and we nailed twenty pages in one day. She just couldn't believe it, and she disappeared. It was that opening scene between Nigel and Eric. I'd already staged it and laid out the camera spots, and nailed it. So we were ahead by two days the first day!"

The scene crackled not only because of preparation but also because the casting dynamics couldn't have been better. "Eric and Nigel got along famously," Penn reports. "It was Eric saying, 'Wait a minute, wait a minute, I'm number one on the call sheet,' and Nigel saying, 'Eric, my dear boy, take the little bottle out of your mouth.' They loved each other, they really did. They had a deep devotion."

Stoltz agrees. "In no time we were having a little competition as to whom Arthur liked better, who was the more *important* actor, that sort of thing. We were so relaxed that we started clowning with each other, and started a friendship which made the work process a delight. The entire process was a joy from start to finish, and it was entirely due to the tone Arthur set."

Stoltz kept a journal that records Penn's process, including the interrogation scene that jumped the company two days ahead: "On the first day of rehearsals, we sat around a table and easily read through the script, asking a few questions, but 'no acting.' Arthur is very complimentary, 'that's terrific fellas, really nice . . . ' Then we broke for lunch, ate together, and got to know each other a little bit. It was like being at a nice dinner party with very smart and interesting people. Who also dressed well."[5]

After lunch Penn toured the sets with the actors, then returned to the table for another read-through. Almost immediately he told them, "Okay, fellas, let's take it off the page." "By this," Stoltz explained, "he meant for us to look at the page when we needed to, but mainly to get the feel of the lines and look at each other, to connect with each other. 'If a line's not perfect,' Arthur said, 'so what. Nice and easy, but don't worry about lines.'" When the read was finished, Penn dismissed the cast, cautioning them, "Now *don't work on it at home*. Just let it breathe."

Over the next few days, as rehearsals continued, differences in acting method emerged between the American Stoltz (playing British) and the British Hawthorne (playing Afrikaans). "Nigel wanted to know exactly which piece of paper he'd pick up and from where, and what it meant to him," Stoltz wrote. "As I was the prisoner, I simply had to stand still and respond, which was not as easy as it sounds. As we ran through the scenes, Arthur walked around us, almost as if he were in the scene himself, and found how to shoot it, letting the actors and the content determine where the camera should go. This got us used to having a third presence (in this case Arthur, soon the camera) as we work. After each run-through he would say, 'very nice, very nice, kid' to me, and, 'very nice, very nice' to Nigel, like a calm, non-judgmental presence. He was like a conductor, trying different crescendos and tempos. We'd run through each scene two or three times completely. Arthur to me: 'keep with the disdain, the snooty British stuff. That works well.' It's always what 'works well,' or 'perhaps this might be worth trying.' Never a negative word is spoken. Never 'pick up the pace'; always 'dig into him more.'"

In addition to being both an actor and a producer, Louis Gossett Jr. found that he had a third, even more visible role during the shoot: international celebrity. "I had been offered other things to do in South Africa, but I decided not to go until Mandela was free and they started to deal with apartheid," Gossett explained. In 1993 apartheid was dismantled, and in 1995 the Truth and Reconciliation Commission was established to integrate the country. In that year, *Inside* rolled. Continues Gossett, "So I said, okay, I'll come. This was probably one of the first films produced in free South Africa."[6]

Gossett was fêted wherever he went, and it affected his professional duties. "He was up nights, a lot of parties," Penn reports gently. "He was visiting Mandela and was politically very involved with South Africa, but he wasn't paying attention to his acting as well as he could have—until I got him on the set. When he realized that he was playing with two heavyweights, you could feel him get up on his toes: 'Holy shit! This is where I'm playing, this is big leagues.'"

As the questioner, Gossett personifies not only the backstory of his character as a black South African but his own history, as only someone who starred in *Roots* can bring to the role. "I play this character that's in prison at the beginning, and we're all terrorized in there, including Eric Stoltz, the Caucasian sympathizer," he related. "And then fade out, fade in. Mandela comes out, I now become in charge of the prison, and I want to charge the man who did all that terror, the killing of all those prisoners [Hawthorne]. We have our little discussion—he thinks he's going to be free—but he gets charged. It's a nice psychological drama."[7]

Inside is made even more compelling by Penn's full use of the medium. Most startling is his use of sound. When Marty Strydom (Stoltz) is first incarcerated, he is left alone in his cell with only his imagination to decipher the noises he hears around him: beatings, screams, moans, and the pervasive din of prison life; the viewer shares not only his cell but also his fears. "I loved that," Penn beams conspiratorially. "That aspect attracted me a great deal. There's some shots where the prisoners were singing, and we dollied back down the empty hallway and we panned from one closed steel door to another, and the song goes on. There are things in it where I really felt, 'This is good filmmaking.'"

Having seen America's civil rights struggle firsthand, Peggy and Arthur Penn could note the differences between American and South African race relations once restrictions were supposedly lifted. "By the time we were there, Nelson Mandela was out of prison," he says. "It was right before the Truth and Reconciliation Commission was formed [1995] and, with Lou Gossett, who was sort of a hero, we were able to travel. We had a full Zulu crew. We had no difficulty. The whites were, themselves, liberal whites, mostly movie people, so we didn't encounter hostility. It was still there; everybody had a tale. Peggy is a considerable student of the Truth and Reconciliation Commission, and she was amazed at the human progress of people who would ordinarily conceive of themselves as victims requiring justice and instead are able to forgive and accept apology. It's really quite remarkable."

Coming after the tensions of *The Portrait*, *Inside* restored Penn's directorial confidence, and he enjoyed the camaraderie of professionals. "We became such good friends, Nigel and his partner, Trevor Bentham. We saw each other again in New York, and then I got word that he was mortally ill.[8] I called them in England and couldn't get through. Terrible."

Hawthorne's performance as the guilty colonel is at once imperious and disingenuous, shrewd and naive, arrogant and even vulnerable—a remarkable palette that kept his costars on their toes. Gossett matches him step-by-step, allowing his questioner first to be angered by this cagey animal, then become increasingly measured as he gets wise to his tricks, finally pouncing in a way that is not revenge but justice. It's a lesson not only in the banality of evil but in the skill of a fine actor.

Penn and Elkins delivered *Inside* to Showtime for network notes, "which he told us in advance he wasn't going to take and wasn't going to listen to," remembers Jerry Offsay, adding, "and then he begrudgingly said, 'You know, you might have a crumb or two of a right idea' and made some small changes in it." The changes chiefly concerned clarifying a plot point about a prisoner whom Stoltz hears being tortured but who may be faking it as a spy for the apartheid regime.

While shooting *Inside* in Johannesburg in 1995, Penn took part in one of the most unusual commemoratives in film history—in fact, one that celebrated the very beginning of film itself a hundred years earlier. He and thirty-nine other world-class directors were invited by a consortium of French companies to make short silent films using one of the original Cinematographe cameras built by Auguste and Louis Lumière in 1895.

"It was shot at the same time I was getting *Inside* ready, and I had a day where I wasn't shooting," Penn says, "so we set this up on the grass outside the studio and shot it. We were asked to confine ourselves to exactly the same circumstances," Penn explains, "the length of time, the mobility of the camera, it naturally had no reflex viewing—you looked through it and put a cap on it and cranked—and it was 'Do whatever you want.'" Like the Lumière brothers, the filmmakers had to use seventeen-meter (fifty-two-second) 35mm loads, no sound, and no more than three takes.

"I told my wife and she urged me to do it," he later recalled. "She asked what I would choose as a subject. I pondered that, and then I told her of a vision I had of a pregnant woman lying on an elevated table, while beneath her on a lower shelf a figure swathed in white gauze sat up as liquid dripped from the figure above onto him. The single shot would begin on the swathed figure and moved up to the woman's pregnancy and then to her face, and she would regard the lens and turn away. My wife said, 'What is going on in your head? Where did that come from?' I had no answer."[9]

Speaking in the documentary that was made about it (*Lumière and Company*), Penn responds to the off-camera interviewer: "Why do I make films? Well, for two reasons. One: I can't help it. That's the kind of work I like to do most in the world. And second of all, I feel I have to do something like that. I don't know whether it will be film or cinema or video or theater, but something. And is cinema mortal? I think if we're mortal, cinema will be mortal. If we live—if the human race lives—then cinema will live. I'm not so sure about either one."

"The crew arrived and set up," Penn said. "The camera, made beautifully of wood, had a handle and a lens. It weighed twelve pounds. We tried several rehearsals. The camera back was open so I could see the figure through the lens. The body of the camera was filled with drive gears and a shutter; it was a camera and a projector as well. Then the film went in, the back was closed, and the operator cranked as we took three takes. That was our limit as this was a special film coated with the same emulsion as was used by the Lumières. When it was developed, there was a movie. As I touched that camera, I sensed a palpable connection to the magic of motion pictures. It was a moment of reverential emotion. Here was the instance of our film lives carrying back to the time of creation."[10]

After *Inside*, Penn became more involved with the Actors Studio until late 2000 when Edwin Sherrin—at the insistence of TV producer Dick Wolf—offered him the post of executive producer on Wolf's flagship TV series *Law & Order*. Sherrin had been running the show for nearly a decade and was eager to branch out. The two men had met during *Monday After the Miracle*. Sherrin is married to actress Jane Alexander, who starred as Anne Sullivan, and whom he had directed to acclaim in *The Great White Hope* on Broadway in 1968. Taking over *Law & Order* as executive producer in 1993, he polished it into a marvel of mass production. Each episode takes eight sixteen-hour days to shoot, and the company works five-day weeks. There is no time to experiment or deviate from the formula.

Penn's tenure as show runner did not go well, as Sherrin had suspected. "I thought that Arthur's experience as a feature filmmaker, and his very thorough demand for aesthetic freedom and kind of piercing through to what he considered to be the truth of an event, would not lend itself to the production of television episodics," he ventures. "I thought it was great that Arthur wanted to do it, and I think that the company was very excited by it, but I think it was not a good marriage."

Penn painfully agrees. "Ed painted rather a glorious picture of the job—you know, you shoot the show, it goes out to California, they do a rough edit, send it back, and you do the finished edit. [It was] nothing like that. Nothing. First of all, the show is written out there under their supervision, which is really not their supervision, it's the head writer. And in this case they had a head writer who managed to alienate all the other six or eight writers, who were all ready to quit, and the scripts kept getting worse and worse. I would then send them out to be edited, and they came back, 'That's not *Law & Order.* We have our way.' And they do. They have their way.

"I was out of my depth," he concedes. "There is a way of thinking about television when you're in television that's different from the way you think when you're doing a play. I remembered television as a naive 'Let's-do-this-and-we'll-put-this-together' medium where there was improvisation going on all the time. I was the wrongest person in the world to do it because of my reliance on improvisation."

After thirteen episodes, Penn and Wolf agreed to abrogate their deal, and the director left. In the meantime, Sherrin had the idea to bring in Penn's son, Matthew, who eventually took over as show runner until he, like Sherrin, sought other opportunities. Matt Penn has become one of TV's most skilled directors.

In late 2001, Penn directed an episode of the ensemble courtroom series *100 Centre Street* titled "The Fix." It was his last screen credit, and it made him, at seventy-nine, one of the oldest working DGA members. "The reason I did it," he says, "was that I wanted to experience the digital multiple camera aspect that resembled live TV." In planning some of the shoot, executive producer Sidney Lumet conspired happily with his old colleague to re-create the days when they were calling shows on live

TV. "Sidney knew what I wanted, which was to see how close we could get back to our old control room. They had a little multiple-camera control room setup, and I watched the scenes, came out, did what had to be done, went back, and did a take."

Recent years saw Penn entering that phase of an artist's career in which he is honored not only for his work but also for surviving long enough to celebrate it. Beginning in the mid-1990s, he received awards and retrospectives from Berlin, Edinburgh, Harvard University, Savannah, the Los Angeles Film Critics Association, New York's Anthropology Film Archives, and the Berkshire International Film Festival, among a mounting number of other recognitions. Although a directing Oscar eluded him despite three nominations, the New York division of the Academy of Motion Picture Arts & Sciences belatedly fêted him in 2005.[11]

The 2006 career achievement award from the Directors Guild of America was the occasion for Penn to reflect, before his peers, "Mine has been a checkered career. Movies and theater, back and forth, a dozen Broadway plays and fifteen feature films. But I must confess an unfulfilled ambition: I wish I had been bolder. Too often I censored myself. That's a terrible thing. It's the very obverse of creating. To you on the edge of your careers as filmmakers, don't hold back. Let us see your human secret. It's your gold: share it."[12]

Penn modestly underestimated his achievements. He spent his life and career avoiding mediocrity, yet saw it prevail in a world where innovation threatens the status quo. Such is the risk of being visionary.

Never one to wallow in the past, Penn was forced, by the conversations for this book, to do just that. As was earlier stated, both he the author are uneasy analyzing films too closely. Too many things come about as much by accident as by intent, and while a director is responsible for what *stays,* anyone familiar with the controlled chaos of filmmaking knows it's hard to control what *goes* in.

Critics have endlessly observed, for example, that Penn's films are about outsiders. But that's facile; all drama is about outsiders, whether physically, emotionally, or morally. A character doesn't have to be a fish in order to find himself out of water. Drama follows Newton's First Law: an object in motion remains in motion unless an external force is applied to it. Conflict is the external, disengaging force, and drama is the result. Besides, Penn's films are only a third of his career, even if they are the most visible.

"The interesting thing," he mused, "is that I can't detect the similarity in the films until they're done and well behind me. Each time I think I'm doing an absolutely brand-new film. It's only with hindsight of fifteen years or so that I detect that there are very simple, clear lines between the films. I don't think of them as films about alienation. I think of them as yarns."[13]

Arthur Penn's career defines the role of the artist in society. At various times he was a television director dabbling in movies, a stage director returning to television, a filmmaker seeking Broadway in order to escape Hollywood, and a teacher removing himself entirely from the workplace to pass along knowledge of all three.

Penn's gift was that he was a collaborator and not a dictator, and an auteurist but not a solipsist, something that baffles the ideologues but nurtures all who had the privilege of working with him. An "Arthur Penn film" is not one man's vision but the result of inspiring everyone to do his and her best.

"Arthur in a very real way changed American film," praises his longtime friend, screenwriter Walter Bernstein. "He tied into the zeitgeist of the sixties and was always looking for an edge. He has guts. The combination of violence and compassion is the example of an Arthur Penn film. I think he was extremely influential to European filmmakers."

In 1970 Penn spoke at the American Film Institute in Los Angeles. *Bonnie and Clyde* and *Alice's Restaurant* had made his reputation; *Little Big Man* was poised for release and would burnish it. Ahead lay *Night Moves, Sly Fox,* and his stewardship of the Actors Studio. That day at the AFI he was at the height of his Hollywood clout, yet had no hesitation criticizing the studio dinosaur and challenging the young filmmakers who, he feared, yearned to ride it. "I would counsel you to resist that as hard as you can," he cautioned. "Explore the ways around filmmaking that don't involve the majors, particularly at a time of massive change in filmmaking. It clearly lies with you and those of my generation that have the guts—and I don't necessarily align myself with them—to bust it open. I think there will be a significant change six months from now. Keep your eyes and ears open to those winds of change. I think they're more important than those that are entrenched in the real estate out here."[14]

They gave him warm applause. But over the next thirty years, these same upstarts would redefine the studio system into a factory that manufactured a brand of movie that couldn't be farther away from the contemplative films that Penn and his peers struggled to make.

But that's the stuff of hindsight. The accidental life of Arthur Penn is an event lived in time-present: seizing opportunities, creating others, considering many more, yet viewing each through the lens of the human experience.

"Nobody is prepared for success," he once confessed. "It happens overnight. And when it does, you're suddenly living in a manner, not only to which you're not accustomed, but which you don't deserve. I don't mean to be moralistic or socialistic about it. We lean over backward to live as simply as possible, given the situation we're in. I mean, I don't want to knock it, but it gets to be unwieldy."[15]

Wrap

They say that the artist himself is least able to judge his own work, but that rejects the very nature of the creative process. An artist deconstructs before he constructs, and often destroys in order to discover. On May 20, 1968, Arthur Penn delivered these remarks at a symposium at Dartmouth College. Both reflective and prescient, they offer remarkable insight, not only regarding Penn himself but also the self-examination he clearly performed while writing them.

I am an outsider to American film. I never envisioned myself as being a film person. I went to film very seldom as a child. I experienced a terrifying horror movie at about age six; I don't remember where it was. I always thought of the theater as being my métier and it was only somewhat by accident that I found myself making film, because along came live television and I had a brief experience with that. And then was invited to make a film at Warner Bros., and I made one, and I was bewildered by what I encountered. And that's what I am here to describe, because those things that bewildered me in film-world continue to bewilder me, and continue, in a certain sense—at least in my sense—to describe the character of American film.

For instance, I was very startled that the people in Hollywood referred to motion pictures as "an industry" and to the films themselves as "product." That came as a staggering insight to me, and I wondered about that. I've since read about it, and there's no mystery to it: there's a long history of nepotism and to the growth of a new industry out there, and, in the course of the growth of an industry whose technology is as complex as that of motion pictures, there began to be established certain technical norms which were, in terms of light and film and sound, as being of the highest level, and that began to be the glossy Hollywood product. That had a twofold purpose. One was to improve the technique of the material. But the other was to find a place for the nephews and son-in-laws so that they wouldn't disturb the process if the process was meticulously as evolved as that.

Oddly enough, roles were cut out that didn't particularly involve the personality of the person filling that role. By that I mean that they used to talk about "Send me a writer." I recall hearing the story from Clifford Odets that during one of the temporary crises on a movie set, the word went out, "Send me a writer" and a young man arrived, and the producer said, "How much do you make?" and the young man said, "seventeen fifty" and the producer shouted, "I told 'em to send me a writer," meaning that if he didn't make thirty-five hundred a week, he wasn't a writer.

You could get a director who was hired under long-term contract to make films; that was his job. You could get stars who were beautiful machines that you could wind up and they would say the lines and they all belonged to the studio. It was a highly familial, but clearly structured, organization.

That was the Hollywood that prevailed up to the incursion of television. Television invaded the domain that Hollywood had occupied with great privilege and no competition, and it terrified them. At the same time, in the period shortly after the Second World War, film of an extraordinary character was beginning to be made in Europe, and it was starting to be imported into the United States. A small part of the American consciousness was beginning to be touched by those films, and the major flow of the Hollywood film was beginning to be severely interrupted, if not diverted, by the development of television.

What happened, of course, is that Hollywood retracted. Instead of trying to make a new kind of film, it just reduced the number of the same kind of films it had been making all along. It wasn't until the Hollywood film as film was suddenly overwhelmed by European film that it came to the point where it is now, and that is a kind of crossroad where a highly industrialized, highly technical film industry is confronted with the alternatives of continuing as it has in the past, making films for television, or returning to a kind of pre–Industrial Revolution condition, which is a kind of craft guild in which each man is permitted to make his own film.

That dilemma confronts the studios constantly, and it confronts the American filmmaker constantly. Because the American film is the only film which is not, at least in part, subsidized. Every other film of every other nation in the world is subsidized in part or in whole by some part of the national culture. That is not true in this country of a medium which is profoundly expensive. Shockingly expensive. So experimentation and freedom are not as readily available to the American filmmaker as might be available in other countries. The dilemma which confronts us at this moment is whether American motion picture companies are willing to subsidize a kind of anarchy which unseats the familiar power structure.

The norms I spoke about before have, in a certain sense, depersonalized American film to the degree that it has removed that look which we now associate with the European look: that is, the characteristic odd, bizarre cutting of the Godard film; the kind of lengthy, deeply personal, introspective film of Antonioni; the flamboyant brilliance of a Fellini film. These things were not possible within the existing Hollywood norm. And I don't mean only a technological norm, but the concept of "norm" as a state of mind.

It was to that that I found myself placed in opposition from the first day I walked on a movie set to make a film, and it is that norm that has continued to haunt us to this very hour in American filmmaking. In that sense, even the French directors find themselves beginning to cry out against the spirit of experimentation in American film and the intrusion of American filmmaking on the filmmaking of other countries. Chains of [European] distribution have now been bought, in part or in total, by American film industries, and that is beginning to be felt by Godard or Truffaut, and the cries of pain are getting to be more and more audible. Before this, they couldn't understand why we just couldn't go out and make what we wanted to make; they had no comprehension of our concept that a film had to be committed to paper and that paper had to be filtered through a series of descending intelligences until, finally, we arrived at a point where somebody would write a check, in a very sizeable amount, for a film which his daughter or son would want to see, and if the son or daughter took after the father, so much the better.

What we found ourselves doing was designing films for an audience that was predetermined, that had had a backlash upon the film industry, and structured clichés and visual concepts which were so interchangeable as to remove the personal from decisions. A director could be changed in the course of a film. A cameraman could be changed in the course of a film. Even an actor could be changed and very little difference would be made.

Now we are at a different crossroad and a different kind of film will emerge, but I think that crossroad is a crossroad of our culture as a nation and part of the world. A confrontation of whether or not we will be mobilized into a kind of impersonal unity, or allow ourselves the privilege of disparate and individual choices, is a profound one in all forms of art but, most peculiarly, that form of art which is the motion picture, because it involves ever so many people and so expensive a medium.

How good is my next picture going to be? Yes, I get that from the critics a lot. "Well, it wasn't as good as his last picture." That's relatively easy to comfort yourself with. Cole Porter said every show he wrote after his first show, they always panned it, and then, the next show he would write, they would write, "Well, it certainly wasn't as good as his last show." And that's the way he went through life, writing one great song after another but always getting panned for his show not being as good as the last show.

I'm not saying that one doesn't have good films, less good films, and some lousy films. But you don't have a thousand percentage hitters in baseball, either. That's how the game is played. Nobody bats a thousand.

Arthur Penn Credits

Films

Note: Penn's films are generally available on DVD or VOD with the exception, at this writing, of *Visions of Eight*.

The Left Handed Gun (1957). Teleplay: Gore Vidal; script: Leslie Stevens.

The Miracle Worker (1962). Writer: William Gibson.

The Train (1964) (uncredited; scenes only). Book: Rose Valland; screen story and screenplay: Franklin Coen and Frank Davis; Nedrick Young and Howard Dimsdale; Walter Bernstein (uncredited).

Mickey One (1965). Writer: Alan Surgal.

The Chase (1966). Play: Horton Foote; script: Lillian Hellman, Michael Wilson, Ivan Moffat, Horton Foote.

Bonnie and Clyde (1967). Writers: Robert Benton and David Newman; Robert Towne (uncredited).

Alice's Restaurant (1969). Song: Arlo Guthrie; script: Venable Herndon and Arthur Penn.

Little Big Man (1970). Book: Thomas Berger; script: Calder Willingham.

Visions of Eight (1973). Documentary. Sequence: "The Highest."

Night Moves (1975). Writer: Alan Sharp.

The Missouri Breaks (1976). Writer: Thomas McGuane; Robert Towne (uncredited).

Four Friends (1981). Writer: Steve Tesich.

Target (1985). Story: Leonard Stern; script: Don Petersen and Howard Berk.

Dead of Winter (1987). Book: Anthony Gilbert (Lucy Beatrice Malleson; uncredited); script: Mark Shmuger and Mark Malone.

Penn & Teller Get Killed (1989). Writers: Penn Jillette and Teller (né Raymond Joseph Teller).

Lumière and Company (1995). Documentary.

Television

Note: Television credits are still in the process of rediscovery as kinescopes and paperwork resurface. Gratitude is expressed to the Paley Center (formerly the Museum of Television and Radio), www.producersshowcase.org, and www.filmsaroundtheworld.com for important access.

1952

Colgate Comedy Hour (National Broadcasting Company), April 27 (debut). Penn served as floor director (multiple episodes).

1953

Desert Cafe (Gulf/First Person Playhouse), July 3. Writer: Robert Alan Aurthur.

The Death of the Old Man (Gulf/First Person Playhouse), July 17. Writer: Horton Foote.

The Comeback (Gulf/First Person Playhouse), July 24. Writer: David Shaw.

One Night Stand (Gulf/First Person Playhouse), July 31. Writer: Robert Alan Aurthur.

Tears of My Sister (Gulf/First Person Playhouse), August 14. Writer: Horton Foote.

Crip (Gulf/First Person Playhouse), August 21. Writer: Stewart Stern.

A Prophet in His Land (Gulf/First Person Playhouse), September 4. Writer: Doug Johnson.

A Gift from Cotton Mather (Gulf/First Person Playhouse), September 11. Writer: Paddy Chayefsky.

The Happy Rest (Goodyear Playhouse), October 4. Writer: N. Richard Nash.

John Turner Davis (Philco/Goodyear Playhouse), November 15. Writer: Horton Foote.

The Strong Women (Philco/Goodyear Playhouse), November 29. Writer: Paddy Chayefsky.

The Glorification of Al Toolum (Philco/Goodyear Playhouse), December 27. Writer: David Shaw.

1954

Buy Me Blue Ribbons (Goodyear Playhouse), February 28. Writer: Sumner Locke Elliott.

The Broken Fist (Philco/Goodyear Playhouse), March 27. Writer: David Shaw.

The King and Mrs. Candle (Philco/Goodyear Playhouse), April 18. Writer: Sumner Locke Elliott.

The Joker (Philco/Goodyear Playhouse), May 2. Writer: N. Richard Nash.

The Lawn Party (Goodyear Playhouse), May 23. Writer: Tad Mosel.

Adapt or Die (Philco/Goodyear Playhouse), June 13. Writer: Harry Miles Muheim.

Man on the Hunt (Justice), August 19. Writer: George Bellak.

Star in the Summer Night (Goodyear Playhouse), August 22. Writer: Tad Mosel.

Man on the Mountaintop (Philco/Goodyear Playhouse), October 17. Writer: Robert Alan Aurthur.

State of the Union (Producers Showcase), November 15. Writers: Howard Lindsay and Russel Crouse.

Beg, Borrow or Steal (Philco/Goodyear Playhouse), November 28. Writer: Jay Presson Allen.

Catch My Boy on Sunday (Philco/Goodyear Playhouse), December 12. Writer: Paddy Chayefsky.

1955

The Assassin (Philco/Goodyear Playhouse), February 20. Writer: Bernard Woolfe.

My Lost Saints (Philco/Goodyear Playhouse), March 13. Writer: Tad Mosel.

The King and Mrs. Candle (Producers Showcase), April 22 (musical adaptation). Writer: Sumner Locke Elliott.

The Pardon-Me Boy (Philco/Goodyear Playhouse), May 15. Writer: J P Miller.

The Miss America Story (Philco/Goodyear Playhouse), September 4. Coverage of the Miss America Pageant.

The Battler (Playwrights '56), October 18. Story: Ernest Hemingway; script: A. E. Hotchner and Sidney Carroll.

The Heart's a Forgotten Hotel (Playwrights '56), October 25. Writer: Arnold Schulman.

Daisy! Daisy! (Playwrights '56), November 22. Writer: Sumner Locke Elliott.

The Waiting Place (Playwrights '56), December 20. Writer: Tad Mosel.

1956

Lost (Playwrights '56), January 17. Story: Burton Roueche; script: Arnold Schulman.

Return to Casino (Playwrights '56), February 14. Writer: Mann Rubin.

Adam and Evening (Playwrights '56), March 13. Writer: Arnold Schulman.

The Undiscovered Country (Playwrights '56), March 27. Writer: J P Miller.

Nick and Letty (Playwrights '56), June 5. Book: Lonnie Colman; script: Nelson Gidding.

Missouri Legend (Goodyear Playhouse), October 7. Writer: Ernest Kinoy.

1957

The Miracle Worker (Playhouse 90), February 7. Writer: William Gibson.

Invitation to a Gunfighter (Playhouse 90), March 7. Story: Larry Klein and Hal Goodman; script: Leslie Stevens.

Charley's Aunt (Playhouse 90), March 28. Play: Brandon Thomas; script: Leslie Stevens.

The Dark Side of the Earth (Playhouse 90), September 19. Writer: Rod Serling.

1958

Portrait of a Murderer (Playhouse 90), February 27. Writer: Leslie Stevens.

1968

Flesh and Blood (National Broadcasting Company), January 26. Writer: William Hanley.

1993

The Portrait (Turner Network Television), February 13. Writer: Lynn Roth; play: Tina Howe.

1996

Inside (Showtime), August 25. Writer: Bima Stagg.

2001

"The Fix" (*100 Centre Street*; A&E), November 5. Writer: David Black.

Plays (Broadway/Off-Broadway only)

The Lovers (1956) (consultant). Writer: Leslie Stevens.

Two for the Seesaw (1957). Writer: William Gibson.

The Miracle Worker (1959). Writer: William Gibson.

Toys in the Attic (1960). Writer: Lillian Hellman.

An Evening with Mike Nichols and Elaine May (1960). Writers: Mike Nichols and Elaine May.

All the Way Home (1960). Book: James Agee; script: Tad Mosel.

In the Counting House (1962). Writer: Leslie Weiner.

Lorenzo (1963). Writer: Jack Richardson.

Golden Boy (1964). Play: Clifford Odets; musical book: William Gibson.

Wait Until Dark (1966). Writer: Frederick Knott.

Sly Fox (1976). Play: Ben Jonson; adaptation: Stefan Zweig; writer: Larry Gelbart.

Golda: A Partial Portrait (1977). Writer: William Gibson.

Monday After the Miracle (1982). Writer: William Gibson.

Hunting Cockroaches (1987). Writer: Janusz Glowacki.

One of the Guys (1990). Writer: Marilyn Suzanne Miller.

Fortune's Fool (2002). Writer: Ivan Turgenev; adaptation: Mike Poulton.

Sly Fox (2004) (revival). Writer/revisions: Larry Gelbart.

Notes

1. A Boy of Two Cities

1. Referring, of course, to William Penn (1644–1718), a Quaker who founded Pennsylvania under charter from King Charles II. And speaking of Penns, many people mistakenly assume that Arthur Penn is related to actors Sean, Michael, and the late Christopher Penn. The Penn boys are Irish and are scions of director Leo Penn (1921–1998) and actress Eileen Ryan (1928–).

2. Ethical culturalism is a movement founded in the United States by Felix Adler (1851–1933) advocating that human behavior should be governed by a system of ethical beliefs instead of religious convictions.

3. Not to be confused with the famed Neighborhood Playhouse in New York City, where acting teacher Sanford Meisner and his acolytes developed their application of the Method.

4. Irving Penn's biographies make no mention of this first wife, noting only that in 1950 he married Lisa Fonssagrives, née Anderson. She was born May 7, 1911, in Sweden and married Ferdinand Fonssagrives in 1935, divorcing him in 1950 to marry Irving. They had a son, Tom. Lisa died in 1992 at the age of eighty-one, Irving on October 7, 2009, at ninety-two.

5. This quotation is from Jerome Charyn, *Movieland: Hollywood and the Great American Dream Culture* (New York: New York University Press, 1996).

2. The Theater of War

1. Jon Krampner, *The Man in the Shadows: Fred Coe and the Golden Age of Television* (Piscataway, NJ: Rutgers University Press, 1997); plus interview.

2. The combative Chayefsky—later the author of *Marty, Network*, and other classics—had been shot in the ass when, according to legend, a building was bombed while he was sitting on the toilet. He preferred using the technical term "penetrating wounds of the left and right buttock," undoubtedly to make it sound less ignominious.

3. So named as homage to the original company founded in 1887 by André Antoine to present experimental drama by Becque, Zola, and others.

4. The trials were held November 10, 1945, through April 13, 1949.

5. The first trials were held in the Palace of Justice in the American sector of occupied Berlin. Later sessions were held throughout Germany.

3. The Teachable Moment

1. The popular, multivolume, child-friendly encyclopedia first published in America in the 1920s.

2. See also Josef Albers, *Interaction of Color* (New Haven, CT: Yale University Press, 1971).

3. Unaired interview excerpt from the documentary *Buckminster Fuller: Thinking Out Loud* (1996) by Karen Goodman and Kirk Simon.

4. Ibid.

4. Up at Eight, Off at Nine

1. Jerry Lewis, interview with Sam Denoff, October 27, 2000, available at the Archive of American Television, Academy of Television Arts and Sciences, www.emmytvlegends.org.

2. The coaxial cable also doomed sophisticated programming. "When we first started," notes Carl Reiner of *Your Show of Shows* and *Caesar's Hour,* which lampooned foreign movies, Broadway plays, and urban life, "it was New York and Chicago, and then [came] the coaxial cable. When we went into smaller cities, they had never seen foreign movies. They didn't know about satire. Most of America preferred to see Lawrence Welk." Since the lowest common denominator was larger and more attractive to advertisers, it was inevitable that TV would become what TV has become.

5. The Edge of Chaos

1. Despite his avowed indifference, Foote earned screenplay Oscars for *To Kill a Mockingbird* and *Tender Mercies.*

2. Krampner, *The Man in the Shadows.*

3. As a stage play retitled *The Death of Papa, The Death of the Old Man* debuted February 8, 1997, at the Paul Green Theatre at the University of North Carolina with Ellen Burstyn, Matthew Broderick, and Hallie Foote.

4. *The Philco Television Playhouse* spanned and defined television's golden age. It ran from 1948 to 1955 and featured adaptations

and original dramas directed by, in addition to Penn, Vincent Done-hue, Robert Mulligan, Gordon Duff, Delbert Mann, and others. Its premieres included *A Trip to Bountiful* by Horton Foote; *Marty, Bachelor Party,* and *The Catered Affair* by Paddy Chayefsky; and Gore Vidal's *Visit to a Small Planet* and *The Death of Billy the Kid,* the latter of which became *The Left Handed Gun.* In 1951 the show acquired an alternate sponsor, the Goodyear Tire & Rubber Company, on whose weeks it was called *The Goodyear Theatre.* In 1954 Philco dropped out and Alcoa Aluminum joined Goodyear for *The Alcoa Hour.*

5. Quotation from Gorham Kindem, *Live Television Generation of Hollywood Film Directors: Interviews with Seven Directors* (Jefferson, NC: McFarland, 1994).

6. February 22, 1994, museum panel.

7. Newman and Hotchner became friends and years later began the Newman's Own product line, which gives all profits to charity.

8. The makeup artist on the show was Dick Smith, later renowned for his latex appliances.

9. Mosel, via Jon Krampner, *Female Brando: The Legend of Kim Stanley* (New York: Backstage Books, 2006).

10. Unpublished transcript of Schickel-Penn interview for the 1995 documentary *Arthur Penn.*

6. Built for Television

1. Quoted in Kindem, *Live Television Generation,* 102.

2. The success of the news division was chiefly thanks to Edward R. Murrow and his "Murrow Boys": William L. Shirer, Charles Collingwood, Bill Shael, and Howard K. Smith. Popular radio shows were *Jack Benny, Ozzie & Harriet, I Love Lucy* (aka *My Favorite Wife*), *Gunsmoke, Amos 'n' Andy,* and *Fibber McGee and Molly.*

3. Seminar, Museum of Television and Radio, Beverly Hills, CA, October 3, 1996.

4. Because of its significance, *The Miracle Worker* will be addressed separately, in chapter 9.

5. January 1, 2000, interview with Prairie Miller, *Star Interviews.*

6. Brandon Thomas's 1892 play was a staple in touring, summer stock, and community theater. Two male college students persuade a third to dress in drag as an aunt to appease school rules by chaperoning them and their dates, but then the real aunt shows up. The role has been played onstage by Etienne Giradot, José Ferrer, and Louis Nye and in movies by Jack Benny and Charles Ruggles. Its 1948 Broadway musical iteration, *Where's Charley?* memorably starred Ray Bolger (as did the 1952 film), who sang, "Once in Love with Amy."

7. Interviewed by Henry Coleman on October 21, 1998. Courtesy

Archive of American Television, Academy of Television Arts and Sciences.

8. Geraldine Page, Elizabeth Patterson, Ned Glass, and Rudy Bond also appeared. Hunter was nominated for an Emmy.

9. Penn, interview with Henry Coleman, October 21, 1998.

10. The Southern California Gas Company was not mollified. The next year the company leveraged its advertising dollars to force CBS to allow it to place a technician in the audio booth to bleep any mention of Nazi gas chambers from Abby Mann's Holocaust drama, *Judgment at Nuremberg.*

11. Peggy Penn, "The Second Half of Joy: A Memoir by Peggy Penn." The author gratefully acknowledges Mrs. Penn's generosity and contribution to this work, here and elsewhere.

12. For her facility with language, see her poetry collection, *So Close* (Fort Lee, NJ: CavanKerry, 2001).

13. The production she auditioned for was *The Pardon-Me Boy,* which aired May 15, 1955.

14. Eileen Ryan played Masha, Peggy Maurer played Irini, and Carol Gustafson played Olga. Later Peggy played Masha in a second production. Also in the cast, which Ross directed at the Fourth Street Theatre in April of 1955, were Leonardo Cimino, Shirley Gale, George Ebeling, and Frances Cheney.

15. Now best known for playing the husband of Gertrude Berg on the series *The Rise of the Goldbergs,* Loeb was forced from his career by the Blacklist and eventually, unable to find work, he committed suicide.

16. "Of all the rising actresses whom I have seen in the New York theatre, Miss Maurer seems to me easily the most poetic. . . . [She] will be remembered as one of the loveliest and most exact Chekhovian performances within memory." Richard Hayes, "The Stage," *Commonweal,* October 1956.

17. Harold Clurman, *The Fervent Years: The Group Theatre and the 30s* (New York: Knopf, 1945).

18. Gig Young (1913–78) played countless likable second leads in romantic comedies, finally earning respect as the sleazy emcee in *They Shoot Horses, Don't They?* (1969), which won him an Oscar.

19. Jacqueline Presson (1922–2006) took the name "Jay" to disguise her gender as a writer. She married Lewis M. Allen in 1955 to become Jay Presson Allen. Her substantial credits include *The Prime of Miss Jean Brodie, Prince of the City, Cabaret, Travels with My Aunt,* and *Marnie.* Gaby Rodgers appeared extensively in golden age TV dramas. Her few film roles include the film noir classic *Kiss Me Deadly.*

20. *Lost* was scripted by Arnold Schulman from a story by Burton Roueche. It aired January 17, 1956, on *Playwrights '56*.

21. *The Spot on the Wall* was released in July of 1958 as *I Bury the Living*. A cemetery owner discovers he can cause a living person's death by sticking a pin into a cemetery map of his or her reserved grave.

7. Kid's Play

1. Blangsted's numerous credits include *Rhapsody in Blue, Rio Bravo, P.T. 109, Summer of '42,* and the *Maverick* TV series. He also edited—and was then ordered to truncate—the 1954 *A Star Is Born*.

2. The show aired July 24, 1955, on *Philco Television Playhouse*. At this writing all kinescopes are presumed lost.

3. William Henry Bonney was also known as Henry McCarty and Henry Antrim.

4. Fred Kaplan, *Gore Vidal: A Biography* (New York: Doubleday, 1999).

5. Paul Newman made his screen debut for Warner Bros. in *The Silver Chalice* (1954), a self-serious drama about the artisan who crafted a commemorative cup of Jesus and the disciples at the Last Supper. His antipathy toward the film was such that, when it hit TV in 1966, he bought ads in the Hollywood trade papers apologizing for it.

6. American Film Institute seminar, Los Angeles, January 30, 1970.

7. W. T. Orr (1917–2002) produced such profitable series as *Cheyenne, Sugarfoot, Surfside 6, 77 Sunset Strip, Maverick, Bronco, Bourbon Street Beat, The Roaring Twenties, Lawman, Hawaiian Eye,* and later, *F Troop*.

8. Penn's comments adapted from his DVD commentary. Similar themes resurface in *Bonnie and Clyde*.

9. Titled *The Kid* and dated November 15, 1956. Newman was always presumed to play Billy, but Richard Boone, Lee J. Cobb, Richard Anderson, Steve Hill, Karl Malden, and Art Carney were all initially considered for Garrett.

10. Stevens's *The Lovers* ran May 10–12, 1956, at New York's Martin Beck Theatre. Penn was not the credited director. Last billed in the cast was a young actress named Joanne Woodward, later Mrs. Paul Newman.

11. Kaplan, *Gore Vidal*. Vidal subsequently regained rights in his screenplay and in 1989 got it produced for Turner Network Television as *Gore Vidal's Billy the Kid*. Ironically, TNT was later bought by Warner Bros.

12. Trilling was Warner Bros. head of operations.

13. Partial quote from Harvard Film Archive seminar, Cambridge, MA, February 1, 2008.

14. This was based on events Penn had seen in the war.

15. The camera looks through the steamed glass to the street below, and Billy draws circles where each person will take position. The film then dissolves forward in time to the actual event.

16. "The line" is the imaginary line between the two actors nearest to the camera. Crossing it on a cut confuses the audience by scrambling the actors' eyelines.

17. Schickel-Penn interview.

18. A famous late-1800s photograph of Bonney shows him standing with a Model 1873 Winchester rifle to his right and wearing a holster on his left hip, leading to the conclusion that he was left-handed. Later analysis of the rifle led to the revelation that, for a century, the photograph had been reversed and that Bonney was, in truth, a righty.

19. "For now we see through a glass, darkly; but then face to face: now I know in part; but then shall I know even as also I am known" (1 Corinthians 13:12). The passage refers to a mirror, not tinted glass.

20. Philip K. Scheuer, "Arthur Penn and Fred Coe Just Finished *Left Handed Gun,*" *Los Angeles Times,* August 4, 1957.

21. Eric Sherman and Martin Rubin, *The Director's Event* (New York: Atheneum, 1970).

22. Courage was a veteran music arranger whose occasional forays into composition include the fanfare for the original *Star Trek.*

23. Penn, DVD commentary.

24. Those seeking closure, irony, or both might want to note that long after Jack Warner sold his studio and refused to retire, he made 1972's *Dirty Little Billy* starring Michael J. Pollard as a bumbling stoner version of Billy the Kid. It was Warner's last film.

8. Four for the Seesaw

1. November 14, 1968, to February 15, 1969, at Lincoln Center's Vivian Beaumont Theatre with Anne Bancroft, Frank Langella, René Auberjonois, and Susan Tyrell.

2. The Austen Riggs Center is an open psychotherapeutic community in Stockbridge, Massachusetts. Established in 1919, it is highly regarded for its noncoercive environment and close alliance between its staff and its residents. In 1994 it was integrated with the Erik Erikson Institute.

3. *The Cobweb* (New York: Knopf, 1954) was filmed by MGM with Lauren Bacall, Richard Widmark, and Charles Boyer.

4. The new house was in Stockbridge, Massachusetts, about a mile from the Riggs Center.

5. William Gibson, *The Seesaw Log* (New York: Knopf, 1968).

6. Considered a neo-Freudian, Erikson articulated eight stages of psychosocial development in which one's personality is shaped by one's increasing skill in resolving conflicts. He also coined the phrase *identity crisis.*

7. She has published numerous papers, including "Creating a Participant Text: Multiple Voices, Narrative Multiplicity and Writing" (with Marilyn Frankfurt, *Family Process*, 1994); "Letter Writing in Family Systems" (*The Family Therapy Networker*, 1991); "Rape Flashbacks" (*Family Process*, 1985); "Chronic Illness: Writing Voices and Trauma" (*Family Process*, 2001); and the book *Joined Imaginations: Writing and Language Therapy* (2009).

8. Robin Wood, *Arthur Penn* (New York: Praeger, 1969).

9. Apparently there were limits. While *Seesaw* was running, Laurence Olivier contacted Gibson about doing it in London opposite his future wife, Joan Plowright. Queried Gibson, "Why do you want to do this play?" and Olivier answered, "Well, we like to make money, don't we?" Because Penn wanted to direct it in London, however, Gibson turned Olivier down.

10. Kindem, *Live Television Generation*, 128.

11. Robert Wise—not generally known for comedies (*West Side Story, The Sound of Music, The Day the Earth Stood Still*)—directed from Isobel Lennart's (*Funny Girl, The Sundowners*) adaptation.

9. Three Miracles

1. Helen Keller, *The Story of My Life* (New York: Doubleday, Page, 1903).

2. John Albert Macy married Anne Sullivan in May of 1905, and the three of them—Anne, John, and Helen—lived together in Wrentham, Massachusetts. Tensions produced by this arrangement and its shifting interdependencies are dramatized by Gibson in *Monday After the Miracle* (see chapter 15).

3. Dorothy Herrmann, *Helen Keller: A Life* (Chicago: University of Chicago Press, 1999).

4. Wood, *Arthur Penn* (edited).

5. Penn's trademark tennis shoes were the result of slipping off the stage once while rehearsing a play. Thereafter, the director favored traction over tradition.

6. Patty Duke, *Call Me Anna* (New York: Bantam, 1987).

7. *Weekly Variety*, August 16, 1961.

8. Not knowing that Penn and Gibson were making the film

themselves, François Truffaut had tried to buy the rights. Rebuffed, he made a temperamentally similar film, *The Wild Child,* in 1970, carping to Charles Thomas Samuels in *Encountering Directors* (September 1 and 3, 1970) that Penn's film was inferior to Keller's autobiography because Gibson both wrote and produced it, while defending Penn for "translating another man's idea."

9. American Film Institute seminar, January 30, 1970.

10. Super-grainy blown-up footage and echoey audio conjures Annie's terrifying youth in the almshouse.

11. Schickel-Penn interview (interpolated).

12. Interpolated from Gary Crowdus and Richard Porton, "The Importance of a Singular, Guiding Vision," *Cineaste* (1993).

13. Ross Baker, with Fred Firestone, eds., *Movie People: At Work in the Business of Film* (New York: World, 1972).

14. Quoted in Krampner, *Female Brando.*

10. The King of Broadway

1. Hammett served five and a half months in 1951 for refusing to give the FBI a list of names of members of the Civil Rights Congress, of which he was secretary. Upon his release, he revealed that he had never had such a list.

2. Literary license in her autobiographical trilogy *An Unfinished Woman, Pentimento,* and *Scoundrel Time* inspired rival writer Mary McCarthy to charge, on a TV talk show in 1979, "Every word she writes is a lie, including *and* and *the.*" Hellman sued McCarthy for defamation, and the litigation ended only when Hellman died in 1984.

3. Molly Penn was born March 10, 1962.

4. *The Tumbler* by Benn W. Levy, also starring Rosemary Harris, William Mervyn, Donald Moffat, and Martha Scott. It lasted five performances at the Helen Hayes Theatre in New York, February 24–27, 1960.

5. He to star in 1939's *Wuthering Heights,* she to script *Dead End* and *The Cowboy and the Lady.*

6. Clifford Odets, an icon of the left-leaning Group Theatre, named names on May 19 and 20, 1952, after promising Hellman over dinner the night before that he would not do so, boasting resolutely that he was "a man of the Left." It was Kazan who persuaded Odets to testify to save his career, as Kazan had done on April 10, 1952.

7. As proof of just how eclectic *Omnibus* could be, one of the series' second unit directors (*Mr. Lincoln, Pt. 1,* 1952) was Stanley Kubrick.

8. *Take Two: Mike Nichols and Elaine May* (produced by Julian Schlossberg; directed and edited by Phillip Schopper; PBS, *American Masters,* 1996).

9. *An Evening with Mike Nichols and Elaine May* ran at the John Golden Theatre from October 8, 1960, to July 1, 1961. Scenic design is credited to Marvin Reiss.

10. Recognizable as old-fashioned thin-frame chairs with curlicue backs.

11. According to Theodore H. White in *The Making of the President: 1960* (New York: Atheneum, 1961), Nixon's people asked for "two tiny spotlights ('inkies' in television parlance)" to brighten shadows under his eyes. He also used Lazy Shave, a pancake makeup beard cover.

12. Hewitt adds a chilling sidebar: "Many years later when Kennedy was assassinated I was doing a show and we got Nixon on it. He was being made up by the same gal who came to Chicago [for the first debate] whose services he wouldn't use. And I said to him, 'You know, Mr. Nixon, if you'd let Frannie [Arvold] here make you up four years ago, you mighta been president.' You know what he said, without a beat? 'I mighta been dead now, too.'"

11. The Little Play That Could

1. Krampner, *Female Brando.*

2. In a career stretching nearly fifty years, the well-respected Cantor (1920–2001) was variously a press agent, manager, and producer.

3. Hays's Broadway credits begin in 1956 and include *The Tenth Man, Gideon, Sunday in New York, A Cry of Players* (William Gibson), *In the Counting House* (directed by Penn), *Two by Two,* and *The Gingerbread Lady,* among many others. He was five times nominated for the Tony. Not to diminish Hays, but Jo Mielziner's impressionistic sets for *Death of a Salesman* had drawn attention in 1949.

4. Campbell Scott was born July 19, 1961.

5. J. Wesley Zeigler, "The Play That Wouldn't Die," *Arena Stage Program,* twelfth season, 1962–63.

6. *All the Way Home* would run from November 30, 1960, to September 16, 1961.

7. Mosel is fond of noting that the only other instance to date of both a play and its source material winning Pulitzer prizes is James Michener's novel *Tales of the South Pacific* and Rodgers & Hammerstein's musical *South Pacific.*

8. The flops were *In the Counting House* and *Lorenzo* (see chapter 16).

12. Train Wrecks

1. Penn quoted in Kate Buford, *Burt Lancaster: An American Life* (New York: Knopf, 2000).

2. Lancaster was assisted on *The Leopard* by up-and-coming director Sydney Pollack, but their efforts were both disowned by Visconti and rejected by U.S. critics. *Il gattapardo* was not restored for American release until 2004.

3. This paragraph from American Film Institute seminar, Los Angeles, October 7, 1970.

4. Patrick McGilligan, ed., *Backstory 3* (Los Angeles: University of California Press, 1997).

5. Walter Bernstein immediately resigned from the film and declined screen credit for his work. In the commentary track for the film's 1994 laserdisc release, Frankenheimer said that Nedrick Young and Howard Dimsdale wrote the script he shot, not Coen and Davis, but that Young and Dimsdale (both of whom had been blacklisted) were denied credit in Writers Guild of America arbitration.

6. Inference drawn from author's interview with Lancaster, September 20, 1986, plus Penn's report that Lancaster had been seen in Paris as though waiting for a signal.

7. Bernstein quotes Lancaster, "Frankenheimer is a bit of a whore but he'll do what I want." (Buford, *Burt Lancaster*.)

8. American Film Institute seminar, October 7, 1970.

9. Interview with Richard Combs, National Film Theatre, date unknown.

10. Although he is known primarily for writing three films, none of which lived up to the promise of their scripts (*Little Fauss and Big Halsy*, 1970; *The All-American Boy*, 1973; and *The Hamster of Happiness*, aka *Second-hand Hearts*, 1981), Charles Eastman was revered as a writer and uncredited rewriter. He is also the brother of Carol Eastman, aka Adrian Joyce, writer of *Five Easy Pieces* (1970).

11. *Honeybear, I Love You.*

12. Columbia Pictures' press notes for *Mickey One*.

13. Michael Wilmington and Gerald Peary, "Interview with Warren Beatty," *Velvet Light Trap* (Winter 1972).

14. Unsigned production item, *New York Times*, January 10, 1963.

15. Schickel-Penn interview (interpolated).

16. Combs interview.

17. American Film Institute seminar, January 30, 1970 (interpolated).

18. Beatty was named corespondent in Caron's divorce action from her husband, Peter Hall, in February 1965.

19. Kamatari Fujiwara (1905–85) appeared in more than a dozen films for Akira Kurosawa, including *Yojimbo* (1961) and *Kagemusha* (1980).

20. That is, Mickey One's self-destructiveness.

13. Brandeux

1. Christopher Andersen, *Citizen Jane* (New York: Henry Holt, 1990).

2. For years there has been confusion over whether the film is based on Foote's 1952 play or his 1956 novel. In 1955 Foote's lawyer urged him to novelize his play (New York: Rinehart, 1956) in the belief that it would secure him additional copyright protection.

3. Spiegel also purchased rights to two of Foote's one-act plays, *John Turner Davis* and *The Midnight Caller*, intending to fold them into the drama. A vestige is the boy who is orphaned when Bubber kills the motorists in *John Turner Davis*.

4. Peter Bart, *New York Times*, June 20, 1965.

5. Comments at Harvard Film Archive seminar.

6. Penn contends that Spiegel also had Hellman writing an adaptation at the time she was working with him on *Toys in the Attic* in early 1960.

7. Hellman's quote is from Andrew Sinclair, *Spiegel: The Man behind the Pictures* (Boston: Little, Brown, 1987). Moffat is known for *Giant* and *Tender Is the Night*.

8. Ibid.

9. Comments at Harvard Film Archive seminar.

10. June 20, 1965.

11. Some of Surtees' work can be seen in the title sequence modified by famed titlist Maurice Binder of James Bond film fame. LaShelle's many credits include several for Billy Wilder: *The Apartment, The Fortune Cookie*, and *Irma LaDouce*, among others.

12. Prior to filming, the Shurlock Office cautioned against the expressions "son of a bitch," "bastard," and "How is she in bed?" They also warned, "Please avoid any undue brutality" in a scene where a black man is beaten by three men, but raised no objection to Calder getting pummeled.

13. Film is normally shot at twenty-four frames per second, so a slightly reduced rate speeds the action without becoming jerky. Conventional fights are shot from an angle that looks as if the fist is making contact, but in fact the recipient jerks his head back and winces. Thuds are added later.

14. *Elliot Norton Reviews*, c. January 1971, WGBH-TV, Boston.

15. Last fragment from Schickel-Penn interview.

16. August 11–16, 1965, saw the Los Angeles neighborhood of Watts go up in flames in reaction to a police arrest of two brothers on suspicion of drunk driving. Community resentment of the police, fueled by decades of institutionalized racism, exploded. By the time the shooting and looting stopped, thirty-four people were dead and a

thousand were wounded, and between $50 and $100 million in property was damaged, almost all of it in Watts itself.

17. In 1962 Fanny Lou Hamer, in a civil rights action coordinated with SNCC, attempted to register to vote in Mississippi. She and those with her were beaten by police and jailed.

18. Kastner's productions include *Where Eagles Dare, Angel Heart, 92 in the Shade, Equus, Harper,* and dozens of others. In the early 1970s, the Nixon administration created an IRS loophole allowing investors to claim two and a half times the amount of their actual investment as a leveraged shelter against anticipated income. Until the dodge was rescinded by the Carter administration in 1976, upwards of $150 million was raised at a time when the average movie budget was $4 million. For the first time in Hollywood history it actually made fiscal sense for a studio to green-light risky projects that might lose money legitimately rather than by dint of sleazy bookkeeping.

19. "Production Services" was what financing entities were called.

20. Combs interview.

21. Clayton is based on real-life regulator (assassin) Tom Horn.

22. Lloyd Shearer, *Parade,* December 7, 1975.

23. August 24, 1975.

24. Thomas McGuane, *The Missouri Breaks,* Marlon Brando's copy, dated June 20, 1975, containing revisions through July 20, 1975.

25. *Time Out London,* retrospective story, May 21–28, 2003.

26. Ibid.

27. Jack Nicholson had just won the Best Actor Academy Award for *One Flew Over the Cuckoo's Nest.*

28. Nicholson interview, behind-the-scenes featurette.

29. William Wolf, *Cue,* May 15, 1976.

30. Combs interview.

31. This is charted in Peter Biskind's gleefully lurid chronicle *Easy Riders, Raging Bulls* (New York: Simon & Schuster, 1998).

14. Foggy Mountain Breakthrough

1. Wood, *Arthur Penn.*

2. For example, Jean-Luc Godard: "A motion picture should have a beginning, a middle, and an end, but not necessarily in that order."

3. Two remarkable books stand out: Mark Harris, *Pictures at a Revolution* (New York: Penguin, 2008), and Susanne Finstad, *Warren Beatty: A Private Man* (New York: Harmony Books, 2005).

4. Penn, interview with Philip Porcella, August 30, 1976.

5. Soon after they met in 1930, Clyde went to jail for burglary. Bonnie smuggled him a gun for an escape, but he was recaptured.

When Clyde was released in 1932, he rejoined Bonnie, and the film story picks up.

6. John Toland, *The Dillinger Days* (New York: Random House, 1963).

7. Patrick Goldstein, "Blasts from the Past," *Los Angeles Times,* August 24, 1997.

8. Ibid. In Harris, *Pictures at a Revolution,* Benton quotes $75,000.

9. Both described in Goldstein, "Blasts from the Past."

10. Ibid.

11. Ibid. (One wonders if there is any connection between this story and Jack Warner's account of begging David Belasco for *Girl of the Golden West.*)

12. Harris, *Pictures at a Revolution.*

13. Tom Luddy and David Thomson, "Penn on Penn," in *Projections 4* (London: Faber & Faber, 1995).

14. The scene in which Bonnie and Clyde encourage an evicted farmer and his handyman to shoot out the windows of their repossessed home is Penn's contribution.

15. Benton, interview with Philip Porcella.

16. Robert Towne, interviewed at American Film Institute (Joseph McBride, ed., *Filmmakers and Filmmaking,* vol. 2 [Los Angeles: J. P. Tarcher, 1983]).

17. C. W. Moss is a combination of two Barrow gang members: Henry Methvin and William Daniel "W. D." Jones, originally called Wallace Duffy Jones in the script. Jones was still alive when the film was made and sued Warner Bros., apparently without results. (Ann James, "Bonnie and Clyde Driver Loses Life to Shotgun Blasts," *Texas City Post,* August 31, 1974). The gang also included Raymond Hamilton, Joseph Palmer, Ivan M. "Buck" Barrow, and, by association, Buck's wife, Blanche.

18. Goldstein, "Blasts from the Past."

19. Benton, interview with Philip Porcella, c. 1978.

20. Warren Beatty's copy of script, dated 1967, USC/Warner Bros. Archive. ©Warner Bros.

21. Beatty and Weld had briefly appeared together in the TV series *The Many Loves of Dobie Gillis* in 1959–60. Michael J. Pollard also appeared.

22. Weld's then husband was playwright-screenwriter Claude Harz, to whom she was married from 1965 to 1970. Their daughter, Natasha, was born in 1966.

23. Comments to the author at the November 17, 2005, tribute to Penn by the Academy of Motion Picture Arts & Sciences in New York.

24. Beatty's script.

278 Notes to Pages 155–170

25. Gary Crowdus and Richard Porton, "The Importance of a Singular, Guiding Vision: An Interview with Arthur Penn," in *The Cineaste Interviews*, vol. 2, ed. Gary Crowdus and Dan Georgakas (Urbana, IL: Lakeview, 2002).

26. Ibid.

27. The six films the two collaborated on are *Bonnie and Clyde, Alice's Restaurant, Little Big Man, Visions of Eight, Night Moves,* and *The Missouri Breaks.*

28. Allen playfully disputes this, explaining, "I was not an overnighter. First place, I had a family!"

29. Greenberg worked again with Penn and Allen on *Alice's Restaurant* and *The Missouri Breaks.* He won an Oscar for editing *The French Connection* (1971).

30. The original budget was $1,655,137.50. Beatty and Penn were to get 40 percent of "net profits," which were defined as 2.9 times the cost of the picture. After ten years, either side could buy out the other. Latest domestic box office rentals: $22,800,000.

31. Crowdus and Porton, "The Importance of a Singular, Guiding Vision."

32. Joe Morgenstern, "A Thin Red Line," *Newsweek,* August 28, 1967.

15. Golden Boys

1. Sammy Davis Jr., Jane Boyar, and Burt Boyar, *Sammy: An Autobiography* (New York: Farrar, Straus & Giroux, 2000).

2. William Gibson, *Golden Boy: A Memento* (New York: Atheneum, 1965).

3. From 1960 to 1968, Davis was married to May Britt (Maybritt Wilkins). He was also married to Loray White from 1958 to 1959, and subsequently to Altovese Gore from 1970 to his death in 1990.

4. Davis, Boyar, and Boyar, *Sammy.*

5. Philip Langner, Marilyn Langner, and Armina Marshall produced *Golda* under the aegis of the Theatre Guild, which was founded in 1919 by Lawrence and Marilyn Langner and Marshall.

6. There is also speculation that Meir was involved with a Palestinian banker named Albert Pharaon.

7. Undaunted, Gibson returned to Jerusalem, where he reworked his play into a one-woman show called *Golda's Balcony*. It ran 493 performances, from October 15, 2003, to January 2, 2005, at the Helen Hayes Theatre. Tovah Feldshuh won wide acclaim for her performance as, subsequently, did Valerie Harper, and the play remains a touring favorite. It was directed by Scott Schwartz.

16. Curtains

1. Richard Lippe and Robin Wood, "An Interview with Arthur Penn," *CineAction!* Spring 1986.

2. Other sources present its translated title as *A Poor Gentleman.*

3. Barry Singer, interview with Alan Bates and Frank Langella, *New York Times,* March 31, 2002.

4. Bates died on December 27, 2003. Praises Schlossberg, "He never missed a performance. I had no idea, and apparently no one else did, either."

5. Ron Dicker, "*Fool* Lures Director Back to Broadway," *Hartford Courant,* February 20, 2002.

17. Hippie Sunset

1. Actually, he said, "History is *more or less* bunk."

2. *Alice's Restaurant Massacree,* ©1966, 1967 (renewed) by Appleseed Music Inc. All Rights Reserved.

3. Ibid.

4. Arlo Guthrie's commentary track for the *Alice's Restaurant* DVD.

5. Ibid.

6. Alice Brock is an artist and gallery owner in Provincetown, Massachusetts (www.alicebrock.com). Ray, twelve years her senior, died of a heart attack in Virginia in 1979.

7. Venable Herndon (1927–99) wrote the plays *Bag of Lies, Independence Night, Sugar Mill, Tom Thumb,* and *Until the Monkey Comes,* as well as several unproduced screenplays.

8. The budget for the film was $2.3 million.

9. Comments at Harvard Film Archive seminar.

10. Guthrie, *Alice's Restaurant* DVD commentary.

11. Dede Allen, interview with Philip Porcella, 1976.

12. Guthrie, *Alice's Restaurant* DVD commentary.

13. Now a grandfather, Arlo Guthrie has reportedly declined to be tested for the presence of the Huntington's gene. Although there is a fifty-fifty chance that he carries it, as of this writing the disease has not presented.

14. Joseph Gelmis, *The Film Director as Superstar* (New York: Doubleday, 1970).

15. Guthrie, *Alice's Restaurant* DVD commentary.

18. Little Big Mensch

1. Tony Crawley, "Arthur Penn on Personal Experiences," *Movie Scene* 1 (March 1985).

2. Michael Lindsay, "An Interview with Arthur Penn," *Cinema 5,* no. 3 (1969).

3. Penn, *Elliot Norton Reviews.*

4. Ibid.

5. Ibid.

6. Richardson wrote the plays *Lorenzo,* which Penn directed in 1963, and *Xmas in Las Vegas,* which Fred Coe directed on Broadway in 1964.

7. Comments at Harvard Film Archive seminar.

8. Script extract by Calder Willingham, ©1970 Cinema Center Films.

9. Allen, interview with Porcella.

10. Crawley, "Arthur Penn on Personal Experiences."

19. A State of Great Disorder

1. David L. Wolper with David Fisher, *Producer: A Memoir* (New York: Scribner, 2003).

2. The Milliken camera was operated by Atze Glanert at six hundred frames per second, requiring a rotating prism instead of a pulldown sprocket system to expose film speeding nonstop through the gate. Traditional cameras shoot at twenty-four fps.

3. Arthur Penn, *Action!* (Los Angeles: Directors Guild of America, 1972).

4. Tag Gallagher, "Night Moves," *Sight and Sound* 44 (Spring 1975).

5. Charyn, *Movieland.*

6. *The Dark Tower* was a swipe at Universal Pictures' executives' office building, known derisively in the film community as the Black Tower. The final title had nothing to do with Bob Seger's song "Night Moves."

7. Alan Sharp, *Night Moves* (New York: Warner Paperback Library, 1975). The game was played in 1922 in the "B" Haupturnier preliminary to Bad Oeyenhausen between Bruno Moritz and K. Emmrich. It was a queen sacrifice followed by three knight moves, driving the king into a corner, but Moritz missed it. Sharp: "I'm very pleased that, even though it's incomprehensible from the viewer's point of view, we got the title out of it as well."

8. The Senate Watergate Committee started meeting on May 17, 1973, and issued its report on June 27, 1973.

9. Allen, interview with Porcella.

10. Gallagher, "Night Moves," 87.

11. The Baltimore bench speech: "I was pretty proud of myself, the way I tracked him down. I followed all the clues—followed him job to job, city to city—finally found him in Baltimore in a rooming house on Hibiscus Avenue. Went up to his door—little card there with his

name on it. Somebody pointed him out to me. He was in a park, on a bench, sitting there, just a little old guy reading the funny pages out of a paper, mouthing the words with his lips. I just sit there for a while, and watched, and then went away. It was something I was just never very proud of: standing six feet away from my father and then just walking away. Trouble is, after the first six feet it's hard to tell whether you're jumping or you're falling." (©Alan Sharp).

20. Sly Foxes

1. *Foxy,* a musical adaptation of *Volpone* set in the Klondike in 1896 and starring Bert Lahr and Larry Blyden, played 72 performances in 1964. It had a book by Ian McLellan Hunter (who was still blacklisted in Hollywood), lyrics by Johnny Mercer, music by Robert Emmett Dolan, and was directed by Robert (Bobby) Lewis.

2. It was to Penn that Gelbart said what has become his most frequently quoted wisecrack. Stuck in Boston trying to save the musical *The Conquering Hero* (based on the Preston Sturges film *Hail the Conquering Hero*), Gelbart was overjoyed to receive a visit from the Penns. When Arthur asked, "How's it going?" Gelbart's reply was "If Hitler's alive, I hope he's out of town with a musical."

3. Lew Grade ran Associated Television, a commercial rival to the BBC, and was known for having wrested control of the Beatles' songs away from the Beatles.

4. Published stage directions indicate that the chest is to be placed stage left; that is, not at the foot of the bed.

21. The Studio

1. Interestingly, there's seldom discussion about the playwright's responsibility to provide material for the actor to do his job.

2. Michael Ellison, "Stars to Make Method Work at Actors' Studio," *Guardian,* June 21, 2000.

3. Stanislavski died in 1938 in Moscow.

4. Newman said of Strasberg, "I found everything that he was teaching fascinating, but I could never really make it work for me" (Ellison, "Stars to Make Method Work").

5. In *Two for the Seesaw,* Bancroft entered her apartment carrying grocery bags and rushing to answer a ringing phone. It gave her an object as well as an obstacle and instantly established her character.

6. Actor-writer-producer Lipton remains a controversial figure. At once a celebrity and an exhaustive interviewer, he also is the subject of mockery for his ingratiating manner. Guests go on *Inside the Actors Studio* knowing they'll be among friends.

7. It's anybody's guess how Kazan, who named names to HUAC, got along with Mankiewicz, whom archconservative director Cecil B. DeMille tried unsuccessfully to depose from the Directors Guild presidency during the same era by challenging his loyalty.

8. "These," says Penn, "in distinction from the Studio, charged students and eventually became very lucrative for his heirs."

22. A Sea of Mud

1. John Brady, *The Craft of the Screenwriter* (New York: Simon & Schuster, 1981).

2. Ibid.

3. The screen credit reads "Sidney Aaron," the writer's actual first and middle names.

4. Schickel-Penn interview.

5. Lippe and Wood, "An Interview with Arthur Penn."

6. Unsourced interview (possibly Tom Milne) with Penn, conducted via correspondence, while he was prepping *Monday After the Miracle* in South Carolina. Courtesy Paul J. Cronin.

7. Interviewed by Carmine Amata, "Penn/Tesich/Georgia's Friends," *Films and Filming,* May 1982. Steve Tesich died on July 1, 1996, of a heart attack. He was fifty-four.

8. Combs interview.

9. Hackman and Fay Maltese were married from 1956 to 1986 and have three children. In 1991 he married Betsi Arakawa.

10. Lippe and Wood, "An Interview with Arthur Penn."

11. Anthony Gilbert is the pen name of Muriel Roy Bolton.

12. In 2006 Shmuger was named chairman of Universal Pictures. In October of 2009 he was ousted.

13. Interview with author, January 13, 1987.

14. Luddy and Thomson, "Penn on Penn."

23. Back to Basics

1. Krampner, *Female Brando.*

2. Ms. Peck acted in only a handful of roles after *The Portrait,* but in 2006 she produced, with Barbara Kopple, the award-winning documentary on the Dixie Chicks, *Shut Up and Sing.*

3. Penn to Peck fax, June 18, 1992.

4. Ibid.

5. These and other journal selections are courtesy of Eric Stoltz.

6. Interviewed by Felicia Mabuza-Suttle for the Africa Channel, February 11, 2008, and produced by the author.

7. Ibid.

8. Sir Nigel Hawthorne died on December 26, 2001, of a heart attack while battling pancreatic cancer.

9. Comments upon receiving Directors Guild of America honors, Directors Guild of America Theater, New York, October 12, 2006.

10. Ibid.

11. Participating in the November 17, 2005, event were actor Estelle Parsons, writer Walter Bernstein, producer Julian Schlossberg, Academy president Sidney Ganis, and Academy New York events chairman Arthur Manson; Melanie Griffith and Dustin Hoffman sent video messages; and *Night Moves* was screened. Family and many of Penn's colleagues were in attendance. The event was arranged by Patrick Harrison. The author emceed.

12. Acceptance remarks, October 12, 2006.

13. Penn, interview with Porcella.

14. American Film Institute seminar, January 30, 1970.

15. American Film Institute seminar, October 7, 1970.

Selected Bibliography

Berle, Milton, with Haskel Frankel. *Milton Berle: An Autobiography.* New York: Delacorte, 1974.

Biskind, Peter. *Easy Riders, Raging Bulls.* New York: Simon & Schuster, 1998.

Brady, John. *The Craft of the Screenwriter.* New York: Simon & Schuster, 1981.

Brenman-Gibson, Margaret. *Clifford Odets: American Playwright—The Years from 1906–1940.* New York: Atheneum, 1981.

Brode, Douglas. *The Films of Dustin Hoffman.* Secaucus, NJ: Citadel, 1983.

———. *The Films of the Sixties.* Secaucus, NJ: Citadel, 1980.

Brooks, Tim, and Earle Marsh. *Complete Directory to Prime Time Network TV Shows, 1946–1979.* New York: Ballantine, 1979.

Buford, Kate. *Burt Lancaster: An American Life.* New York: Knopf, 2000.

Cawelti, John G., ed. *Focus on Bonnie and Clyde.* Englewood Cliffs, NJ: Prentice-Hall, 1973.

Charyn, Jerome. *Movieland: Hollywood and the Great American Dream Culture.* New York: New York University Press, 1996.

Chekhov, Michael. *On the Technique of Acting.* New York: Quill, 1991.

Coles, Robert. *Erik H. Erikson: The Growth of His Work.* 2nd ed. Boston: Little-Brown, 1970.

Dick, Bernard F. *Hal Wallis: Producer to the Stars.* Lexington: University Press of Kentucky, 2004.

Erikson, Erik H. *Childhood and Society.* 2nd ed. New York: Norton, 1963.

———. *Life History and the Historical Moment.* New York: Norton, 1975.

Fagan, Myron C. *"Red Treason on Broadway."* Hollywood: Cinema Educational Guild, 1954.

Finstad, Susanne. *Warren Beatty: A Private Man.* New York: Harmony Books, 2005.

Fonda, Henry (as told to Howard Teichman). *Fonda: My Life.* New York: New American Library, 1981.

Foote, Horton. *Collected Plays (The Trip to Bountiful, The Chase, The Traveling Lady, The Roads to Home).* Lyme, NH: Smith & Kraus, 1996.

———. *Selected One-Act Plays.* University Park, TX: Southern Methodist University Press, 1989.

Gallagher, Tag. "Night Moves." *Sight and Sound* 44 (Spring 1975).

Gibson, William. *The Cobweb.* New York: Knopf, 1954.

———. *Golda: Notes on How to Turn a Phoenix into Ashes.* New York: Atheneum, 1978.

———. *A Mass for the Dead.* New York: Atheneum, 1968.

———. *The Miracle Worker.* Hollywood: Samuel French, 1956.

———. *Monday After the Miracle.* New York: Atheneum, 1983.

———. *The Seesaw Log.* New York: Knopf, 1968.

Goldman, William. *The Season: A Candid Look at Broadway.* New York: Harcourt, Brace & World, 1969.

Grobel, Lawrence. *Conversations with Brando.* New York: Hyperion, 1991.

Hagen, Uta, with Victor Frankel. *Respect for Acting.* New York: MacMillan, 1973.

Harris, Mark. *Pictures at a Revolution.* New York: Penguin, 2008.

Hellman, Lillian. *Toys in the Attic.* New York: Random House, 1959.

Herndon, Venable, and Arthur Penn. *Alice's Restaurant.* New York: Doubleday, 1970.

Hilliard, Robert L., and Michael C. Keith. *The Broadcast Century.* Stoneham, MA: Focal, 1992.

Himelstein, Morgan Y. *Drama Was a Weapon: The Left-Wing Theatre in New York, 1929–1941*. Piscataway, NJ: Rutgers University Press, 1963.

Kaplan, Fred. *Gore Vidal: A Biography*. New York: Doubleday, 1999.

Kazan, Elia. *A Life*. New York: Knopf, 1988.

Kindem, Gorham. *Live Television Generation of Hollywood Film Directors: Interviews with Seven Directors*. Jefferson, NC: McFarland, 1994.

Krampner, Jon. *Female Brando: The Legend of Kim Stanley*. New York: Backstage Books, 2006.

———. *The Man in the Shadows: Fred Coe and the Golden Age of Television*. Piscataway, NJ: Rutgers University Press, 1997.

Lewis, Jerry. *Jerry Lewis in Person*. New York: Atheneum, 1982.

Lewis, Robert. *Method or Madness?* New York: Samuel French, 1958.

Logan, Josh. *Josh: My Up and Down, In and Out Life*. New York: Delacorte, 1976.

McArthur, Colin. *Underworld USA*. New York: Viking, 1972.

Meisner, Sanford, and Dennis Longwell. *On Acting*. New York: Vintage Books, 1987.

Mosel, Tad. *All the Way Home*. Hollywood: Samuel French, 1961.

———. *Other People's Houses: Six Television Plays*. New York: Simon & Schuster, 1956.

Parish, James Robert. *Fiasco: A History of Hollywood's Iconic Flops*. Hoboken, NJ: John Wiley & Sons, 2006.

Peary, Danny. *Cult Movies 3*. New York: Simon & Schuster, 1988.

Penn, Arthur. *Action!* Los Angeles: Directors Guild of America, 1972.

Ross, Frank. *The Agency: William Morris and the Hidden History of Show Business*. New York: Harper Business, 1995.

Schickel, Richard. *Second Sight*. New York: Simon & Schuster, 1972.

Schickel, Richard, and John Simon, eds. *Film 67–68*. New York: Simon & Schuster, 1968.

Sherman, Eric. *Directing the Film.* Boston: Little, Brown, 1976.

Sherman, Eric, and Martin Rubin. *The Director's Event.* New York: Atheneum, 1970.

Sinclair, Andrew. *Spiegel: The Man behind the Pictures.* Boston: Little, Brown, 1987.

Taylor, Al, and Sue Roy. *Making a Monster.* New York: Crown, 1980.

Thomey, Todd. *Glorious Decade.* New York: Ace Books, 1971.

Trager, James. *People's Chronology.* New York: Henry Holt, 1992.

Vineberg, Steve. *Method Actors: Three Generations of an American Acting Style.* New York: Schirmer Books, 1991.

Wake, Sandra, and Nicola Hayden, eds. *The Bonnie & Clyde Book.* New York: Simon & Schuster, 1972.

Wilder, Gene. *Kiss Me Like a Stranger: My Search for Love and Art.* New York: St. Martin's, 2005.

Wilk, Max. *The Golden Age of Television.* New York: Delacorte, 1976.

Wood, Robin. *Arthur Penn.* New York: Praeger, 1969.

Zierold, Norman. *The Moguls.* Los Angeles: Silman-James, 1969.

Credits

Excerpts from Peggy Penn, *The Second Half of Joy: A Memoir by Peggy Penn* appear courtesy of Dr. Penn.

Excerpts from Eric Stoltz's journal of the making of *Inside* appear courtesy of Mr. Stoltz.

Excerpts from Henry Colman's interview with Arthur Penn; Morrie Gelman's interview with Martin Manulis; and Sam Denoff's interview with Jerry Lewis appear courtesy of the Archive of American Television (http://EmmyTVLegends.org).

PLAYBILL used by permission. All rights reserved, Playbill, Inc.

Every effort has been made to trace copyright holders of photographs. The author apologizes for any errors or omissions and would be grateful to be notified of any corrections that should be incorporated in future reprints or editions of this book.

As used throughout, Oscar®, Oscars®, Academy Award®, and Academy Awards® are trademarks and service marks of the Academy of Motion Picture Arts and Sciences.

Index